MW01053271

Catholic and Mormon

CATHOLIC AND MORMON

A Theological Conversation

STEPHEN H. WEBB
AND
ALONZO L. GASKILL

OXFORD
UNIVERSITY PRESS

OXFORD

UNIVERSITY PRESS

Oxford University Press is a department of the University of
Oxford. It furthers the University's objective of excellence in research,
scholarship, and education by publishing worldwide.

Oxford   New York
Auckland   Cape Town   Dar es Salaam   Hong Kong   Karachi
Kuala Lumpur   Madrid   Melbourne   Mexico City   Nairobi
New Delhi   Shanghai   Taipei   Toronto

With offices in
Argentina   Austria   Brazil   Chile   Czech Republic   France   Greece
Guatemala   Hungary   Italy   Japan   Poland   Portugal   Singapore
South Korea   Switzerland   Thailand   Turkey   Ukraine   Vietnam

Oxford is a registered trademark of Oxford University Press
in the UK and certain other countries.

Published in the United States of America by
Oxford University Press
198 Madison Avenue, New York, NY 10016

© Oxford University Press 2015

All rights reserved. No part of this publication may be reproduced, stored in
a retrieval system, or transmitted, in any form or by any means, without the prior
permission in writing of Oxford University Press, or as expressly permitted by law,
by license, or under terms agreed with the appropriate reproduction rights organization.
Inquiries concerning reproduction outside the scope of the above should be sent to the
Rights Department, Oxford University Press, at the address above.

You must not circulate this work in any other form
and you must impose this same condition on any acquirer.

Library of Congress Cataloging-in-Publication Data
Webb, Stephen H., 1961– author.
Catholic and mormon : a theological conversation / by Stephen H. Webb and Alonzo L. Gaskill.
pages cm
ISBN 978–0–19–026592–2 (hardback : alk. paper)
1. Catholic Church—Doctrines.   2. Church of Jesus Christ of Latter-day Saints—
Doctrines. 3. Mormon Church—Doctrines.   4. Catholic Church—Relations—Church
of Jesus Christ of Latter-day Saints.   5. Catholic Church—Relations—Mormon
Church.   6. Church of Jesus Christ of Latter-day Saints—Relations—Catholic
Church.   7. Mormon Church—Relations—Catholic Church.   I. Gaskill,
Alonzo L., author.   II. Title.
BX1753.W37 2016
280'.042—dc23
2015003398

1 3 5 7 9 8 6 4 2
Printed in the United States of America
on acid-free paper

Contents

Introduction

HOW DID WE GET HERE?

RELIGION IN AMERICA is rife with one-dimensional labels, misleading generalizations, and sweeping statements. Because Catholics and Mormons stand out in a country that is still heavily dominated by Protestantism, they are especially vulnerable to spiritual typecasting—and many of those oversimplifications are uncannily similar. Theologically, both traditions have been accused of putting more emphasis on the role of works than grace in the drama of salvation. Ecclesiastically, both have complex and exclusive rituals that can be easily misunderstood and disparaged. And historically, their loyalty to the American democratic experiment has been held in suspicion, if not contempt.

Religious beliefs and practices need to be carefully analyzed in order to replace caricature with full-bodied characterizations. Even where there is a grain of truth in a generalization, caution is required, since generalizations can easily turn into prejudice and bigotry. Here too Mormons and Catholics share a remarkably parallel list of affronts and denunciations. Catholics blindly follow the Pope and Mormons worship Joseph Smith. Catholics put Mary above Jesus while Mormons give as much devotion to a Heavenly Mother as the Heavenly Father. Catholics substitute the early creeds for the Bible while Mormons replace the Bible with the Book of Mormon. Catholics borrowed their rituals from pagan practices while Joseph Smith raided the ceremonies of Masonry for many of his ideas. Catholics have large families and Mormons have multiple wives. Catholics have a fixation with Rome while most Mormons live in Utah.

None of these statements is true, even the last one (most Mormons these days live outside of the United States). There is and always has been more to Catholicism than the pope and the Blessed Virgin, and Mormonism certainly cannot be defined by polygamous practices abandoned long ago or by the geographical boundaries of Utah. These two churches, with their authoritarian hierarchies, elaborate rituals, and heavenly matriarchs, do not fit easily into American predilections for egalitarian organizations, informal worship, and pragmatic beliefs, which is just one reason they both stand to benefit from a mutual dialogue. The best way to deal with stereotypes and misinformation, we believe, is to jump right into more fundamental and weighty issues. There is so much these traditions can learn from each other that it would be a shame to dwell on the many ways that they have been misunderstood by others.

Nothing less than the most significant issues that impact Christian identity are at stake in this dialogue. After all, both Catholicism and Mormonism have ambitiously universal views of the Christian faith. Catholicism speaks with the oldest and largest voice of any church, and reserves the right to put into words the consensus positions on every theological topic, while Mormonism aims to restore Christianity to an unsurpassable fullness in ritual, belief, and practice. On the surface, those identities contradict each other. Catholicism is a continuous tradition, committed to the conservation of the earliest, ecumenical creeds, while Mormonism teaches that the landscape of Christian history is riddled with sin and apostasy and is in need of radical revision and spiritual healing. Mormonism looks to modern-day prophets and a renewal of apostolic authority to connect Christianity to traditions that precede and trump the making of the creeds.

How could these traditions have anything to say to each other when they seem to be going in such different directions? Indeed, how can they exchange information and observations on their respective versions of the Christian faith when they so often find themselves competing for converts? The media has not been slow to cover the tensions that can arise when Mormonism spreads into places where the Catholic Church has been long established.[1] If these demographic trends continue, there will be more opportunities for mutual suspicion and thus a greater need for mutual understanding.[2]

In reality, Mormons and Catholics have much to share—and they are much closer to each other than many assume. Their moral teachings, for example, are broadly consonant, and that provides a strong foundation for institutional collaboration on social issues of public significance.[3] While it is true that they can appear to be far apart in their philosophical and metaphysical commitments, probing beyond the theological surface reveals unexpected connections that can be cast into frameworks for intellectual accord. Perhaps most importantly, theological traditions have the most to learn from alternative viewpoints that challenge the doctrines they hold in highest esteem. We think that readers will be very surprised by how close Catholics and Mormons are on a number of the most basic theological topics and how relevant their differences are for deepening the nuances and richness of the Christian faith.

Dialogues between Latter-day Saints (LDS) and Protestants have been somewhat common in recent years. Craig Blomberg and Stephen Robinson's *How Wide the Divide: A Mormon & an Evangelical in Conversation* really opened the door to a discussion that theretofore had seemed too taboo to entertain. LDS scholar Robert L. Millet has spent years nurturing the dialogue between Protestants and Mormons. Among other things, Millet co-authored (with Gerald R. McDermott) *Claiming Christ: A Mormon–Evangelical Debate* and (with Gregory C. V. Johnson) *Bridging the Divide: The Continuing Conversation between a Mormon and an Evangelical.* Although not a dialogue in the proper sense of the word, Richard J. Mouw's *Talking with Mormons: An Invitation to Evangelicals* seeks to engage Protestants in a civil discussion with Mormons and is itself a contribution to sincere attempts at dialogue.[4] What is curious, however, is the absence of significant and civil dialogues between Latter-day Saints and Roman Catholics. Such conversations are largely non-extant. That is surprising, both because the Catholic Church (particularly since Vatican II) has really sought to reach out to what they used to term their "separated brethren" of the various Christian denominations and also because Mormonism (albeit numerically small) is a decidedly present faith readily encountered.

While Latter-day Saints and Catholics have worked together well for many years on social issues and on humanitarian initiatives, they have kept their distance—theologically speaking—from each other. For us, that is disheartening. And, it seems fare to note, such a stance may actually run counter to the official position these two great faiths have taken regarding other Christian Churches. For example, Elder M. Russell Ballard (of the LDS Quorum of the Twelve Apostles) counseled members of the faith: "Get to know your neighbors. Learn about their ... views. ... Our pioneer ancestors were driven from place to place by uninformed and intolerant neighbors. They experienced extraordinary hardship and persecution because they thought, acted, and believed differently from others.

If our history teaches us nothing else, it should teach us to respect the rights of all people."[5]

Similarly, Vatican II's *Decree on Ecumenism* counsels Roman Catholics: "We must become more familiar with the outlook of our separated brethren. Study is absolutely required for this, and it should be pursued in fidelity to the truth and with a spirit of good will. Catholics . . . need to acquire a more adequate understanding of the respective doctrines of our separated brethren, their history, their spiritual and liturgical life, their religious psychology and cultural background."[6] Indeed, with the Latter-day Saints building a Temple right in the heart of Rome, church officials in the Vatican will be hard pressed to ignore their new neighbors.[7]

These invitations to take other faith traditions more seriously are clear, and they well articulate the interests shared by the authors of this book. It is quite natural for Catholics and Mormons to have prejudices about each other, but it is equally natural to seek to overturn them. It is not enough to respect the rights and tolerate the opinions of those not of our faith; we need to take positive steps to better understand their doctrine, history, rituals, and cultural background. We—Stephen Webb and Alonzo Gaskill—are converts to our respective faiths, which gives us a firsthand perspective on the dangers of assuming you know enough about another version of your faith to make judgments about it or its people. And we both know intimately the beauty that can be found through looking at another's religious tradition with an open and understanding heart. And so this book is an invitation to the reader to engage in the discussion that makes understanding the goal and asks that personal presuppositions be put on hold, or at least suspended long enough so that the reader can enter into another mode of thought. We have not written this book as a debate. It is an exploration, and, moreover, just the first probes of what should be a long journey into unexplored yet jointly held territory. We hope it can serve not only as an example of theological dialogue but also as an example of just plain good theology.

On our individual journeys—wherein each of us have spent years studying the other's faith—we have discovered that Catholics and Mormons may not be twins, but they are certainly siblings. The closer you look, the more family resemblances you will find. And their similarities go well beyond shared moral values and social concerns. There are so many deep correlations to be found among their beliefs precisely because they claim the same God and the same Lordship of Jesus Christ. As members of a family do, Catholics and Mormons pull together when things get tough—as they have on numerous occasions. As different branches of a family tree, they can also feel threatened by the very things they share. Yet they can also learn from each other as they meet and interact. We feel that there is much that Catholics and Mormons can learn about each other through a frank and open dialogue. And, in the process of learning about each other, there is much that they can learn about themselves. So let's begin!

Catholic and Mormon

I

Authority

Stephen

The Protestant Reformation came to an end for me one day in the spring of 2004. I was teaching the history of the Reformation to a class of college students who were almost equally divided between Catholics and Protestants, with a handful of the religiously confused or uncommitted and an agnostic or two thrown in for good measure. I began the course that semester with three questions. I wanted everyone, but especially the Catholics, to be ready to tell me, at the end of our time together, whether they would have joined the Reformers. I wanted the Protestants to tell me what they were still protesting against. And I wanted all the students, even those who were skeptical or noncommittal, to be able to tell me if they thought the theological fuss was worth it.

When we got to the end of the semester and I reminded the students about these questions, one of them raised his hand.

"Prof. Webb," he said, "shouldn't you be willing to answer these questions too?"

That made perfectly good pedagogical sense to me. It had long been a principle in my philosophy of teaching that professors should never ask questions that they themselves are not willing to answer. So I replied as efficiently as I could in order to get my views out of the way and steer the conversation back to the students.

"As for the first question, I wouldn't have joined the Reformers. I'm pretty conservative about social change and skeptical about radical challenges to the status quo. I respect religious authority too much to call for a religious revolution. Speaking as a Protestant with regard to the second question, I don't think the issues the Reformers were protesting are still alive in the Catholic Church. So I guess I don't have any personal grudges against Catholicism. I admit I protest in my own way against secularism and atheism, but not against Catholicism. And as for the third question, about the social and theological results of the Reformation: socially, as you know, it led to chaos, war, and the rise of the modern nation-state to fill the vacuum left by the end of Christendom, while theologically it led to incredible intellectual confusion resulting in the fragmentation of the church we see today. So no, I guess I don't think it was worth it, for the world or the Church."

I realized immediately that I had said way too much. It is not good pedagogy to answer the questions you ask the students before they have had time to formulate their own answers. Besides, I was afraid that my thinking out loud had come across as more conclusive and vehement than I had intended, which made me worry that it would overly influence my students. I usually liked to keep them on their toes by being unpredictable in my classroom opinions, but they now knew exactly what I thought. More important, though, I now knew exactly what I thought.

I had answered the questions in a way that surprised me. It was a case of not knowing what I thought until somebody put me on the spot with questions I had asked others but had not yet asked myself. Once the words were out, I knew that I could not disown them. I was caught off guard and had said what I really think before I had a chance to qualify or soften my remarks. I had known that the Reformation was over for me in my heart, but now I knew it was over in my head.[1]

The reason I had hesitated in coming to this conclusion before that moment was simple enough. If the Protestant Reformation was really over, then shouldn't I stop protesting and make peace with my original home? That is, shouldn't I become a Roman Catholic? That was much easier said than done. It was one thing to say that Protestantism had worn out its welcome in the modern world or that it had achieved all of its goals. It was a completely other thing to actually take the steps toward becoming Catholic. After all, I was raised with the typical anti-Catholic prejudices that were still in circulation in my youth. Those prejudices usually came down to one basic question: How could I submit myself to the authority of the Pope?

How could I do anything else? Consider the following analogy. Imagine that you grew up in a large family with a father who was occasionally verbally abusive toward the older children. (Sadly, for some of you this will be a reality rather than a hypothetical scenario, but please stay with me.) Let us say that your older sisters spent years trying to persuade your father to improve his behavior. After that strategy failed, your older brothers confronted your father and then left the house altogether, declaring that your father had forfeited his parental rights and authority. They told you when they left that your father did not really love them and that he demanded too much from them instead of just supporting them in their decisions and actions. You are not so sure about their judgment, since your father has done nothing personally against you and you believe that parental authority cannot very easily be denied. Nevertheless, you follow your older siblings out of the household and into a new family structure. One of the brothers claims to be the new leader of the family while others contend with him for that title. Eventually, the tensions among your siblings become unbearable, and the family splinters into various factions, many of which are hardly on speaking terms anymore.

Years later, you discover that your father was innocent of some of the charges your brothers made against him. You also learn that he has apologized for the abuses and changed his ways. Some of your younger brothers and sisters remained with him and they love him dearly. They tell you he has been a good father, protecting and providing for them, indeed, sacrificing greatly on their behalf. You now realize that your father loved you all along and that your older brothers have actually committed many of the same deeds that they alleged against your father. Now assume that your father is still alive and wants you back in his family. What do you do?

Ok, I admit it. I have set up this analogy to lead you, dear reader, to the answer that I want you to give. Once again I have gotten myself into bad pedagogy, and it does not help matters much to confess what I have done. I have created a situation where the answer is obvious, and major decisions about religion (or anything else, for that matter) are rarely so simple. Nonetheless, this is the situation that best describes how I thought about my own personal decision. Given the way I came to understand the history of the Reformation, my decision was natural and inevitable. I was the younger brother in this story, and although I loved my older brothers and learned so much from them, I decided to go back to my father. I accepted his authority and began longing for the day when our entire family would be healed and reunited.

Description led to action. After lecturing on the Reformation for years, I had developed a narrative of what had happened in the Christian break-up, and once I imagined myself as a character in that story, I knew what I had to do. The Protestant Reformation had broken up the unity of the Christian Church in order to advance certain theological and practical reforms. Theologically, it emphasized the importance of grace in new and exciting ways. Practically speaking, it sought to end various abuses of power linked to false promises about grace. The genius of the Protestant Reformation, and the reason it was so successful in creating new churches that remain vital to this day, is that it subordinated its criticism of church corruption to its construction of a theology of grace. If grace is free, then the Roman Catholic Church was wrong to be involved in so many activities that appeared to be selling grace to the masses. Many groups and individuals had called for reform prior to the Reformation, but Martin Luther and company were different because they had a positive message to go along with their dire prognosis of Rome's questionable practices.

The problem is that I had concluded that many of the Protestant criticisms were exaggerated and distorted and that the Catholic Church had never stopped preaching the message of grace. Moreover, it seemed to me that Rome had cleaned up its objectionable and corrupt practices. True, Protestantism had opened up new avenues of religious energy and spiritual insight, but it had also become mired in just as many questionable beliefs and practices as medieval Catholicism. When I added up all of those points with the most crucial one—that I believed Jesus Christ wanted His church to be united in one institutional body to reflect His own unity with the Father—I was led to a simple conclusion. I had to return to Rome whether I welcomed it or not—because I knew that Rome would welcome me.

The only alternative, it seemed to me, was to reject the idea that Christianity needs authority and that institutional authority is a legitimate, indeed, a necessary expression of God's will for His people. To return to my family analogy, I had concluded that, regardless of all the arguments about what my father did or did not do to my brothers and sisters, fatherhood itself was not the problem. Some men might not be good fathers, but fatherhood was still a tradition I was not ready to abandon. Someone else in that situation might have decided differently. They might have come to the conclusion that they did not need a father anymore, indeed, that paternal authority in general is an obsolete form of power. Families, that person might decide, should be free to create their own structures of authority, or to live without any form of authority at all.

There are churches that deny the necessity for institutional authority. My grandfather came from a family of devoted Quakers. They believed that Christianity has no need for an ordained class of ministers. In fact, they did not believe in any outward signs of religion, including rituals like the Lord's Supper, which they thought should happen only in the privacy of one's heart, not as a public act of administering bread and wine (or juice) to a congregation. They also believed that their church was the only right way to worship God. My great grandmother, in fact, was known for telling people that "if you are not a Quaker, you are going to hell." They had a lot of strong expressions of authority for being such a small branch on the Christian tree—and a branch that insisted it did not need anything but its own serious intentions to keep growing.

Quakers today are not as certain about themselves as my great grandmother was, but they still believe that the only religious author-ity is the authority that comes from within their hearts, and far from growing, their shrinking numbers have made them little more than a twig on the Christian tree that is impossible to see from a distance. Don't get me wrong. Quakers have done a lot of good in the world, and I am proud of my Quaker heritage. Nonetheless, I cannot accept their view of religious authority. When you make your own heart (that is, your feelings or personal experiences) the source of your religious authority, you have not gotten rid of authority. In fact, you are at risk of becoming an authoritarian, even if you are not as judgmental as my great grandmother.

As Bob Dylan sang in one of the great songs from his Gospel period, "Gotta Serve Somebody":

> *You may be an ambassador to England or France*
> *You may like to gamble, you might like to dance*
> *You may be the heavyweight champion of the world*
> *You may be a socialite with a long string of pearls.*
> *But you're gonna have to serve somebody, yes indeed*
> *You're going to have to serve somebody,*
> *It may be the devil or it may be the Lord*
> *But you're gonna have to serve somebody.*[2]

By somebody, Dylan did not mean yourself. Serving yourself is not a means of escaping the plain hard truth that you have to serve somebody else.

Students of politics have long recognized that structures of authority are necessary in our lives and have given this insight the name of "the principle of sovereignty." Even in a system of government that distributes power among various balanced branches, somebody has to make the call in times of emergency or serious conflict. Legislatures can argue all they want, but somebody has to call for a vote, and once the vote is taken, somebody has to be responsible for enforcing the decision. The sovereign does not have to be a king or queen, but somebody has to be the sovereign. In common language, the buck has to stop somewhere. Anarchy is the only real alternative to the principle of sovereignty, and although anarchy is not taken seriously in any political circles that I know about, it is taken seriously in religious circles. To return to Dylan's song, why can't Christians just serve the Lord and nobody else? The answer is that if you do not have external guidance in serving the Lord, you have to look within, but how can you tell if you are looking at the Lord within or just a mirror of yourself? If authority comes from within, as my Quaker ancestors firmly believed, then everyone is their own master. In the realm of politics, that is impossible, but in the realm of the spirit, such individualism is just as much of a disaster. Christianity cannot survive anarchy any more than any government in the world can.

Most Protestants are not Quakers, of course, and the great majority of Protestants have no difficulty in acknowledging the importance of institutionalized religious authority. Nonetheless, when the Christian world was torn apart by the religious conflicts of the sixteenth century, two consequences followed.

First, nation-states with all of their power took over the role of sovereign authority from the Church. While the Catholic Church used to keep political power in check by being an institution that crossed political boundaries, nations now keep religion in line. Indeed, nation-states have far more power than the Catholic Church ever had.

Second, although many nation-states established official and government-supported churches after the Reformation, the fragmentation of Christendom inevitably led to a radically pluralistic Christian culture. Personal choice began trumping tradition in the lives of many Christians. Rather than simply going to the church that was closest to where you lived, there were multiple church traditions in most communities. People were free to choose among them, which subjected sacred traditions to personal preferences and changing fashions. Religious individualism might not have been the primary aim of the Protestant Reformation, but it was an unintended consequence, and as a fragmented Christianity gradually lost influence in the world, religious individualism turned into theological anarchy. Paganism has come roaring back as a popular form of religion, those who locate themselves in the category of the unchurched are growing rapidly in America, and even atheists want all the perks and advantages of being called a religion. When it comes to religious beliefs, anything goes, and everything traditional is in danger of having come and gone away forever.[3]

Protestants who have hung onto some form of religious authority tend to locate that authority in one of three places. Those on the conservative or fundamentalist wing of Protestantism take an objective view of religious authority by finding it in (and limiting it to) the pages of the Bible. Those on the more liberal or mainstream wing of Protestantism take a subjective view of religious authority by locating it in personal experience or inner thoughts and intentions. Increasingly, a number of Christians in every kind of church locate religious authority in social movements or political agendas.

Take the objective approach first. I agree that the Bible is the inspired Word of God, completely trustworthy regarding anything to do with our salvation, but confining authority to its literal meaning does not do the majesty of the Bible justice. The Bible is trustworthy because it is the record of what God has spoken to us and how God wants to be heard by us. God communicates through the words of the Bible, but He is not limited by them. God speaks to many people in the Bible, but He continues to communicate to believers to this day. The Bible teaches us how to listen to His plan for our lives, but it does not silence God, nor does it deafen us to His continuing presence. The Bible is God's Word, but it is not God's only words.

Consider this example. A year after my wife and I started dating, she went off to Germany on a prestigious fellowship and I started graduate school in Chicago. This was before the days of computers and cell phones, so we wrote each other—a lot! Those letters are precious and shaped our subsequent relationship. But it would have been bizarre if, upon her return from Germany, I had told her that I knew so much about her from her letters that I did not need to hear from her face to face. Her letters were her word, and her words were sacred to me. We honor the pledges we made to each other in those letters to this day, but the purpose of those letters was to bring us into an intimate relationship that is ongoing, dynamic, and, we pray, eternal. That is the way the Bible should be. It governs, shapes, and regulates our relationship with God, but it is not a substitute for that relationship. The Bible is a love letter from God, but it would be a shame to love the letter more than God.

The subjective approach is also looking for religious certainty, but it listens to the inner heart rather than the written word. I grew up in an evangelical church that emphasized the singular drama of the born again experience of grace. Salvation was a matter of publicly confessing that Jesus Christ is your lord and savior. It was not enough to say the words. You had to feel them in the right way. Unfortunately, I was never sure that I felt them with sufficient emotional strength. How can you ever know that your heart is right? Feelings are too unstable to provide the foundation for religious authority.

Emotions ebb and flow, but what about the need for social change? Many Christians find themselves united in the aim of making the world a better place. Certainly, loving others and loving God go hand in hand, and the Church should be a school of social justice as well as a training ground for individual virtue. Nonetheless, giving to the poor and defending victims of social prejudice should flow from rather than take the place of the worship of God. Indeed, the means for achieving social justice are so varied and contested that unless justice is grounded in worship, political partisanship will replace the authority of the Church. Moreover, for all the emphasis on social justice, the authority of public action typically comes down to the sincerity of one's intentions. If caring about others is the basis for faith, how do we know when we care enough? And how do we keep from experiencing pride in our actions and thus nullifying their spiritual value?

It took me several years after my classroom confession that the Protestant Reformation was over for me to get up the nerve to become Roman Catholic, which I finally did on Easter 2007. When a Protestant becomes a Catholic, Catholics call it "coming home," or, more officially, being received into full communion with the Roman Catholic Church. Catholics recognize Protestants as their brothers and sisters in Christ, but they mourn their status as separated from the Church that looks to the Bishop of Rome for direction and guidance. From the Catholic perspective, Protestants do not convert to a new religion when they "come home." Instead, they return to the core tradition that has tried its best to remain true to everything that Jesus taught His disciples. To me, however, becoming Catholic felt like a trip to a new land, not a visit to the old neighborhood. I was not used to the dignity, quiet, and splendor of the Catholic Mass, and I am still learning to appreciate its myriad details and depths.

Becoming Catholic was an adventure for me, but I never could have anticipated how my journey to Rome would also take me deep into the spiritual geography of Mormonism. After I became Catholic, I found myself able to appreciate for the first time how Joseph Smith (1805–1844), the Mormon Prophet, also struggled with the problem of religious authority in his search for a more comprehensive and integrated form of the Christian faith. I had thought about Mormonism before, but it was only after my conversion that I was struck by how deeply affected Joseph was by the fragmentation of Christendom (Latter-day Saints often refer to him by his first name, so I will follow that practice here). When he was growing up, Joseph did not know any Catholics, but he knew a lot of Protestants, and their competing claims and polemical disputes rankled his soul. He seems to have internalized the spiritual pain of Christian divisions more than any other man of the nineteenth century. In times of religious crisis, saints and prophets often hear God speak directly to them, which is what Joseph claims happened to him. I want to save the question of God speaking directly to people after the time of the Bible for later in this book (chapter 4). That is a topic worth pondering in a section of its own. For now, I want to say that I see the life and theology of Joseph Smith emerging out of the social and theological anarchy of the Protestant Reformation. He desperately sought church unity, and he thought that he had to leave Protestantism behind in order to find it. Joseph came to the same conclusion that I did back in 2004. He too realized that the Protestant Reformation was over.

In his own account, Joseph lived at a time that was full of "unusual excitement on the subject of religion." The Methodists brought revivalism to upstate New York, but the increase in religious fervor had the unintended effect of magnifying theological differences. In his words, "great multitudes united themselves to the different religious parties, which created no small stir and division amongst the people, some crying, 'Lo, here!' and others, 'Lo, there!' Some were contending for the Methodist faith, some for the Presbyterian, and some for the Baptist." Three Protestant churches competing for members hardly sounds like radical religious pluralism to our modern ears, but Joseph took the call of Christian unity seriously, and the theological differences he found in these churches were startling. He was especially sensitive to the fact that "the great zeal manifested by the respective clergy, who were active in getting up and promoting this extraordinary sense of religious feeling," did not result in lasting social change. The good feeling of revival was replaced by "a strife of words and a contest about opinions." Joseph followed the debates carefully but was left asking himself, "What is to be done? Who of all these parties are right; or, are they all wrong together? If any one of them be right, which is it, and how shall I know it?"[4]

His words poignantly capture the fundamental situation of a divided Protestantism. In later chapters I want to return to Joseph's story to examine how he sought inspiration from God and what kind of revelation he found. For now I think it is enough to say that Joseph believed that God appeared to him and that he felt called to a prophetic vocation. What set him apart, however, from the many mystics and prophets throughout history who have recorded their auditory and visual experiences of God was his sensitivity to the fragility of religious authority and his recognition that the traditions of the Church needed to be re-established on the grounds of a renewal of the prophetic tradition. In other words, he instinctively understood that religion without authority is merely passing fad or speculative fantasy.

Joseph's principle of sovereignty, to use that phrase, was remarkably democratic, because he had no difficulties in delegating responsibilities and authority. It was also deeply biblical and surprisingly Catholic. To understand these remarks, I need to provide some historical background. Joseph made the most important decisions regarding the structure of the LDS Church after the so-called Zion's Camp march, which was an expedition that Joseph led from Kirtland, Ohio, to Clay County, Missouri, in 1834. The journey's goal was to support, defend, and join Latter-day Saints who had gathered in Missouri to begin the work of building a new Christian community. This American City of Zion was to be a New Jerusalem which would, Mormons hoped, usher in the millennial reign of Jesus Christ. Among other things, rumors that the Saints supported the abolition of slavery led some Missouri residents to organize militias and attack the Saints. Joseph received a revelation calling for an expedition to "redeem Zion" and 200 men, women and children marched through Illinois and Indiana to Missouri. Once there, Joseph tried to negotiate for the return of Mormon property and the safety of Mormon settlers, but after the negotiations failed and cholera broke out, he disbanded the camp.

The expedition was a test of faith, but its practical failure also constituted a political crisis for the Saints. Expectations had been high for a resolution of the Missouri situation, so when Joseph returned to Ohio, he met disappointment, frustration, and resistance. This was a moment ripe for a new political and social arrangement. A lesser man of God would have asserted his sovereign authority over his flock in order to silence critics and ban outsiders. Instead, Joseph reached deep into biblical and early Christian sources to share his power with others. He received a message from God that "there has been a day of calling, but the time has come for a day of choosing, and let those be chosen that are worthy."[5] Joseph relied on the advice of three of the witnesses to the Book of Mormon to call upon twelve men, all of whom had been part of Camp Zion, to constitute what he called the first Quorum of the Twelve Apostles. He then called seventy men to be members of what Mormons call the Quorum of the Seventies. The details of these groups have changed over the years, but the First Presidency, the Quorum of the Twelve Apostles, and the Quorum of the Seventy, are still the basic structure of the general hierarchy of the LDS Church.

The numbers twelve and seventy were obviously not a random choice. Twelve is the number of disciples that Jesus chose to lead his religious movement. Seventy is more obscure to most Christians, but it is drawn from Luke 10:1, where Jesus appointed seventy men to go two-by-two spreading the Gospel. And in fact, Joseph instructed the twelve and the seventy to take the Christian message to those who have not heard it, even into foreign lands. They had priestly authority to instruct others in the faith and to perform all that needed to be done for their salvation.

Joseph did not seek his own advantage through these appointments. Instead, he empowered others in a remarkably self-effacing manner. He sent his most trustworthy followers away from his presence, indeed, in many cases, he sent them overseas. Nonetheless, he remained in charge of the LDS Church. He was the President of the Church and head of what Latter-day Saints call the "First Presidency" (the presiding hierarchical quorum of Mormonism).

What is significant to me is that Joseph was reconstituting the apostolic unity that provided the original organizational foundation of the New Testament Church.[6] He did not refer to himself as a new Peter, but that is what he looks like from the Roman Catholic perspective. His leadership was both confident and collegial. He treated the other Apostles as brothers, not as their ruler, let alone a tyrant. He consulted with them, encouraged them, but in the end, he was the one who gave them their tasks and missions, and they always reported back to him.

His quest for renewed religious authority was not limited to these church offices. He continued to add new scriptures to the books of the Bible, sometimes by providing new translations of the King James Version of the Bible. Yet it was his own prophetic authority that served as the basis for his new religious movement, and he exercised that authority through a very Catholic understanding of the collaboration of the apostles, with one among them at their head, as the model for church structure. And he embraced the Catholic insistence that the Church should be led by priests who must be endowed with spiritual power by the successors to the apostles.

From the Roman Catholic perspective, this reconstitution of their own view of authority will look a bit like a case of "reinventing the wheel." I do not mean that in a derogatory way. The very word "catholic" means universal, so Catholics tend not to be surprised when other Christians come to agree with them about what Christianity is. In fact, Catholics think that every non-Catholic church imitates, in its own incomplete way, the basics of the Catholic faith. In Joseph's day, and in his part of the world, the universal features of the Catholic faith had been neglected and mishandled, but the pieces were still there, waiting to be put back together.

The reason this Catholic connection is not better understood is that the history of Mormonism has long been restrained by Protestant scholarship. Protestants dominated the American religious scene in the nineteenth century just as they dominated the historical interpretation of America throughout the twentieth. From the perspective of the centrist culture of the Protestant social establishment that emerged in the nineteenth century and held sway throughout the twentieth, Mormonism was a bizarre conglomeration of irrational beliefs and superstitious practices, a relic of more exuberant and irrational times. But what if Mormons were not trying to be Protestants? What if Mormons were trying to create a more authoritarian, ritualized, and sacramental version of the Christian faith? What if, that is, they were reinventing Roman Catholicism for a time and place where Catholicism was all but unknown—and to the extent that it was known, it was as misunderstood as Mormonism?

To see this point, imagine a society that invents the wheel and then forgets all about it. Few vestiges of its impact remain when, all of a sudden, somebody comes along and discovers how great wheels are. That person is to be congratulated and celebrated for his breakthrough. He has done a great good for his society. Just because somebody else beat him to the idea long ago does not mean that he has not been inspired to make what to him was a new discovery. Of course, if the original inventor of the wheel and his descendants had done a better job of using and preserving it, then the genius of the new inventor would not have been needed.

Let us modify the story a little bit. What if the original inventor of the wheel had been driven out of his society, but his descendants flourished elsewhere. Wouldn't the new inventor and his friends be curious what the older inventor had done? At the very least, the two groups could compare notes on how useful their shared technology is.

Joseph reinvented the theological wheel of apostolic succession (the idea that the leadership of the church should be in the hands of men who are spiritual heirs of the original ministry of the twelve apostles) and the Petrine Primacy (the idea that Jesus singled out Simon Peter to hold the first place of honor and authority among the apostles). That should not cast him in a negative light to Roman Catholics. Indeed, it should affirm Catholics in their understanding of religious authority. I see no reason why Catholics cannot believe that Joseph was inspired by the light of Christ to seek an institutional authority that was basically a tribute to the Roman Catholic Church. Catholics should welcome the Saints as younger brothers and sisters in Christ who were, throughout the nineteenth century, struggling to resolve the problems inherent in Protestantism by drawing from the wisdom and example of the ancient Roman Church. And Mormons could likewise look to Catholics for guidance and inspiration, given that Catholicism is the one Christian tradition (along with its sister tradition, Eastern Orthodoxy) that has tried the hardest to remain in continuity with the authority of the original twelve.

Protestantism shattered the unity of the body of Christ, and Joseph tried to put it back together again. Nothing in Joseph's day and age would have prompted or encouraged him to turn to Rome as the source of what he sought. So he made his own Roman way. And nothing is stopping Mormons from looking to Rome for collegiality and dialogue today.

Alonzo

I was reared in the Greek Orthodox tradition—a faith I deeply love for the beauty of its liturgy and its conservative approach to theology. As a practicing Orthodox, I felt my faith's theological mantra could be something like: "If it was doctrinally good enough for Jesus and the ancient Church, it should be good enough for us today!" Growing up in the post-Vatican II era, when Catholicism had suddenly begun to feel more closely aligned with Protestantism than Orthodoxy, I liked the antique feel of the forms of worship and theology of the Greek Orthodox tradition. To me, there was something very ancient about it—some undeniable effort to avoid the branches and cling to the trunk—which made me feel secure in my faith.

Like Stephen, I have experienced religious transitions and transformations in my life too—and for me these changes have also been related to the question of religious authority. Theologically speaking, I am somewhat of an oxymoron: raised Greek Orthodox, converted to Mormonism, educated in theology at a liberal Catholic University and a conservative Protestant Seminary—now a professor of world religions at Brigham Young University. Am I coming or going? On paper, it is a bit hard to tell!

Because, like Roman Catholics, the Eastern Orthodox believe in Apostolic Succession, my epiphany regarding religious authority was quite different from Stephen's. Historically, I see the need for the Reformation and the Catholic Counter Reformation. By the fourteenth century, things had in many ways gone awry. Yet, with Stephen, I must agree—during the Catholic Counter Reformation, the Church of Rome made many of the changes insisted upon by men like Wycliffe, Tyndale, and Luther. In a sense, the Protestant Reformation did what it needed to do. Latter-day Saints are wont to say that the Reformation was inspired of God. For Mormons, Deity's hand was in the details for at least two reasons. First, it provoked some internal reforms, ending many years of abuses and corruption. But second, the Reformation also broke the hold Catholicism had on the world—it made it acceptable to be a Christian and yet not a Catholic. That is in no way intended to be a polemic against Catholicism. Rather, it is a statement about the beauty of the age in which we live. The ability to exercise our agency—to choose to worship how, where, or what we may. That ability to choose was paramount for Joseph Smith. What he proposed, by establishing Mormonism, was so radical that had the Reformation not taken place, Joseph's message would not have been heard.

The Reformation certainly provoked moral reform in the Catholic Church. But the Councils of Trent and Vatican I pushed back on Reformation theology—as did the Catholic Counter Reformation of the sixteenth and seventeenth century. It was really Vatican II that made sincere efforts to move the Church to a position that would be acceptable—theologically and ecclesiastically—to mainstream Protestantism. After Vatican II, the Church suddenly felt more Protestant—in its worship forms and in its teachings. Thanks to John XXIII and Paul VI, this was a different kind of Ecumenical Council, with a different purpose and a dramatically different outcome. The previous twenty ecumenical councils had all been called to combat heresy in the world—heresies outside of the Church. In a sense, the Second Vatican Council (the 21st ecumenical council) sought to look for strengths outside of the church and adjust Catholic teaching to honor and assimilate them. This has long been a frustration to many ultra conservative Roman Catholics, who feel that through Vatican II the Church in many ways "sold out" to the Protestants or outright apostatized.[7]

Is Webb right in claiming that the Reformation is over? I think he is! The queries and concerns of the reformers have largely been answered. And in the centuries since Wycliffe and Luther, the Catholics have made the major changes asked for. For this LDS outsider, Vatican II was Rome's attempt to offer the olive branch to the Protestants. Indeed, it seems evident to an outsider that one of the major outcomes desired by that council was the reunification of Catholics and their separated brethren. A great deal of what came out of Vatican II should appease most Protestants. And yet, it did not really work. Very few of the "separated brethren" rejoined; and a number of conservative Catholics headed for the door.

Like the Catholic Counter Reformation or the Council of Trent, Mormonism was somewhat of a response to the Protestant Reformation. As Stephen has shown, Joseph Smith was reared in a Protestant milieu—and was greatly troubled by the fractured nature of Christianity. Ironically, most Christians do not seem that bothered by how void of unity the faith founded by Jesus is. But Joseph was bothered—as are Stephen and I. As Roman Catholic scholar, Robert P. George, has noted:

> Christian division is a scandal. It is contrary to the express will of Christ. Nothing more profoundly impedes the fulfillment of our Lord's Great Commission to go forth into the world and make disciples of all nations. Division among Christians is a stumbling block to many people to whom the gospel is preached. They ask: "How can I know that the Christian gospel is true if Christians themselves cannot agree about the fundamental points of its meaning? Whose gospel shall I believe: that of the Catholics? the Eastern Orthodox? the Protestants?—which Protestants? the Anglicans? the Methodists?—which Methodists? the Lutherans?—which ones? the Presbyterians?—PCUSA or PCA? the Baptists?—Southern or American? On what authority am I being asked to choose? On what basis am I to decide?"[8]

As a religion, Christianity is in an awful way! We are terribly fragmented. Attempts at reconciliation, such as Vatican II, have not succeeded. What are we to do? For Mormonism, the crisis of religious authority is the primary cause of our dilemma.

While in graduate school, I was enrolled in a class taught by a rather prominent Roman Catholic scholar. He was curious about why a Mormon was taking a graduate degree at a Catholic university. He invited me into his office, where he asked me countless questions. He was particularly drawn to the teachings of Joseph Smith—as the prophet had taught things which resolved some long-standing doctrinal concerns this renowned academic had struggled with for many years. That being said, while behind closed doors this man was fascinated by the teachings of my faith, nevertheless, publicly he treated me with a great deal of condescension because I was a Latter-day Saint. He would take jabs at my religion in class, in front of the other students. On one occasion, unprovoked, he noted to our class: "Mormons are a lot like the earliest Christians—primitive and naïve." I remember thinking: "Wow! I know I'm supposed to be offended by that comment. But the fact that a scholar of this caliber is acknowledging that my faith is a lot like the early Christian Church is hardly offensive to me. If I had to choose to be like someone (doctrinally, or otherwise), would it be Augustine or Jesus? Aquinas or the Twelve Apostles? If we Mormons are really like the 'primitive' ancient Church, we must be doing something right!" For Joseph Smith, the great crisis in Christianity arose because of the loss of the Apostles after the death of Jesus. History bears out the fact that the Church, after the death of Jesus—and particularly after the death of the Apostles—began to fragment. There were numerous brands of Christianity in the second and third centuries. Joseph Smith believed this was largely due to the loss of universal authority: the loss of a prophet or apostles to lead and guide the Church.

Do not misunderstand me. There is no denying that Bishops continued to exist after the death of the Apostles, and for Catholics this resolves the crisis of Apostolic Succession. But for Joseph—and for Mormons—the continuity of the office of the Bishop still left a void of religious authority in the Church. Because the New Testament records Bishops existing at the same time that the Apostles existed, Latter-day Saints see those two priesthood positions or offices as distinct from each other. Thus, while Roman Catholics would trace their Apostolic Authority or Succession through the Bishops of Rome, Latter-day Saints hold that John was the last of the Apostles—and that apostolic (or universal) authority was lost at the end of the first century. Bishops continued to run local congregations and had authority to do so. But the apostles were gone. And Christianity, from a Mormon perspective, was run on a local level until around the time of the pontificate of Pope Leo I (d. A.D. 461), when a degree of universal authority was reintroduced into the church by Roman Catholicism. So, the view of Roman Catholicism has traditionally been that Apostles and Bishops are synonymous[9]—and that there has been an unbroken line of bishops since the days of Peter, each of which held apostolic authority. For Latter-day Saints, on the other hand, the view has been that Apostles and Bishops are two different offices within the Church, and that the apostolic office was lost at the end of the first century, leaving Bishops to run their individual stewardships, but leaving the Church without a universal head. From the perspective of Latter-day Saints, Leo the Great sought to reintroduce a sense of "universal authority" into the Church through his pontificate—something not consistently present after the death of the Twelve and prior to the fifth century.

So what really was Joseph Smith doing? What was he trying to accomplish by starting The Church of Jesus Christ of Latter-day Saints that April morn of 1830? These questions are at the heart of Mormonism—and at the heart of the crisis of religious authority in Christianity today.

In Joseph Smith's understanding, the various offices of the priesthood—the various vocations within the Church—each hold a different level or type of authority and stewardship. In LDS ecclesiology, the highest level of priesthood "authority" or "power" is resident in an apostle. Peter was given "the keys of the kingdom of heaven" by which he had the power to "bind on earth" and "in heaven" (Matthew 16:19). Mormons do not see their bishops—or bishops in any denomination—as having that level of power. They certainly acknowledge that the apostles of old had it. But, in LDS thinking, with the death of the last apostle that power to "bind" or "seal" on earth and in heaven was lost. Part of what those "keys" represented, Latter-day Saints believe, is the ability to receive revelation for the entire Church—the universal Church. Peter had that ability, along with his brethren in the Twelve. The bishops upon the earth at the same time as Peter did not.

For Joseph, a "reformation" of the Church was not sufficient. Things of a divine nature had been lost—priesthood "keys" and the power to receive revelations for the world. What Joseph was engaged in was a "restoration" of primitive Christianity. He, through heavenly manifestations, was returning to the earth not just lost ideas but lost powers. Through angelic ministrations akin to those of the biblical era, Joseph received a restoration of the lost "keys" or "powers" resident in the ancient Church.

He was not "changing" what was had in the Church of his day: he was "restoring" what was lost from the Church of antiquity. Just as Judaism by the first century had lost some of its prophetic zeal while being occupied by foreign powers, Christianity by the fourteenth century was in need of reform but was facing too many conflicting reform movements. In response to the religious decline of Judaism, God sent Jesus to get things back on target. And Jesus "restored" many lost truths and powers. In response to the problems the reformers saw, Latter-day Saints believe God sent Joseph to "restore" many lost truths and powers. Thus, Mormonism is not just another denomination of Christianity. It is a restoration of primitive or biblical Christianity. And like Roman Catholics, who rely on Apostolic Succession for their claims to authority, members of The Church of Jesus Christ of Latter-day Saints hold that they too have apostolic succession—not from Peter to their current prophet, but from Jesus to Peter, and from the resurrected Peter (appearing as one of many angels) to the Prophet Joseph Smith, and from Joseph's successors to the current prophet and apostles. One LDS leader shared an experience he had with a Roman Catholic scholar, which well highlights the LDS view of things.

Many years ago a learned man, a member of the Roman Catholic Church, came to Utah and spoke from the stand of the Salt Lake Tabernacle. I became well-acquainted with him, and we conversed freely and frankly. A great scholar, with perhaps a dozen languages at his tongue's end, he seemed to know all about theology, law, literature, science, and philosophy. One day he said to me: "You Mormons are all ignoramuses. You don't even know the strength of your own position. It is so strong that there is only one other tenable in the whole Christian world, and that is the position of the Catholic Church. The issue is between Catholicism and Mormonism. If we are right, you are wrong; if you are right, we are wrong; and that's all there is to it. The Protestants haven't a leg to stand on. For, if we are wrong, they are wrong with us, since they were a part of us and went out from us: while if we are right, they are apostates whom we cut off long ago. If we have the apostolic succession from St. Peter, as we claim, there is no need of Joseph Smith and Mormonism: but if we have not that succession, then such a man as Joseph Smith was necessary, and Mormonism's attitude is the only consistent one. It is either the perpetuation of the gospel from ancient times, or the restoration of the gospel in latter days."[10]

Catholics and Latter-day Saints alike understand the need for the Reformation. And yet, we also both share a concern that some of the fall-out of the Reformation was a loss of Christian cohesiveness. In addition, because of the Reformation, Protestantism has largely lost a sense of apostolic authority. That concept of "keys"—mentioned by Christ, believed by Catholics to be held by the pope, and believed by Mormons to be held by the prophet—has largely been lost among our "separated brethren." Whereas Catholics still seek a universal Church, and Latter-day Saints predict the return of one, Protestants seem largely unconcerned about unification—with Catholicism, or with the other branches of Protestantism.

Joseph Smith grew up in a Protestant environment. The denominations he knew and interacted with were Protestant. As far as we know, he was unacquainted in his early years with Catholicism, its teachings and history. Would it have made a difference if he had known some Roman Catholics, or had frequented the Mass? It seems highly unlikely. You see, Joseph's fixation was with the ancient Church—in doctrines but also in authority. Particularly in authority! Joseph was looking for apostles and prophets—not just in name, but in roles and experience. He was looking for a Church that claimed "the gift of tongues, prophecy, revelation, visions, healing, interpretation of tongues, and so forth" (*Article of Faith* 7). He was looking for "the same organization that existed in the Primitive Church, namely, apostles, prophets, pastors, teachers, evangelists, and so forth." He was looking for a faith that believed "all that God has revealed, all that He does now reveal, and" that expected that God would "yet reveal many great and important things pertaining to the Kingdom of God" (*Article of Faith* 9). Thus, had Joseph known of the details of Catholicism, he would likely have been a bit less disheartened by all of the division he saw in Protestantism, but he would have nevertheless still struggled with what he perceived as the absence of part of the ancient Church in the modern Church. Joseph still would have sensed that a "reformation" (where the pope was called a prophet, cardinals were called apostles, and parish priests were called bishops) was not enough. God needed to "restore" those ancient "keys" or powers (along with doctrines) Joseph believed had been lost—a loss which resulted in the fragmentation of the church in the second and third centuries and also led to the Protestant Reformation.

Now, Stephen and I both see the need for apostolic authority—apostolic succession. We both see the dangers in the continuation of the fragmentation which the Protestant view on authority allows. However, I suppose we differ in at least one way. For Stephen, his conversion to Catholicism was a "return home" from his wilderness journey. He had come back to a much more ancient version of Christianity than he had been a part of—only to a version of it that had reformed itself. I, on the other hand, left a faith that believed in Apostolic Succession (i.e., Greek Orthodoxy), to join a Church that also believed in it. Why? Because, like Joseph, I longed for the faith of the Hebrew Bible and Greek New Testament—a faith that included "prophecy, revelation, visions, healing . . . and so forth" (*Article of Faith* 7). The authority was paramount for me—before and after my conversion. But the idea of living prophets and apostles was simply the fruit that evidenced to me—as they did to Joseph Smith—that I was in a place where that authority truly existed.

So, to reiterate Stephen's questions: "Did Joseph reinvent the wheel?" Is the LDS view of authority an "imitation" of the Roman Catholic model? No, not really! Joseph would have firmly agreed with the Catholic position that a "true" and "living" faith must have authority—apostolic authority. But his definition of that is slightly different than what he would have found in nineteenth-century Catholicism—or even in the twenty-first-century Church. Joseph would not have argued that he was "reinventing the wheel." Rather, he would have claimed that Jesus had given him the "wheel" back. And the version of the wheel that his good, earnest, and faithful brothers and sisters in Christ had was just not quite the one Jesus invented in the first place.

Now none of this is to be taken as an attack on Catholics, Protestants, or members of the Eastern Orthodox community. What I had hoped to do here was to describe how our positions are in many ways similar and in other ways different. But our goal is not to imply that one tradition should be respected and another should be discounted. On the contrary, what Christianity needs more of is mutual respect and a spirit of contemplation. In my own experience, becoming an LDS Christian has, in many ways, caused me to love and appreciate Catholicism in a way I did not prior to my conversion. It has made me more aware of the tremendous good that faith has done for Christianity, and for the world (and what God has done through it). I have prayed regularly (since his elevation) for Pope Francis—in the hope that God would use him for the good of the world. I would hope those of other Christian denominations would also pray for those not of their faith—that we might have unity and that God, through us, might accomplish His will.

Webb is right: Catholics and Mormons should see each other as relatives rather than enemies; as friends, not foes. Protestants and Eastern Orthodox are also are brothers in Christ. We all have things we can learn from each other: from our successes and our failures. For example, even on the subject of authority, each of us can learn from the Protestant experiment. Erasing a need for authority—for apostolic hierarchy—as the Reformation did, causes a fracturing of the faith; a fracturing that looks as though it will never be healed. From the Catholic experiment that we call Vatican II, a lesson can be learned regarding what Christians want and need. Where Rome loosened up on requirements, standards, and dogmas—even on whether there is salvation outside of the Church—more left than came into the newly calibrated faith. Those who truly wish to be religious want a hierarchy that offers certainty about authority, obedience, salvation, morality, and the like. From the Orthodox experiment, found in the ecumenical patriarch, we can learn how numerous denominations can be functionally independent and yet very united. Fifteen denominations running their own show, while acknowledging an ecumenical patriarch, is a model for Christian cooperation.

As Christians, there is so much we can learn from each other—on the subject of religious authority, but on other lessons of life and faith. And like Jesus, who openly ate with those considered "sinners" by the world, we too should be open to sit at the table of fellowship with those who believe differently than we: to hear what they have to say, to look for beauty in their traditions, to notice what God has done through them, and to build bridges in our common cause.

Stephen

Comparing Mormonism to Catholicism is in some like ways comparing David to Goliath. There are about 15 million Mormons in the world compared to around 1.2 billion Catholics. The Catholic Church is not just the big kid on the block. It owns the block and then some. More than one out of every six people on the planet is Catholic. Perhaps that is one of the reasons I find the Mormons so fascinating. Americans love to "root for the underdog," and Christians should not need to be reminded that they began as underdogs. The early Christians numbered only a few hundred, growing to several thousand in their early years. They constituted a small drop in the Roman Empire's very large bucket. Nonetheless, look at what they accomplished! Numbers can be deceiving, and small numbers especially so.

Membership in The Church of Jesus Christ of Latter-day Saints might be small compared to the Catholic Church, but the ideas behind the Saints are very large. Indeed, I think those ideas are large enough to merit the very big claim that Mormonism, Catholicism, and Eastern Orthodoxy represent the main options when it comes to thinking about the authority of the Christian faith.

Actually, I think Mormonism and Catholicism are less like contrasting alternatives than complementary versions of each other. Since all agree that the Roman Catholic Church is much older than the Latter-day Saints, and since the Catholic Church was for the most part identical with or at least the source of much of Western culture for so many centuries, it should not be surprising that every subsequent Western Christian tradition borrows from some aspects of Rome's many riches and resources. When I started thinking about Mormons and Catholics with regard to religious authority, I was really surprised by how similar they are. Bred in the bones of Catholicism is the idea that the Christian Church should be one, united, and comprehensive. Those who have joined other churches are separated from us (to speak as a Catholic), but they are not bad people nor are they wrong about everything they believe. Separation is not divorce. The word "separation" suggests a situation that is temporary, giving the parties time to work out their problems and achieve a reconciliation. Those who are separated have part of the truth but not its fullness. Catholics hope and pray for the eventual reunification of all branches of the Christian faith. (I will discuss why Catholics should but do not officially treat Mormons as "separated brethren" in chapter 5.)

I actually grew up in a church that was a product of nineteenth-century restorationist impulses. My church was part of the Stone-Campbell Movement, which emerged during the Second Great Awakening as an effort to unify Christianity on the basis of New Testament models of authority. Many Protestant traditions seek Christian unity by skipping over ancient rituals and diverse practices and going straight to a literal interpretation of the Bible. The restoring impulse of the Saints is different. They want a form of Christianity that is full of tradition, not a church that is wedded to the Bible alone. They are not primitivists, in the sense of wanting to live their Christian faith in the most stripped-down, streamlined, and simplistic manner. Neither are they romantics who imagine that a perfect organization of Christianity once existed and can never be achieved again. The Saints want to embody here and now the fullest expression of Christianity's truest possibilities. That is why I would suggest that the Saints have a catholic imagination in the sense of a small "c," since catholic means universal. The Saints do not want to be one sect among many. The Saints are not interested in carving out a theological niche to occupy. As Alonzo says of Joseph, for him, reformation was not enough. The Saints want it all. They are robustly imaginative and doctrinally comprehensive in their retrieval of the ancient church. They look back in order to have the widest possible horizon of what the future of Christianity can be.

What also sets them apart from other restorationist movements is that they do not just look back at the Bible. The restorationist church I grew up in was fundamentally Biblicist. Everything had to come from the Bible and only the Bible. Of course, we lived in a world that had all sorts of theological positions and practices not found in the Bible, which kept us busy trying to show that everything we believed had biblical precedent. The problem is that my church taught double predestination, biblical inerrancy, and forensic justification (the idea that salvation is a change in our legal status before God, not a change in our capacity to become more righteous), all of which are theological ideas not found explicitly in the pages of the New Testament. The Saints go back not to the Bible alone but also to the fullness of biblical traditions and early Christian practices, as that fullness is expounded and amplified in various revelations to Joseph Smith. The LDS version of theological fullness is not identical with the Catholic version, of course, but the emphasis on fullness is common to both traditions.

Both Mormonism and Catholicism can be stereotyped and misunderstood because of their commitment to the Gospel in all of its fullness. Both can appear baroque and ungainly to outsiders. Both are complex rather than simple forms of Christianity and both manage to preserve their complexity within a strongly hierarchical structure of authority.

Alonzo is right to emphasize how much disunity there was in the early church and the fact that it took a long time for the Bishop of Rome to emerge as the unifying church office. Several questions are important for our discussion.

First, would there have been more unity if the Bishop of Rome had not emerged as the Pope (the father) of all the faithful? I think the answer to that question is obvious. The Papacy kept the church united in times of incredible social, political, and cultural turmoil. This unity was preserved for centuries even in the midst of tensions between Western and Eastern forms of the faith as well as the challenges from those who rejected the early creeds. This does not mean that Popes were without flaws or that unity did not have its price. Yet, without the development of some kind of centralized authority, disobedience in the church would have been devastating to its globalizing mission, and heretical groups like the Gnostics would have been much more successful at claiming to represent the teachings of Jesus.

Second, was this centralization of authority in the Bishop of Rome biblically justified? As Alonzo points out, Peter was indeed given the keys to the kingdom of heaven. He was selected by Jesus Christ to be the leader of the Apostles. The historical evidence is clear that he ended up in Rome and that the Roman bishops traced their lineage as well as their claims to authority to him. It is possible that the Apostle Paul appointed a leader of the Roman Church before Peter's arrival, a man named Linus, which is why his name shows up on some lists as the first Pope. Other lists put him in the third position after Clement. The Catholic Church teaches that he came after Peter, who was the first Bishop of Rome. Whatever the order of Popes, the idea that Jesus gave Peter special authority and that he in turn passed that authority down to subsequent leaders of the Roman Church is hardly controversial. Nonetheless, it is one thing to say that subsequent Bishops of Rome claimed a lineage from Peter and it is another thing altogether to say that this lineage had continuous authority, which leads us to the next question.

Third, was this apostolic succession unbroken? The Latter-day Saints believe it was not, that, in fact, there was a great falling away (or apostasy) from early church teachings. Catholics believe that Bishops appointed other Bishops by laying their hands on them and praying for the Holy Spirit to guide them as they carried on the original mission of the Apostles. Even if there was not a literal laying on of hands from the first Bishops to all the rest, throughout every generation of church authority (and surely there was not!), the Catholic idea is that the office of the Bishop of Rome was in continuous occupation (at least the continuity was sufficient to preserve the ideal of apostolic succession) and that the holders of that office were guided by the Holy Spirit to play the role that Peter played among the original twelve.

This third question is where the Saints and Catholics divide, but it is also the question that can bring them together as they seek to better understand each other. As Alonzo points out, the Saints identify apostolic authority with revelation and spiritual power. Mormons, however, are not Pentecostals. They do not demand of their Apostles the display of spiritual gifts like tongue speaking, faith healing, and emotional exuberance. The earliest Mormons did display many of these spiritual gifts, like other Christians at that time, but as the Latter-day Saints grew and became more organized, apostolic authority was increasingly identified with the capacity to receive revelation, not the manifestation of unusual spiritual gifts like glossolalia. Joseph was a prophet because God spoke to him and he was true to what God told him, and because he was a prophet, he was authorized to appoint a new set of Apostles. Mormonism shares with some Protestants the idea that at some point in early Church history the original mission of the Apostles lost energy and focus and was distorted by foreign (Greek and Roman) influences. What is new about Mormonism is its connection of apostolic authority with revelation and its subordination of the office of the Apostles to the prerogative of a Prophet.[11]

The LDS view of succession, as Alonzo points out, runs from Peter directly to Joseph, skipping over centuries of Christian martyrs, missionaries, miracle workers, and yes, popes. This view of apostolic succession makes perfectly good sense given the LDS understanding of revelation. Mormons and Catholics alike believe that Jesus revealed His plans for the Church to the Apostles, but Mormons believe that those plans were not fully executed because the bond between apostolicity and revelation grew weak to the point that it was broken altogether. Even the best-laid plans go awry without ongoing communication from above, which is why God revealed those plans anew to Joseph, who in turn had the authority to appoint a new set of Apostles.

What is interesting is that Catholics and Mormons are in agreement that not all divine revelations are recorded in the Bible. Catholics believe that there are traditions that have been handed down from the Apostles through oral communication. They include infant baptism, the doctrine of the Trinity, purgatory, and Mary's perpetual virginity. None of these teachings are found explicitly in scripture, though Catholics believe that they are implied there and that they do not contradict scripture. Moreover, there are a variety of practices, like the permission to take an oath and resting on Sunday rather than Saturday that became the tradition of the Church even though they are not found in the Bible. Catholics accept the fact that their tradition evolves and changes, but Catholics do not believe that the Bishops of the Church are authorized to receive new revelations about the essentials of the faith beyond what the Bible and tradition jointly teach. The leadership of the Church is charged with interpreting, defending, and promoting revelation, and the Church has the responsibility of systematizing the content of revelation by the discipline of theology and the development of catechisms, but even the Pope cannot add to or subtract from the deposit of the faith found in the Bible and tradition.

So when the Saints say that revelation ceased with the end of the apostolic era, Catholics for the most part agree, although they do not think that revelations of a biblical magnitude began again with Joseph Smith. Two further distinctions need to be made. The first is the distinction between spiritual power and divine revelation. Catholics believed that spiritual power never left the Church after the apostolic era. Christians continued to work miracles and there were plenty of martyrs during the period of the Roman Empire who faced death with supernatural courage. Catholics take these displays of spiritual power as evidence that the Holy Spirit was guiding the Church (and has never abandoned the Church).

The other distinction is between biblical (or public) revelation and what Catholics call private revelation. Some Protestants argue that all genuine miracles ceased at a certain point in Church history, but Catholics stand firmly with Mormons in opposition to this view. Like Mormons, Catholics believe that God has not ceased speaking to people up to and including the present time. In fact, if Catholics were to accept the validity of Joseph's visions of God, they would put those visions in this category (but more on that in chapter 4).

Another comment on terminology is needed here. The Saints make a strong distinction between the office of an Apostle and the position of Bishops, whereas Catholics (and most other Christians) reserve the title Apostle to the first selected followers of Jesus (and their immediate replacements, including Paul, who was the "Apostle to the Gentiles"), although sometimes missionaries were called Apostles (Saint Patrick was called the Apostle to Ireland). Moreover, most Christian traditions, if they use the title of Bishop, use it as the name of a church leader who is in a position of authority over a number of priests and their local congregations and thus think of Bishops, following Catholic tradition, as exercising the same kind of authority as the Apostles exercised over the men they called to assist them. The Saints reserve the title Apostle for the President of the Church (and his two counselors) and the members of the Quorum of Twelve Apostles. LDS Apostles are thus the rough equivalent of the Pope and the Bishops of the Catholic Church (with the Quorum of the Twelve functioning in some ways analogously to the Cardinals of the Catholic Church). Both churches agree, however, that without these offices, which are grounded in the decisions of Jesus, there would be no legitimate authority in the Church.

A Catholic could go as far as this concerning the ministry of Joseph: He was a modern visionary not content to keep his revelations to himself. He wanted to reinvigorate the Church not through a revival of spiritual power alone but also through a restoration of proper authority. He lived in a milieu that had lost sight of the connection between Christian authority and the office of the Apostles. And he saw that the Protestant leadership all around him had, for the most part, turned its back on the reality of God's continuing revelations (what Catholics call private revelation) to ordinary people. In all of these ways, he was a true follower of Jesus who was seeking the structures of authority that already existed in the Catholic Church. Evidence of this claim can be found in the fact that his successors in the Latter-day Saints, called the Presidents of the Church, rarely claim to have revelations themselves. The LDS Presidents have become defenders, protectors, and promoters of the deposit of revelation that Joseph received. They function, in other words, in ways very similar to the Pope. They do not add to the truth of their Church but interpret, explain, and refine it.

So, should Mormonism try to play the role of David to Catholicism's Goliath? Both Mormons and Catholics worship the Messiah who came in the lineage of David, and both try to stand apart (and against) the Goliath of modern godlessness. A better question would be to return to the issue of religious unity and to phrase it in the pragmatic idiom that the Saints themselves often use in explicating the significance of their beliefs. Is acknowledging Joseph Smith's prophetic vocation more likely to bring unity to Christianity than acknowledging the primacy of the Bishop of Rome? I can hear skeptics say, "Most likely, neither!" I can hear devout Mormons point to the amazing growth of their Church, yet I can also hear Catholics point out that the only church with the institutional reach, theological breadth, and practical experience to make unity possible is the one centered in Rome. For my part, I wonder just how far a Catholic openness to Joseph and a Mormon openness to Rome would take the longing for Christian unity.

Alonzo

Over the years I have met a number of Christians dismissive of Mormonism based on its size or age. However, with Stephen I acknowledge that those are meaningless measures of a faith's "truthfulness" or "validity." First-century Christians were, by comparison to their contemporaries, small—particularly when compared to Judaism, out of which they had grown. Thus, though Latter-day Saints are miniscule when compared to other Christian denominations (out of which they have grown), as Stephen has often said to me, "look at what the Latter-day Saints have accomplished." Like the early Christians who were outnumbered by their Jewish and Pagan neighbors, but who grew at a rapid rate, Mormonism has done the same thing—and has had an influence rather out of proportion to its age and size.

In his response, Stephen suggested that Mormons do not go back to the Bible for their Christianity but, instead, to Joseph Smith's amplifying revelations and "prophetic authority." I would challenge, or at least nuance, that claim. Do Mormons look to other things in addition to the Bible for their fullest understanding of the Christian message? Absolutely! In this regard, they are much like Roman Catholics or Eastern Orthodox Christians with their comfort in allowing "tradition" and "scripture" to walk hand in hand, guiding the Church and defining the doctrine.[12] So also for Mormons, there is definitely a sense that the Bible is not the sole source for authoritative teaching or understanding about Jesus's message to the world. But Latter-day Saints certainly do not shy away from the Bible. They do not ignore it. They absolutely believe in the Holy Bible and its inspired nature and message. But they are also much like first-century Christians on this matter. Whereas many Protestants today go solely to the Bible for answers about God, salvation, or Church policy, had the first-century Christians done this they would have continued to do things like requiring circumcision for Gentile converts to Christianity—as that is what the Bible of their day taught. Jesus and His Apostles were inspired by the Spirit to introduce ideas, practices, and doctrines which were not in the Bible of their day (i.e., the "Old" Testament). They did not rely upon "ancient scripture" for their faith but upon "new revelation." That was the foundation for the teachings of the Church in the first century. What guided them was not the "New" Testament. It did not exist in their day. And it was not the "Old" Testament that determined their doctrine—as they largely used it as a proof text to show that Jesus was the Christ. But they saw its content and requirements as largely fulfilled and superseded by Jesus and His teachings—and the words of Christ's successors or Apostles. The "New" Testament was not the source for Christian doctrine. The acts of the Apostles created that document. The "Old" Testament was not the source, for Christ's words—and those of His Apostles—superseded that text. For the ancient Christians, the Bible did not make the Church, but the Church made the Bible. So it is with members of The Church of Jesus Christ of Latter-day Saints. They love the Bible. They cite is constantly. They revere its witness of Jesus. And they hold it to be the word of God. But like the ancient Christians, LDS Christians "believe all that God has revealed, all that He does now reveal," and they "believe that He will yet reveal many great and important things pertaining to the Kingdom of God" (*Article of Faith* 9). This certainly sets them apart from their Catholic brothers and sisters—and from contemporary Christianity in general. Stephen mentioned that Catholics largely believe that revelation to the Church ceased at the close of the Apostolic era, but that "private revelations" continued—constituted by personal promptings and epiphanies to individuals, but not to or for the Church as a whole. Mormons would acknowledge many of these "private revelations" as real and legitimate gifts from God to spiritually receptive, obedient, and truth-seeking followers of Christ. But for Latter-day Saints, in the prophetic arena God is the same yesterday, today, and forever. Mormons look at the historical practice—in both the Old and New Testaments—of God speaking through Patriarchs, Prophets, and Apostles; and Mormons hold that as significant, important, and even paramount. These ancient prophets were men who had more than just "private revelations." Thus, while LDS Christians believe in "private revelations"—including to those outside of their faith—they also hold that God's pattern has always been to provide for the Church individuals (like Moses, Isaiah, Ezekiel, Peter, and Paul) who were visionaries in the ultimate sense of the word. These were individuals who entertained angels, saw visions, and received direct revelations from God for the whole Church—the catholic (or universal) church. Joseph Smith once noted:

> You will admit that the word spoken to Noah was not sufficient
> for Abraham . . . but for himself he obtained promises at the hand
> of the Lord, and walked in that perfection . . . Isaac, the promised

seed, was not required to rest his hope alone upon the promises
made to his father Abraham, but was privileged with the . . . direct
voice of the Lord to him. If one man can live upon the revelations
given to another, might I not with propriety ask . . . have I not an
equal privilege with the ancient saints? And will not the Lord hear
my prayers, and listen to my cries as soon as he ever did theirs,
if I come to him in the manner they did? Or, is he a respecter of
persons?[13]

Joseph also taught: "God said, 'Thou shalt not kill;' at another time He said,
'Thou shalt utterly destroy.' This is the principle on which the government of
heaven is conducted—by revelation adapted to the circumstances in which
the children of the kingdom are placed."[14] Mormons staunchly believe in
the biblical model of presiding authorities who hold a calling and vocation
over and above that of the laity—and a significant part of that calling is that
they have visions and revelations for the Church as a whole. While there is
little question as to the holiness and spirituality of men like Pope Francis,
traditionally Catholic popes have not seen themselves as prophets in the
sense Moses or Isaiah were. Yet that is exactly what Mormons are claiming Joseph Smith and his successors are. And if there were ever a time in
which modern revelation of biblical proportions was needed in the Church
and world, it is now! LDS Christians believe Mormonism is simply a return
to the Christianity of the Bible—when the heavens were perceived as open
and God dispensed revelation akin to that given to Old Testament prophets
and patriarchs, and to New Testament apostles. That is not a criticism of any
other denomination; just a frank acknowledgment of where we differ from
most of our brothers and sisters in Christ.

     I must clarify; with Stephen, I fully agree that the Catholic Church
has played a role in God's plan. During some of the darkest and most
difficult days—between the first century and the Reformation—it was
largely the Roman Catholic Church that preserved for us biblical texts,
truths about Jesus and His divine mission and ministry, and many
of the rites of the ancient Church. Consequently, I would not argue
(as some unfortunately have) that Catholics are "the Church of the
devil" ·or that the pope is the anti-Christ. From my perspective, such
claims ignore history and evidence a real absence of Christian civility
and love. Setting aside the handful of unrighteous rogues who have
occupied Peter's See, Christianity and the world are decidedly better
because many righteous popes have presided over the largest Christian

denomination. (I am frank to say, I believe Pope Francis's pontificate will exemplify this.) And much would have been lost had such men not sacrificed and served as the presiding figure for the majority of Christianity. All that Latter-day Saints are arguing is that some things were lost after the close of the New Testament era. And these things have been restored by God in recent days. Those who know LDS doctrine know that they are decidedly different on this point. Even the Roman Catholic Pontiff would reject for himself some of the things Mormonism claims for its prophet.

For all of his humanity, the Prophet Joseph Smith was very much what Latter-day Saints see as the model of what prophets should be: revelatory, visionary, charismatic, and self-sacrificing. Stephen, while acknowledging Joseph's spiritual gifts, suggested that his successors "rarely claim to have revelations themselves." Again, I would beg to differ—at least in a subtle way. Brigham (the second President of the Church) had a revelation (canonized in the LDS Doctrine and Covenants) explaining how the Saints should make their way West. Wilford Woodruff (the fourth President) had numerous visionary experiences and revelations, including the one that ended plural marriage among Mormons. Lorenzo Snow (fifth President) received a revelation which brought a rather dramatic shift in the Church's financial status. Joseph F. Smith (sixth President of the Church) had a vision of the deceased and how they receive the Gospel in the Spirit World. Spencer W. Kimball (twelfth President) received a rather famous revelation expanding priesthood ordination to all worthy men—regardless of race. Gordon B. Hinckley (fifteenth President) received a revelation on temples and how to make them more readily available to members of the Church in areas where there is not a large population of Latter-day Saints. Most of Joseph's successors—at least those who served for a significant window of time—had rather revelatory or visionary encounters. The shift in Mormonism (since Joseph's death) has been less that visions have ceased and more that the prophets and apostles are a bit more cautious about talking openly about spiritual experiences. But there seems to be little question: Joseph's successors still claim revelations and visions. Now, it seems fair to say that Joseph was the architect of the Restored Gospel—and his successors have had more of a role of keeping the ship (Joseph built) on course.[15] But there have been some significant shifts in the decades following Joseph's martyrdom—and each has been associated with revelations or visions.

So, is there any hope that Latter-day Saints will acknowledge the calling or divinely appointed mission of the pope—or any non-LDS religious leader? There certainly seems to be. On February 15, 1978, the First Presidency of the Church released the following declaration: "The great religious leaders of the world . . . received a portion of God's light. Moral truths were given to them by God to enlighten whole nations and to bring a higher level of understanding to individuals."[16] Similarly, an article in the *Encyclopedia of Mormonism* states: "Latter-day Saints believe . . . God inspires not only Latter-day Saints but also founders, teachers, philosophers, and reformers of other Christian and non-Christian religions."[17] So, a Mormon who is aware of his faith's teachings on other religious traditions must acknowledge that God works through receptive people of all denominations—Roman Catholics included. And there are things practicing Latter-day Saints can learn from their brothers and sisters of other faiths. A spirit of condescension, criticism, cynicism—or a "holier than thou" attitude—do much to harm relationships, religious freedoms, and the work of the Lord. Such attitudes are also contrary to the spirit of civility and love taught by Jesus. This rebuke is intended for any and all who struggle on this point—those of my own tradition included. Some years ago I attended a meeting of an interfaith council of which I was a member. One Evangelical brother on the council struggled greatly to accept Latter-day Saints and Catholics as Christians because they differ in doctrine from him. In consequence of his concerns, he radiated a spirit of discomfort and was greatly limited in his ability to contribute—as his fixation was on our differences rather than on our major similarities: a conviction of the divine and salvific mission of the Lord Jesus Christ. If we truly are Christian, we must act more Christlike toward those who believe differently than we. Jesus declared: "A new command I give you: Love one another. As I have loved you, so you must love one another. By this everyone will know that you are my disciples, if you love one another" (*NIV* John 13:34–35). Fixation upon orthodoxy over and above orthopraxy can be a dangerous approach to Jesus's teachings.

Finally, Stephen's analogy of "separation" vs. "divorce" is a meaningful and attractive one. Both he and I ultimately wish that the divide between the various members of the Christian family could be repaired—preventing a permanent divorce—through a bit of "counseling," per se. Truth be told, however, Christianity is less like a married couple who has separated, and more like a husband and wife who have irreconcilable differences, but who—for the sake of their children—have decided to remain living under the same roof, seeking to be cordial one with another, all the while feeling a great deal of frustration that his or her spouse simply cannot see the world as accurately as he or she does. Reconciliation for the Christian Church is a pipe dream—at least prior to the Second Advent. Realistically, it seems the goal most likely to be achieved would be to live in love and tolerance "for the sake of the kids"—and pray that, upon the Lord's return, we can work all of this out.

Stephen

Alonzo has helped me to see that Catholics believe in the continuity of Bishops while Mormons believe in the power of Prophets. Bishops vs. Prophets: Could it be that simple? No, there is much more to discuss (and thus the rest of this book!), but religious differences often come down to alternative sources of authority. Both traditions understand authority as a gift, and both locate the origin of that gift, as far as the Church goes, in the lives of the Apostles. Both traditions acknowledge that the gift of authority needs to be institutionalized in stable, well-defined offices. They also agree on the need for rituals to demarcate a tradition of transmission, so that authority can be handed down from one generation to another. But Bishops (authorized church leaders) for Catholics are necessary (after the New Testament period) to review, assess, and authorize the claims of Prophets (religious visionaries), while religious visionaries simply are the highest church authorities for Mormons.

In other words, from the Mormon perspective, the original Apostles were prophets, and their heirs should be as well. Terminology is tricky, and Alonzo does a good job of explaining why Mormons call their local church leaders Bishops but their general church leaders Apostles. There is an even greater and probably decisive terminological difference. Mormons call their President a Prophet, but Catholics do not call the Pope a Prophet. Why not? Has Catholicism gone too far in severing the connection between church authority and religious visionaries? Where have all the prophets gone in the Catholic Church?

Avery Dulles, before he was raised to the rank of a Cardinal in the Catholic Church, wrote a book on dogma with a chapter titled, "The Permanence of Prophecy in the Church." It is an incredibly relevant chapter for this dialogue. He notes the high standing of prophets in the New Testament (1 Corinthians 14:1–5), but also insists that they were distinguished from and ranked beneath the Apostles (1 Corinthians 12:28; Ephesians 2:20, 3:5, 4:11). Early Christian prophets, Dulles argues, were not official witnesses of the risen Christ. They were also not teachers or theologians. They passed on admonitions and predictions they received from the Holy Spirit. These claims and insights needed to be scrutinized to make sure they harmonized with the faith, since there were many prophets during this period and not a few were false (1 Corinthians 12:3; 1 John 4:3; Mark 13:22). The Church was thus forced (or inspired) to develop rules for distinguishing between genuine and counterfeit prophecies.

Most important, Dulles admits that the early Church began to view prophecy as something belonging to an older era and that this trend pushed prophets into the margins of respectability. Those claiming prophetic status often ended up as heretics or martyrs, like Joan of Arc and Savonarola. After the Reformation, Catholic leaders increasingly resisted the possibility that prophetic voices could legitimately question the Catholic hierarchy. Vatican II redressed some of these problems by giving the whole Church a prophetic function. All Catholics are called to be prophetic witnesses of the faith. Yet Dulles writes, "In spite of the biblical allusions, the conception of prophecy here advanced [by Vatican II] seems to be only a pale reflection of the rich and dynamic charism [this is the preferred Catholic term for gift, drawn from the original Greek word for grace] described in the New Testament." Dulles goes on to say that "Churchmen are always tempted to suppress prophecy, for it is a disturbing element." Moreover, "subsequent history has shown that when prophets are not given their say within the Church, they rise up to condemn it from outside."[18]

This analysis can help Catholics become more sensitive to and appreciative of the Mormon understanding of Joseph as a prophet, yet it is important to note that Dulles identifies prophecy with critique and admonition. He thinks of prophets in terms of Protestant-like criticisms of Catholicism's emphasis on ritual and tradition. Nothing in what Dulles says prepares a Catholic to come to terms with the Mormon identification of the office of the Prophet with the office of the Apostle. There have been countless prophets in the Church since the Gospel was first proclaimed, but Joseph had the heart of a prophet combined with the mind of a pope. Mormons are not just another charismatic group with new theological ideas. They represent the return of the prophet, we could say, in a new, authoritative form. For that reason alone, other Christians should carefully attend to what they have to say.

2

Grace

Alonzo

Luther's declaration of salvation *sola fide* is a thorn in the side of many Catholics and Latter-day Saints alike. Are we saved by grace? That loaded question is a bit like the "yes or no" query: "Have you stopped beating your wife?" No matter how you answer, your position will most likely be misunderstood.

Many of the reformers struggled with what appeared to be a Catholic fixation upon obedience, works, sacraments, and authority. Although the problem seems less of an issue in the post-Vatican II era, prior to that period some Protestants questioned the Christianity of Catholics—assuming that they trusted more in their own works, the authority of the hierarchy, and the organizational Church for their salvation, than in Christ Jesus! Latter-day Saints too have been criticized by many in the evangelical movement for their focus on "keeping commandments" and for their sense that sacraments are, at least in part, salvific.

I many ways, Catholics today seem more Protestant on this topic than they did prior to 1965. However, as recently as last month I had an interaction with a nondenominational Christian who indicated to me that he could not interact ecumenically with Catholics or Mormons because both of those traditions did not place their trust in Christ, but rely upon their own merits for salvation. "They work their way to heaven!" he said.

While I will leave it to Stephen to explain the Catholic view on this matter, suffice it to say, I believe that most Mormons and Catholics would take issue with Luther's view of texts like the Epistle of James. Luther saw it as contradictory with Paul. He perceived it as emphasizing works, rather than grace. He felt it did "violence" to scripture and was "a right epistle of straw" that did not belong in the Holy Bible. Latter-day Saints and Roman Catholics traditionally do not see a contradiction between James and Paul. Rather, contra Luther, they tend to allow James to color or perhaps even contextualize Paul and the Christian doctrine of grace.

In my first two decades of life, as a practicing member of the Eastern Orthodox tradition, I do not believe I ever asked myself: "Am I saved by grace or by works?" I certainly believed heavily in the salvific merit of sacraments—and trusted that God would work the rest out in His own way—regardless of how little I understood about the matter. It was my interaction with the Campus Crusade for Christ folks, and then the Latter-day Saints, that really got me thinking about this question. Am I saved? What would happen to me if I died today? Is salvation achieved through uttering a short prayer? Through efforts at obedience to God's commandments? Through a combination of the two? Or through something totally different? I had never contemplated such important questions—as they had simply never come up in my Greek Orthodox world. Consequently, when they did arise in my conversations with evangelicals and Mormons, I sensed for the first time the importance of the questions but also the depth of the controversy surrounding this foundational theological issue. I am reminded of a comment made by Erwin Lutzer, in his book, *The Doctrines that Divide*, where he wrote: "Sadly, though we have had the New Testament for almost twenty centuries, Christendom still gives us an unclear answer to this question ['Are we saved by grace or by our works?']. Yet our destiny in heaven or hell depends on the correctness of the answer."[1] At nearly 20-years-old I contemplated this for the first time.

A year after I converted to Mormonism I served a full-time mission in Great Britain. Perhaps because of my Orthodox background—but certainly also because of my reading of the New Testament—I entered the mission field with a perspective that would have upset Luther. While my teaching was not fixated on "works," when conversing with Protestants it often went there—and the discussion was seldom productive. I can recall numerous conversations in which, using the Bible, I and a Protestant acquaintance, would throw scriptures around that seemed to support or criticize "works" as a means of gaining salvation. The conversations were never fruitful, and the Spirit was seldom present. I have some sincere regrets about my lack of understanding back then, and my approach to the doctrine of grace at that stage of my life.

I see things differently today than I did more than a quarter of a century ago. That is not to say I am more in alignment with Protestants and less with Mormons. Rather, I think I am more in alignment with God and early Christian thought.

The dilemma, to my mind, is that those who preach *sola fide* do so without context. In other words, though salvation may come solely through faith in Christ, that does not necessarily mean that nothing is required of the "saved" in order to lay hold upon the grace-originating gift of eternal life. The debate tends to take an either/or approach. But, from the perspective of this author, things are not quite as cut and dry as the "works crowd" or the "grace crowd" would have them be.

While The Church of Jesus Christ of Latter-day Saints believes that one's salvation comes in, and through, the atoning blood of Jesus Christ, and in no other way, nevertheless, access to that spilt blood requires a degree of effort. From a Protestant perspective, saying the "Jesus prayer"—asking Christ into your life, to rule and reign as personal Savior and Lord—is expected, if not required, of any and all who wish to be "saved." The prayer itself is not salvific. However, it allows one to lay hold upon God's grace. It allows the believer to access Christ's ultimate gift to us.

There are many scriptures, particularly in the writings of Paul, which seem to emphasize the danger of relying upon works for one's salvation (e.g., Romans 1:17, 3:28, and 11:5–6; Galatians 2:15–16; Ephesians 2:8–10). But Paul, and others, also clearly emphasize the need for those converted unto Christ to perform "works" of righteousness—and these works are traditionally suggested to have some degree of salvific merit (e.g., Romans 2:6; Philippians 2:12; 2 Timothy 4:14; Hebrews 6:4–6 and 10:26–27; 1 Peter 1:16–17; 2 Peter 2:20–21; Revelation 2:23 and 26, 14:13, 20:12–13 and 22:12, etc.). So how is this not a contradiction? Well, first, the condemnation of "works" as "non-salvific" traditionally refers to the "works" of the law of Moses. Paul wishes his reader to understand that in Christ the law is fulfilled; therefore, those sacrifices and ritual acts once mandated by the law are no longer needed, and no longer have power to redeem the practitioner. Second, when the occasional verse refers generally to "good works," there is no condemnation of doing good; only the sense that no amount of personal "works" has the ability to save a sinful man. But this is not a condemnation of holiness; only of believing that one's personal holiness has the power to save.

So what do works of piety accomplish for a Christian? In his classic text, *Early Christian Doctrines*, J. N. D. Kelly, a protestant Patristic scholar, explains:

> Our salvation comes, stated Gregory of Nazianzen [flourished A.D. 372–389], both from ourselves and from God. If God's help is necessary for doing good and if the good will itself come from Him, it is equally true that the initiative rests with man's free will. Chrysostom [flourished A.D. 386–407] similarly teaches that without God's aid we should be unable to accomplish good works; nevertheless, even if grace takes the lead, it co-operates (συμπράττει) with free will. We first of all begin to desire the good and to incline ourselves towards it, and then God steps in to strengthen that desire and render it effective.[2]

Kelly adds: "So Ambrose [flourished A.D. 374–397] states, 'In everything the Lord's power cooperates with man's efforts'; but he can also say, 'Our free will gives us either a propensity to virtue or an inclination to sin.' In numerous passages he lays it down that the grace of salvation will only come to those who make the effort to bestir themselves."[3] Kelly also highlighted Theodoret's (circa A.D. 393–466) view, which was that "while all men need grace and it is impossible to take a step on the road to virtue without it, the human will must collaborate with it. 'There is need,' he writes, 'of both our efforts and the divine succor. The grace of the Spirit is not vouchsafed to those who make no effort, and without that grace our efforts cannot collect the prize of virtue.'"[4] Kelly describes the early Christian view of grace and works as a cooperative one. We need God's grace for salvation, but we need our own works to lay hold upon that grace. The two work hand in hand.

A popular verse in the Book of Mormon seems to contradict this ancient view of the relationship between grace and works. It states: "It is by grace we are saved, after all we can do" (2 Nephi 25:23). For many outside of Mormonism, the emphasis in this passage is on the clause "after all we can do." In other words, those who reject the Mormon view see this passage of sacred scripture as evidence that Latter-day Saints see salvation in their works—in "all they can do"; not in Christ's works and all that He has done. Frankly, some Mormons appear to interpret the verse this way, though that interpretation is erroneous. In context of LDS soteriology, the verse is not emphasizing "all we can do" but, rather, what comes after all we can do. In other words, the verse is best understood to mean: "After all we can do, it is yet by grace that we are saved." LDS doctrine on the relationship of grace and works is simply this: we are saved (and exalted, to use the Mormon vernacular) utterly by the grace of God. Nothing we can do can earn our salvation. Nothing we can do makes us worthy of God's grace or gifts. However (and there is always a "however," isn't there?!?), works have their place. While they earn us nothing, like the ancient Christians, Latter-day Saints believe that they qualify us for the receipt of God's grace. They enable us to access that grace—that incomprehensibly generous gift the Father has in store for all those that believe in His Son. As tired as the analogy is, the following explains the principle well.

> Imagine that you and I were "off" and "on" friends in life. I was more committed to the relationship than were you. Nevertheless, when you were "on," we had some very good times together. You sensed that I loved you deeply and, though I did much more for you than you ever did for me, still, you occasionally "stepped up to the plate" and expressed your love to me. You occasionally paid attention to me, dropped by to chat with me (without any provocation, but just because you wanted to). Sometimes you were really kind to my children. As infrequent as they were, each of these things made me feel loved by you. I had hoped that we could be closer, but such was not to be. Somehow, this really never harmed how I felt about you. My love for you was largely unconditional.
>
> Recently I passed away. In my will, I bequeathed to you a rather large sum of money—say, a billion dollars. This, of course, was the ultimate token of how deeply I loved you—of how much our relationship (as one-sided as it often was) meant to me. The size of the gift was incomprehensible to you. You would never have to work again because of what I had provided. You were shocked, overwhelmed, felt unworthy of such kindness—and yet you were excited beyond words.
>
> While you did not need to be at the reading of the will, in order to receive your inheritance you did need to go to the bank and fill out the paperwork necessary for the transfer of the funds into your personal account. If you did not go to the bank to complete this small task, you would have no access to the substantial gift I had left you. Of course, going to the bank and filling out the paperwork was not payment for the gift. You had not "earned" this present. I had given this to you because I loved you; and in spite of how little you did to nurture our relationship. However, if you chose to ignore what was required by the law to lay hold upon this gift, then you simply would not receive it. There were no strings attached to the present I left for you—just legal requirements for accessing it; for making it yours.

In the LDS understanding of grace and works, this analogy is representative of how these two gospel principles work together. God has given us an incomprehensibly large gift. We are underserving of it. We could not earn it if we worked a lifetime trying. Nor do we merit it because of how we treat Him. Indeed, He offers it out of deep and abiding love for us—and in spite of the fact that we are often only "fair weather friends" to Him. God has revealed the means by which we may lay hold upon salvation—and that means is Jesus! But He asks of us small things—a bit of paperwork, per se—here and there as a means of showing that we love Him, and that we desire to be with Him throughout eternity. According to Kelly, this is the view of the early Church; and it is certainly the LDS view of how grace and works cooperate with each other in God's great plan.

For Mormons, this is how James can say "that faith without works is dead" (James 2:20) and Paul can say "for by grace are ye saved through faith . . . Not of works, lest any man should boast" (Ephesians 2:8 and 9). If we have an actual true and living faith in Christ, our works will manifest that. As Luther is reported to have taught, "works do not save a man, but a saved man does works." Like Luther, James was strident in the connection between works as manifestations of faith. Said he:

> What doth it profit, my brethren, though a man say he hath faith, and have not works? can faith save him? If a brother or sister be naked, and destitute of daily food, And one of you say unto them, Depart in peace, be ye warmed and filled; notwithstanding ye give them not those things which are needful to the body; what doth it profit? Even so faith, if it hath not works, is dead, being alone. Yea, a man may say, Thou hast faith, and I have works: shew me thy faith without thy works, and I will shew thee my faith by my works. Thou believest that there is one God; thou doest well: the devils also believe, and tremble. But wilt thou know, O vain man, that faith without works is dead? (James 2:14–20)

In the Spirit of James and Luther, it seems that uttering the "Jesus prayer" is, in itself, a work which allows one to lay hold of God's grace. The prayer does not have the power to save, but the act of uttering it is a manifestation of one's belief and trust in God and Christ. That manifest faith saves—because it invokes the blessings and grace of God. So it is with obedience to any commandment, sacrament, or teaching of Christ. If we engage with faith and sincerity, these become vehicles for grace. They are not of themselves salvific. But as manifestations of our trust in God and faith in Christ's redemption, they are purveyors of salvation.

As I noted above, during those two years I served as a missionary in Great Britain, I engaged in conversations wherein I stressed works with those who were ardently anti-works. I still feel that many of those with whom I spoke confused Paul's condemnation of the works of the law of Moses with works of holiness. Nevertheless, were I to go back on my mission now, I would preach grace, grace, grace! I would emphasize that salvation is in and through Christ's atoning blood and comes in no other way. I would paint "works" for what I believe they are; token gestures of love to God and Christ, which do not save, but which represent our love for God, or commitment to Him, and our longing to be with and like Him.

Stephen

Catholics and Mormons have been tossed into the same boat by most Protestants when it comes to grace. Both have been charged, convicted, and penalized for believing in works-righteousness.[5] Works-righteousness is short hand for the idea that far from being a free gift, salvation must be earned by doing the right thing, and in the theological realm, putting conditions on grace is a serious crime. My friend Alonzo is right that the history of these terms—grace and works—is hardly stable and their deployment in theological polemics can be confusing. The Protestant Reformers used the category of grace to target every Catholic custom or practice that they found annoying, no matter how trivial or benign. Catholics were guilty of diluting genuine faith with rules for personal behavior as well as corporate worship. Nowadays, however, Protestants are likely to accuse Catholics of being free and easy with grace, while Catholics are likely to look down on Protestants for identifying salvation with a specific set of beliefs and actions. Thus, we have the stereotype of the Catholic who believes he or she can be saved just by going to Mass and the Protestant who believes that nobody can be saved unless they have the correct view of the Bible. These stereotypes extend to the clergy. Protestant ministers are typically held to very high moral and doctrinal standards, and if they violate those standards, they forfeit their status as spiritual leaders of their communities. Catholic priests, by contrast, are the recipients of what Catholics call a charism, a special gift of grace which makes them a priest for life, and there is little (though not nothing!) they can do to forfeit that gift. The Protestant Reformers accused Rome of obstructing God's love with walls made of ethical rules and prescribed behavior, but nowadays it would seem that many Protestants think Rome has so lowered these walls that the laity has nothing to climb.

Are Catholics too liberal with regard to grace? That is what I thought growing up. We evangelicals thought that Catholics had all the fun because, no matter how bad they were during the week, they could confess their sins to a priest and receive forgiveness. My Protestants friends and I were much more bound to moral if not doctrinal rules, and much more concerned about the salvific consequences of violating those rules than the Catholics we knew. In a word, we were more legalistic than our Catholic friends. Although we would have denied it at the time, we worked hard to prove that we merited God's grace.

This whole debate about the relative importance of grace and works, however, is hopelessly skewed because the meaning of these terms is so ambiguous. When I profess that Jesus Christ is my Lord and Savior, is that grace speaking or works? Or is it both—the work of grace?

Besides, this debate emerged in a time when religious practices were out of sync with theological convictions, and that time is long since over. Some historians have argued that the image of God, by the late middle ages, had become too judgmental and menacing, and many Christians were anxious about their chances for happiness in the afterlife. Purgatory, which is the place the saved go to be cleansed of all their remaining sins, became, in the medieval mind, a trap that had the potential to ensnare your soul for an unimaginably long stretch of time. The Church hierarchy set out to assure the faithful that they were indeed saved and that God has only good outcomes in store for the faithful, but good intentions can lead to bad consequences. Popes, bishops, and priests wanted to assuage spiritual anxiety, but they ended up increasing it. Rome sold indulgences to raise money for great art and to fight the Turks, but the indulgences were meant to be a reassurance of grace, not a free pass to get out of hell (or purgatory). Indulgences were like a marriage license. They were not intended to take the place of the marriage, nor were they intended to encourage people to think that they had to pay to get married. Love was the substance of marriage, just as it was the substance of our relationship to God. The indulgence was supposed to be a symbol of that love.[6] That message obviously got lost in the zeal to raise money for good causes. The Protestant Reformers were right to say that the system was so theologically confusing and so easily abused that it was best, at that time, to get rid of indulgences altogether.

The Catholic Church does not talk about indulgences and purgatory much these days, but when it does, it is super clear about what they are. Purgatory is simply that part of heaven where continual growth is made toward the holiness that is required for full participation in the divine.[7] Yes, Catholics believe that spiritual growth does not end at death. People will still have to work through what they have done in this life. People still need grace, even in heaven! Wounds will have to be healed, self-knowledge deepened, responsibility taken, relationships restored, and sinfulness renounced. Indulgences are related to purgatory in the sense that the healing we seek now will, in fact, reduce the amount of healing we will need in purgatory. When we repent of our sins and turn to Christ for forgiveness, we are even now preparing ourselves to enjoy the presence of God, and the more we do that here and now, the less time we will have to spend in purgatory. An indulgence is merely the Catholic Church's way of teaching us what kind of acts of repentance might be best for us as we prepare for the afterlife. An indulgence is an opportunity, not a discount.

Many Protestants will still have problems sympathizing with even the most careful Catholic defense of purgatory and indulgences, but at least they should argue against what Catholics believe today, not what Protestants think Catholics believed five hundred years ago. And they should face the fact that evangelical views of grace have become just as problematic today as the Catholic view of indulgences was five hundred years ago. When I was growing up in an evangelical church, I went through several emotional and mental battles over the status of my salvation. My church emphasized spiritual rebirth through a personal relationship with Jesus Christ. I still believe that is the core of salvation: a personal relationship with Jesus that results in spiritual transformation and growth. In the church of my youth, however, the emphasis was on the experiential quality of this relationship, not its enduring and evolving development. Salvation was portrayed to me as a state (you are either deeply in it or completely out of it) rather than a process (you learn to trust Jesus through the providentially ordered events in your life). Because I was sometimes unsure of the state of my feelings, I had to work hard to make sure that I was not doing anything to stifle my experience of grace. It is as if best friends have to keep doing great things together in order to prove that they are friends or that a married couple has to fall in love every evening after dinner in order to make sure that their marriage is still working. The emphasis on being born again put me on a spiritual roller coaster that never let me off. During my turbulent adolescent years, no assurance of God's love was enough to still my stumbling heart. Even the Calvinist doctrine "once saved always saved" that came out of the Reformation as a direct response to indulgences did not help me. The "always" depended on the "once," and what happened once upon a time was too distant a memory to be either the basis or the product of God's eternal decree.

Today, I think the historical background and theological framework of this mixture of evangelical fervor and Calvinist rigor is intellectually misguided and spiritually self-defeating. Evangelical Churches have heard the criticisms and have matured in their understanding of grace. Holy rollers have gotten off the roller coaster. I know virtually no Christians who do not take a balanced approach to grace and works. Grace is essential for salvation, and it is a gift from God, but grace should result in changed lives. The Protestant Reformers turned the asymmetrical relationship between grace and works into an exaggerated opposition in order to fuel their criticisms of Roman Catholic customs. Nearly all Christians today agree that the faithful are liberated by grace to freely give of themselves to others. Grace and works are thus not in competition with each other, as long as the emphasis and priority is given to grace. You can have works without grace, but you cannot have grace without works.

Of course, my formulation of their relationship could be misguided in various major or minor ways. Does that make me less of a Christian? Does that make God love me less? I am convinced that our destiny in the afterlife does not depend on what we think about the relationship between grace and works. To make that point, I want to develop two scenarios:

First scene: Let us assume that we are saved by grace alone, without any regard to works, as some Protestants believe. If so, then false beliefs will not affect our salvation, assuming, of course, that we believe in Jesus and that believing in Jesus is not itself a kind of work. Take the made-up example of Sam. Sam believes in Jesus Christ, prays for the forgiveness of his sins, and goes to church regularly, but he thinks that he has to avoid major sins and give time and money to poor people in order to be saved. In fact, he worries that he is not doing enough for others, and he thinks that he should pursue a career in social work because that would give him a lot of opportunities to help the needy. He is disappointed in Christians who do not volunteer their time or money to help those who need it, but he is not judgmental toward them. He does, however, vote for politicians based on what they promise to do for the economically disadvantaged. Now, is he going to be damned by God because he has a distorted view of grace? True, he probably has too much pride in the good works he does, and putting complex economic issues at the center of his political commitments might be imprudent, but will he go to hell because he has overvalued the salvific importance of helping others?

Second scene: Now let us assume that we are saved by grace that results in good works, and then take the example of Betty. Betty thinks we are saved by grace alone, and she goes out of her way to deny that works have anything to do with salvation. She is not a bad person. In fact, because she believes in grace, she prays a lot to God and asks God for forgiveness. She goes to church most Sundays and thinks a lot about what a wonderful savior Jesus Christ is. She shares her faith with others but tends to ridicule people she calls "do-gooders." She occasionally volunteers at a homeless shelter, but she gives her tithe to missionaries from her church rather than to programs that directly serve the poor. She thinks you should help others only if it makes you feel better about yourself, not because it has anything to do with your relationship to God. In fact, she sometimes worries that she thinks too much about helping other people, because she is convinced that pride is the root of all sin. She knows in her heart that only God can change people, and thus she thinks that trying to change the world is a sign of disbelief in divine providence. Now, will she be denied entrance into heaven because she thinks that grace does not necessary result in good works? Sure, she is too hard on those who go out of their way to help others, and she is too fatalistic about the fate of the poor. But those are beliefs she sincerely holds, and, since she, like all of us, will have time in heaven to have all her beliefs brought into alignment with Jesus Christ, should wrong beliefs keep her out of heaven altogether?

I will pass over the more clear-cut cases of people who believe in Jesus Christ but think that the freedom of grace means that they can do just as they please, without even trying to love others, and those who believe that only good works will get them into heaven. People in those categories are victims of an either/or mentality regarding grace and works. They think that holding to one means rejecting the other. I have not come across very many, if any people who actually fall into these categories, and I am quite happy to leave their afterlife up to God. In fact, I am more than happy to leave everyone's afterlife up to God. I do not presume to know anybody's heart, nor do I know God's plan for the saved and the unsaved alike. That, in fact, is just my point. The relationship between grace and works is a theoretical question, and I doubt

very much that what position, within biblical reason, we take on theological theories will shape our future with God. Theoretical questions
are important, but they are not that important. Of course, I could be
wrong about this—very wrong. That is why I try to trust in my relationship with Jesus, and hope that God's love for me will make me a better
person. What else can anyone do?

Having said all of this, I agree wholeheartedly with Alonzo that it just
does not make any sense to say that salvation and works are mutually
exclusive or theological incompatible. Even those who say that only a born
again experience will save you are requiring a work for salvation, since
"having a certain kind of experience" is something that we try to do, in
the sense of preparing ourselves by opening our hearts, and thus it is a
"work." As Alonzo rightly says, when you receive a gift, even the freest gift
imaginable, you still have to do something to receive it, even if that just
means showing up and extending your empty hands.

So, on the issue of grace, I think Mormons and Catholics are pretty
much at the same place: the foot of the cross. We both look to Jesus, yet
we both realize that we have to prepare ourselves, through rituals, moral
effort, charity, prayer, Bible study, and gathering with other Christians
both to receive God's grace and to grow in it.

That belief about grace also impacts our beliefs about heaven. Mormons
and Catholics also stand together in their conviction that heaven is not a
static state of perfect, unchanging, intellectual bliss. We believe that just
as we can grow closer to God in this life, we can continue to grow closer
to God in the next.

In sum, what sets Mormons and Catholics apart from some Protestants
is that we see holiness as a journey, not a state. If holiness is a state, you
are either in it or out of it. If it is a journey, then no matter how far you are
in it, you have further to go.

Alonzo

As committed to a cooperative doctrine of grace/works as Latter-day
Saints and Catholics are, one has to wonder, "What is the downside to
all of this?" After all, I would think most evangelicals would be happy
with what Stephen and I have testified to. Catholics and Mormons place
their trust in Christ; and in Him only! We kneel at the foot of the cross of
Christ—pleading for His forgiveness and basking in His love. So, what is
to be concerned about?

Here is my worry: after nearly two decades as a Greek Orthodox, then graduate school at the feet of Catholic scholars, coupled with more than two decades as a Mormon, and many years of teaching world religions and Christian history, I am convinced that the Orthodox, the Catholics, the Mormons, and Protestants are all at the foot of the cross—but for many the weather consists of a very thick fog. By that I mean we each seem to have a pretty pronounced doctrine of grace (including a general understanding that living a life of holiness is a manifestation of our faith in Christ). However, somehow the cross gets obscured. We fear! We doubt! To me, those are signs that we—each of us—get fixated on our own weaknesses and sins and we forget Jesus's perfection, grace, and love for us. Calvinists may be an exception to this, but so many Christians say they believe in Christ and His redemptive act, but then they fret over their weaknesses and failings.

Of course, we should be concerned with the pendulum swinging so far to the left that our trust in Christ leads us to live a laissez-faire brand of Christianity. A few evangelicals (though I think a small number) have suffered from that. Since Vatican II some Roman Catholics have also struggled with "casual Christianity"—though I think less because of an overdeveloped sense of grace and more because the Church has largely lightened up on its public condemnation of sin. (That is not to say that Catholics are "pro-sin"—just less prone to "hell-fire and damnation" discourse than they once were.) Regardless, more and more Christians are living less and less Christ-like lives.[8] This ought to be of concern to each of us. I do not think this "casual Christianity" is evidence that we simply trust more in the grace of Christ. Rather, I fear it may mean that we simply do not care anymore. We do not think about judgment. We do not fear hell. And, perhaps, we simply do not think about spiritual things as often or as deeply as we ought to. I think it is evidence that we love ourselves, but perhaps do not truly appreciate or love God.

While the Lord's gift of grace is a wonderful thing, it can make us an awful lot like a spoiled 8-year-old who expects gifts but seldom says "thanks"—and never really thinks about how generous or kind his father is being by giving them to him when he really does not deserve them owing to his obnoxious and disobedient character. The expectation that you and I attempt lives of holiness in order to qualify for God's grace is, if nothing else, a sort of safety net to protect us from spiritually harming ourselves. Commandments, sacraments, charitable service, and the like, help to blow away the thick fog which obscures the cross. Regaining a view of our suffering Lord, nailed to the cross on our behalf, reminds us that we owe Him so very much for the gracious gift He has freely provided. As Brigham Young counseled, Latter-day Saints must have their "minds riveted—yes, I may say riveted—on the cross of Christ" or their works will be "in vain."[9] How can anyone sincerely contemplate all that Jesus has done and then expect or feel deserving of "cheap grace"?!? It did not come cheaply for Christ and it should not come cheaply to us. We do good and seek to obey because we have our eyes trained on Him attached to Golgotha's cross. When we allow the fog to roll in, that is when we run the risk of forgetting what must never be forgotten by anyone worthy of the name "Christian."

Stephen

My friend Alonzo is too nice to say outright what he hints at in his response to me, so I will say it for him: Roman Catholicism has inherited a goldmine of cheap grace from the Second Vatican Council, while the Latter-day Saints have managed to avoid deflating the value of God's love. Catholicism was once rich in the kinds of social customs and elaborate rituals that can set one group of people apart from everyone else. The Mass was soaked in mystery and you were expected to fast as well as confess your sins to a priest beforehand. Catholics went to their own schools, had their own distinctive art, and did not eat meat (or ate only fish) on Fridays. They stood out. Vatican II changed all of that. The Mass was modernized and various devotional practices were minimized or curtailed, especially practices that offended Protestants. The Church lightened the load, we could say, of being Catholic.

Sociologists have a name for this. They call it the "buy-in cost" of joining any club or organization. One might think that the lower the buy-in cost, the higher the number of members, but it actually works the other way around. If an organization is easy to join, then it is also easy to leave.[10] If it makes no demands on its members, then those members will not go out of their way to identify with its mission. The same is true of churches. If a church aims to entertain, then it has put itself in the position of competing with other forms of entertainment (and religion will usually lose that battle). Christianity thrives when the buy-in cost is high but slumps when the buy-in cost is too low. There is a good reason for that, and Alonzo puts his finger on it: the cross. God gave His all for us, so we should give no less to Him. The cross is of infinite value. It cannot be priced too high, but it can be sold too low. Grace is free, but it is not cheap.

The Saints do a great job of keeping the buy-in cost of Christianity high enough to be challenging but low enough to be inviting. I have heard the Mormons called the "Marine Corps of Christianity." They certainly have not lost the taste for evangelical mission, as so many mainline churches have. They send out their young two-by-two to spread the Gospel, and they require of their members certain social practices, like abstaining from coffee and alcohol—practices that remind them that they are a people set apart by God for greater glory than can be found in this world. While most worship services, including the Mass, have gotten shorter over the years, the Saints still meet for three hours on Sundays and reserve the rest of the day for rest, study, and family time. Catholics have much to learn from the way they have preserved discipline and camaraderie in the church in the face of secular challenges and distractions.

It is common knowledge among church leaders today that more women than men go to church. This happens in just about every denomination, and cheap grace plays a factor in that gender imbalance. Men need to be challenged. They need to be given difficult tasks to accomplish and clear goals to pursue. When spirituality is reduced to a heartfelt emotional response to Jesus, many men lose interest and focus. Mormons involve all of their members, young and old, men and women, by assigning them priestly responsibilities like speaking in church. Mormons know how to organize the religious impulse. As a result, they are one of the few churches that does not suffer from a massive gender imbalance. Another church that is also attractive to men these days is the Eastern Orthodox, Alonzo's previous church tradition. Eastern Orthodoxy is demanding. The Sunday liturgy requires careful attention, and newcomers need much mentoring to learn the traditions. Indeed, the laity is encouraged to submit to spiritual fathers for guidance and discipline, just as Mormon bishops make house calls to offer moral uplift and advice. Roman Catholic priests used to have that kind of respect and standing in the everyday lives of the faithful, but those days are long gone. Maybe Mormons can help Catholics put the sacrifice back into grace.

3

Mary

Stephen

Catholics and Mormons both have a goddess problem. I will leave it to Alonzo to explain the Mormon version of this problem, but I am hoping that, when we compare the two traditions, we can find some lines of convergence (as well as divergence). Given the associations between the word *goddess* and paganism, it is no wonder that Protestants doubt Catholicism's and Mormonism's biblical purity. Yet our goddess elements do little to make Catholicism and Mormonism attractive to New Age questers who connect their spirituality to maternal themes. Perhaps comparing the two traditions can provide some insight and clarity on this vexing topic. Even if sharing a problem does not result in solving it, a little companionship can lighten the load!

I call it a goddess problem, but it has not always been that way. In the days of the Roman Empire, making room in its worship for a feminine presence was a decided plus. Pagans were used to thinking of the divine in both masculine and feminine terms, and the prominent role of Mary in Christianity helped facilitate many pagan conversions.

The place of Mary in the faith was never simple or self-evident. One of the most famous debates in the early Church was ignited when a theologian named Nestorius argued that Mary was the mother of the human part of Jesus, not His divinity. The Christian masses rebelled against this insult to Mary's honor, and at the Council of Ephesus (431), the Church declared that Mary should rightfully be called *theotokos*, which means God bearer or, in common language, the Mother of God. From that declaration on, Mary continued to be elevated in Catholic thought and practice.

It was a short step from being the Mother of God to becoming the Queen of Heaven, where she rules with her Son.

Other titles followed. How could Christ allow His mother's body to rot in the grave when He was sitting at the right hand of the father in heaven? Surely He would spare her the humiliation of death and take her body and soul immediately to heaven when she fell asleep for the last time (thus her death is referred to as a kind of sleep, or dormition). In the Middle Ages, dozens of Cathedrals and hundreds of churches were constructed in her honor. The way her holiness inspired countless people to be witnesses to her Son is hard to describe. It all began to change when the Renaissance artists, inspired by the ancient Greeks to emphasize all things human, began painting her as a humble maiden rather than a cosmic figure of unspeakable beauty and glory. The Protestant Reformers followed suit by denying her any special role in the economy of salvation, other than the virgin birth. The Catholic Church fought back. In 1854, Pope Pius IX announced that it was now official dogma that she was born without the signs of original sin (the Immaculate Conception) and Pope Pius XII announced in 1950 that it was dogma that she was assumed body and soul into heaven (the Assumption). Others pushed for her to be named Co-Redeemer with Christ, but then everything Catholics sought in Blessed Mary, the Mother of the Church, changed with the calling of the Second Vatican Council (1962–1965).

An official document from the council, the Dogmatic Constitution of the Church (also known by its first words, *Lumen Gentium*, or "Light for the Nations"), promulgated by Pope Paul VI in 1964, devoted its last chapter to Mariology. It is a brief chapter, was much debated, and has had important theological consequences.[1] Ecumenical dialogue was in the air, and the Council Fathers were concerned about reaching out to Protestants and Eastern Orthodox. Moreover, the council took place at the height of enthusiasm about the historical study of the Bible. Protestant scholars were confident that they could peel back the layers of time and reveal what the earliest Christians really believed, and Catholic scholars wanted to jump on this bandwagon by drawing a thick line between the earliest teachings of Jesus and later additions to the faith. Roman and Greek contributions to Christianity, in the forms of philosophical thought as well as social and religious customs, were given weighty reappraisals. Anything in Christianity that indicated pagan parallels or influences was treated to careful analysis.

In this theological climate, the Council Fathers decided that it was better to emphasize the way Mary is united to the Church rather than to her
Son. While still affirming her singular contribution to the incarnation,
they cautioned against "past excesses" while resisting the call for new titles
such as Mediatrix, Advocate, and Co-Redemptrix. The Council encouraged the faithful to treat Mary as a model of humble obedience. Written
during the era of space travel, *Lumen Gentium* calls her the "Queen of
the universe," but the attention is focused on her moral actions, not her
place in the cosmological drama of salvation. Mary is the best example of
a Christian because she passively opened her entire self to the love of God.

Debates still rage over the proper interpretation of Vatican II. Some
progressive theologians and priests came to the conclusion that a mini-
malist piety with regard to Mary was an appropriate response. Many
churches in America took down statues of Mary as evidence that Catholics
do not worship her. This was part of a more general trend. Catholic architecture turned in a modernist direction as it dismissed or downplayed the
outward signs that set Catholic churches apart from the functional look of
Protestant places of worship.

Feminist theologians, who were rising in prominence in Catholic
circles throughout the decades following Vatican II, wanted structural
changes to theology, not just architecture. Mary, they argued, had long
been held up as a paragon of outdated and chauvinistic views of feminin-
ity. It was time to retire many aspects of her veneration to the dustbins of
patriarchal history.[2] Ironically, however, the image of Mary that emerged
after Vatican II pleased neither the feminists nor the traditionalists. The
Church made Mary more human by softening her cosmological significance, but to the chagrin of traditionalists, this stripped heaven of its
feminine presence. Moreover, the Church, in its efforts to respond con-
structively to feminism, sought a biblical foundation for the Rome's commitment to the complementarity of the genders. As a result, Rome loaded
even more feminine virtues onto her humanity. Mary was portrayed as
the first Christian and a model for all humanity, but at the end of the day,
she was still the person who said yes to God in a very submissive way.

There are two opposed ways of understanding the increasingly elaborate teachings about Mary in the Catholic Church prior to Vatican II.
First, Protestants typically paint all the Catholic teachings about Mary
with the broad brush of syncretism. They charge Catholics with assimilat-
ing (in sublimated form, of course) the pagan themes of an earth goddess
and a sexualized heaven. Mary, in other words, is where you go to find

Catholicism at its most unbiblical best. Second, Catholic traditionalists argue that all the doctrines about Mary are implied in the Bible and that their development into full-fledged teachings is a matter of legitimate Church authority unfolding their logical implications.

I am something of a Catholic traditionalist, but I actually think these two ways of looking at Marian doctrine are not incompatible, and I agree with the first one as much as the second. Moreover, I think the role of Mary in the Catholic Church is a great way of finding common ground with Mormonism—not necessarily in the details of the teaching, but in the way that the early Church reacted to the wider culture with confidence and creativity. Catholicism and Mormonism are not afraid to recognize and appropriate truth outside of narrow institutional channels. Joseph Smith was a reviver of lost traditions and a hoarder of what other forms of Christianity discarded. He too was sensitive to the needs of the heart for a distinctly feminine presence in heaven. He was open to an evolution of Church teachings that would clarify and expand that which had been originally only implicit or indirect. And my hunch is that the Mormon Church today knows what to do with its own version of a heavenly goddess as little as the Catholic Church knows what to do with its version. What both traditions point to, however, is the longing for a fullness of the divine and a fullness of our desire to be part of that divinity. God is too great to be captured by masculine images alone, and our longing for God is too great to be reduced and restrained to a narrowly masculine understanding of the identity of Jesus. Jesus is indeed the Son of God, and His power and glory have no limits, but Jesus had a Mother, and He loved His mother dearly. So should we.

Another similarity between Catholicism and Mormonism concerns the status of matter, but we will return to this in a later chapter. For now I just want to say that in some interpretations of Mary, her flesh is seen as ontologically altered by the growth of the Son of God in her womb. That is why the thought of her body corrupting in the grave, or her body being born into original sin, is unthinkable for many Catholics. She not only nourished Jesus in her body, but the body of Jesus interacted with her in the most intimate ways imaginable. And not just the body of Jesus: the whole divinity of Christ was inside of her in a way that Christ will never be inside any of the rest of us. She is the first instance of transubstantiation, we could say, taking that word to mean the transformation of matter into a substance capable of conveying the intimate reality of the divine. Mormons too have a very material understanding of God. God is not above and beyond the world, immaterial and thus unimaginable. For Mormons, God is composed of a substance purer than any we have ever directly experienced, but the divine substance is capable of interacting with the physical stuff that makes up the cosmos. Catholics find that interaction to be most tangible, mysterious, and wonderful in the Virgin Mary. Even before His birth, that is, while He was still in Mary's womb, Jesus was filled with the Holy Spirit (Luke 1:15). Mary is indeed unique in her intimacy with God. That is why all generations should call her blessed (Luke 1:48) and why Catholics say, in the rosary, "Blessed are you among women, and blessed is the fruit of your womb" (Luke 1:42).

Alonzo

Unlike Roman Catholics, Latter-day Saints are not typically criticized for their reverence for the Virgin Mary. However, we empathize with our Catholic brothers and sisters because misunderstandings about their sense of reverence for Mary are similar to the misinterpretations about the Mormon appreciation for Joseph Smith. Where the typical Catholic does not "worship" Mary in the way that one worships God; so also, members of the LDS Church do not "worship" Joseph Smith, even though we are regularly accused of doing so. Of course, an entire chapter could be dedicated to what our actions of reverence mean—and what they do not mean. Space restraints will not permit a detailed discussion here. However, a word or two seems appropriate.

For Mormons, Joseph Smith is a modern Moses or Paul. He is a prophetic witness of God who, under the influence of the Holy Spirit, has been used to bring saving truths to a people seeking to know the divine will. Latter-day Saints reverence all scriptural prophets—all of them! Because Joseph is seen as but one more divinely sent and inspired messenger of God, Mormons revere him as they would any of the ancient prophets or apostles. In many ways, Joseph is mentioned more by practicing Latter-day Saints than are, say, Peter or Isaiah. Indeed, some have been critical of Mormons because of how often they "testify" of Joseph Smith and his inspired revelations and visions. One blogger, for instance, claimed that "Mormons speak of Joseph more than they do of Christ, which proves where their true allegiance lies and where they truly place their faith." At the risk of sounding a bit apologetic, my simple reply would be this: Nonsense! Latter-day Saints do not see

Joseph as a savior or messiah. They trust in Christ, and Christ alone for their salvation. So why do Mormons mention Joseph Smith with frequency? The fixation with Joseph is largely because he is what tends to set Mormons apart from other contemporary Christians. The ancient Church of the Old and New Testaments consisted of prophet-believing peoples. They believed in the existence of living and inspired prophets in their day. Though not perfect in their discipleship, Christians of antiquity tended to trust the words and revelations of these inspired prophetic leaders and exercised faith in their commands. With no offense intended, today neither Christianity nor Judaism looks to living prophets—meaning men whose office and experience is akin to that of Moses or Isaiah. The apocalyptic or theophanic has largely been lost from the Judeo-Christian tradition. Certainly many Christians see the pope as a Spirit-directed man. Many may say the same of their pastor or priest. However, few religious leaders today claim revelation on the scale and nature of the biblical prophets: for example, prophecy, revelation, visions, seeing God (as Moses, Isaiah, Paul, and others did), and so on. Again, I am not criticizing my brothers and sisters of other traditions. But I wish to make the point that this is where the Mormon fixation with Joseph Smith comes in. Mormons are prone to "testify" of Joseph's visions and revelations because he is a major part of what sets us apart from other Christians. We, with them, believe in Jesus. We, with them, believe in the Bible. We, with them, believe in the sacrament of the Lord's Supper, repentance, faith, baptism, and so forth. But where Mormons find themselves dramatically unique is in their belief that there are upon the earth today living prophets and apostles who continue to receive visions and revelations (of biblical proportions) for those in the world who are receptive to their message. Because of these prophets and revelations, Latter-day Saints also have a handful of doctrinal differences with other Christians. However, these are merrily appendages to, or the result of, having living prophets. For Mormons, if Isaiah were here today we would honor him and seek to apply his counsel and revelations. Thus, we do the same with Joseph and his successors. We do not worship them, but we reverence the office of prophet—regardless of whom God calls to it (e.g., Moses, Isaiah, Paul, etc.). For this we draw criticism, as Catholics do for their devotion to the only woman God ever called to give birth to a divine being.

Stephen has spoken of the Catholic and LDS "goddess problem." True, we both get negatively critiqued for our perception of the divine exaltation of certain women. However, that may be more of a critique of those who criticize us than it is of our respective faiths. I have to agree with Stephen: this is more of a "goddess advantage" than a "goddess problem."

The concept that there is a feminine side to the divine—or a feminine in heaven—is ancient and certainly has biblical support. (Here I go with the apologetics again!) Of course, we know that among Jewish worshipers at Elephantine there was commonly understood to be a "mother goddess" at Yahweh's side. Scholars have pointed out that the early Israelites engaged in the worship of female deities. Was that a result of a corruption of the faith, or the consequence of ancient prophetic teachings? Who is to say? Certainly, if such ideas were once orthodox, they have been lost. But the Bible suggests the belief in a feminine divine is not a new or new-age idea. One Evangelical scholar noted: "The idea of God as mother has a rich and long tradition in Christian spirituality."[3] The Old and New Testaments hint at the feminine divine. For example, the Hebrew word for one of the most important attributes of God is *rahum*, which is often translated as "compassion," but literally means "womb love." Thus, we find in the Bible God's love painted in feminine terms—using the image of a woman's womb as the metaphor. Similarly, the language of Isaiah 49:15 is curious: "Can a woman forget the baby at her breast and have no compassion on the child she has borne? Though she may forget, I will not forget you!" (*NIV*). Here God is depicted as a nursing mother—a metaphor entirely foreign to men. In Hosea 13:8 God promises: "Like a bear robbed of her cubs, I will attack [your enemies] and rip them open" (*NIV*). God describes divine love as being like what a mother bear feels for her young cubs—including a willingness to do anything to protect her children. Jesus even jumps on the bandwagon in Matthew 23:37, where He states: "Jerusalem, Jerusalem . . . how often I have longed to gather your children together, as a hen gathers her chicks under her wings, and you were not willing" (*NIV*). Thus, even Christ uses feminine language to describe the type of love that He and His Father have for those who profess a belief in them. In a similar spirit, Deuteronomy 32:11–12 states: "As an eagle stirreth up her nest, fluttereth over her young, spreadeth abroad her wings, taketh them, beareth them on her wings, so the Lord alone did lead [Jacob]" (*21st Century KJV*). Again, God is seen in terms that are feminine rather than masculine. God is depicted as a mother eagle teaching, protecting, and supporting her children. Even the Apocrypha's Wisdom of Solomon seems to reference this divine feminine: "She [Sophia (*Gk*) or Hokhma (*Hb*)] brought them over the Red Sea, and led them through the deep waters; but she drowned their enemies, and cast them up from the depth of the sea" (*NRSV* Wisdom of Solomon 10:18–19). In Proverbs 8:22–31, we find Sophia at God's side prior to the creation of the universe, and before the waters and mountains of this earth existed. She is depicted as a co-worker with God and, we learn, He delights in her just as she delights in the newly created cosmos and its inhabitants. Although these are but a few examples, they show that in the Bible God is depicted over and over again as feminine or as mother.

Although our doctrines regarding the feminine divine differ from each other, some Catholic and LDS scholars have gravitated toward passages such as these in support of their variant views of Mary or Mother in Heaven.

The Catholics have a pretty defined Mariology—and have since even before Vatican I. Latter-day Saints, on the other hand, are a bit vaguer on the details surrounding the mother of our Lord. Mary is simply not looked upon with quite the awe and devotion in LDS circles as she is in Catholicism. Nevertheless, her preeminence is acknowledged. Respected ecclesiastical leaders within the LDS Church have spoken of her as the greatest of all female spirits; as one chosen and foreordained to be the mother of the Son of God, after the manner of the flesh.[4] Mormons are taught that they cannot think too highly of Mary and they generally speak her name with reverence.[5] As one Latter-day Saint put it, we cannot but think that the Father would choose the greatest female spirit to be the mother of His Son, even as He chose the male spirit like unto Him to be the Savior.[6] From an LDS perspective, there was no greater honor that the Father of us all could bestow upon any woman. Thus, of those born in the flesh, there is no woman whom Mormons hold in greater esteem than Mary. Consequently, in our doctrine and view of Mary, Mormons might seem to outsiders more Protestant than they do Catholic. Truth be told, however, Latter-day Saints probably fall somewhere between those two traditions.

The place where LDS doctrine most emphasizes "the heavenly feminine" is not in its doctrine of Mary but, rather, in its doctrine of a counterpart to God the Father—whom we refer to as "heavenly Mother." Since the days of Joseph Smith, Latter-day Saints have believed that God had a divine partner—as spouse, if you will. And just as Mormons see God the Father as the creator of our spirits, we also see Mother in heaven as His

partner in that divine parentage. Thus, Eliza R. Snow, an early LDS leader
and poet, penned the following words in her hymn, "Oh, My Father":

1. O my Father, thou that dwellest
In the high and glorious place,
When shall I regain thy presence
And again behold thy face?

In thy holy habitation,
Did my spirit once reside?
In my first primeval childhood
Was I nurtured near thy side?

2. For a wise and glorious purpose
Thou hast placed me here on earth
And withheld the recollection
Of my former friends and birth;

Yet ofttimes a secret something
Whispered, "You're a stranger here,"
And I felt that I had wandered
From a more exalted sphere.

3. I had learned to call thee Father,
Thru thy Spirit from on high,
But, until the key of knowledge
Was restored, I knew not why.

In the heav'ns are parents single?
No, the thought makes reason stare!
Truth is reason; truth eternal
Tells me I've a mother there.

4. When I leave this frail existence,
When I lay this mortal by,
Father, Mother, may I meet you
In your royal courts on high?

Then, at length, when I've completed
All you sent me forth to do,
With your mutual approbation
Let me come and dwell with you.[7]

The last two stanzas of the third verse of Snow's hymn articulate what Latter-day Saints generally believe: that we have a Mother in Heaven who is the mother of each of our spirits.

Mormons openly acknowledge that we know little of the "heavenly feminine"—and we speak little of Her. We do not worship Her, and we do not pray to Her. However, Her existence is understood to be a foundational doctrine for Latter-day Saints. It is foundational because it has strong soteriological implications. Mormons believe in theosis—or God's desire to divinize each of us through the merits of Christ the Lord. In Genesis 1:27 we read: "So God created mankind in his own image, in the image of God he created them; *male and female he created them*" (*NIV*). Mormons hold that men are created after the image of the divine Father and women are created in the likeness of the divine Mother.[8] When God deifies us—making us, through grace, like Him—then men will be more fully after the Father's likeness and women after the Mother's image. Minus the existence of a divine Mother, women seem somehow inferior to men—not fully able to take on the attributes, nature, and likeness of God.

Stephen

I find the Mormon openness to revering the Virgin Mary to be refreshing, welcoming, and hopeful for future dialogue. In fact, this is where Mormons, in my mind, reveal how little immersed they are in Protestant traditions. Many Protestants have something like an allergic reaction to all things Mary. It sometimes seems that Protestants almost define themselves as the anti-Mary theological party, since they suppose that Roman Catholics go too far in honoring her. A Protestant friend once told me that it was unbiblical to praise Mary. Only God can and should be praised, he insisted! Well, I praise people all the time. I praise my children for doing a good job at school or in sports. Praise is a form of celebration, a way of congratulating and acknowledging someone for the gifts they have and what they have done for others. Of all human beings, besides Jesus Christ, of course, who deserves our praise more than Mary? And if there is a feminine dimension to heaven, who would better represent that than Mary?

Like the Mormon reverence for Joseph Smith, the Catholic adoration of Mary is often misinterpreted. In Catholic terms, the honor Mormons pay Joseph would be similar to how Catholics treat the saints (historical figures who, by their exemplary conduct and steadfastness in the faith, are already with God in heaven and can be approached for their prayers and comfort). Death does not separate us from loved ones or from the love of those who are especially close to God. For Catholics, however, Mary deserves a category of her own because she was such a singular person in relation to Jesus. The Catholic Church has technical terms that make all of this clear. The saints are worthy of our deference and respect in actions as well as thought (in Greek, *doulia*, although sometimes rendered *dulia*), but Mary is worthy of our *hyperdulia* (think of a heightened or hyperbolic form of *doulia*). Mary, however, is not to be given the adoration (*latria*, which carries the connotation of worship that veneration does not) that is reserved for God alone.

Alonzo draws from a rich array of history and scripture to establish the ancient roots of the belief in a feminine aspect of the divine. He might be surprised to learn that Pope John Paul II told a crowd gathered in St. Peter's Square in 1999 that God has a feminine side and can be referred to as mother as well as father. Alonzo also mentions the figure of wisdom in the Old Testament, often referred to with the personalized (and feminine) name of Sophia. The tradition of Alonzo's youth, Eastern Orthodoxy, tends to identify Sophia with Mary (as in Maria Sophia), because it is Mary through whom the knowledge and wisdom of God enters the world in its fullest extent. Such speculations, I think, are to be welcomed, and they would be more common and robust today if not for the influence of Protestant theology.

There have been many attempts to fill the void left by Mary's declining influence in the modern world. Think, for example, of the nineteenth-century movement, led largely by Protestants, to establish a Mother's Day in the United States. Is it any coincidence that these Protestant ministers chose a Sunday in May, the month of Mary, to celebrate the "cult of motherhood"? Yet who knows what moral consequences have resulted from the Protestant Reformation's efforts to minimize Mary's role in Christian spirituality. Certainly, the world was a much more brutal, violent, and merciless place in the nineteenth and twentieth centuries, as if masculinity were loosened from the restraints of feminine guidance and direction. Think also about the sexual confusions and excesses that plague the twentieth century and show no signs of diminishing. Men especially have been victims of the absence of a genuine and proper love of Mary. By becoming alienated from their own natural inclinations toward attending to the feminine in the divine, many men have become bereft of heartfelt acknowledgments of the holiness of womanhood.

I suppose where Mormons and Catholics would have a hard time in sorting out a theological consensus on these issues is the way in which Mormons imagine a feminine consort to God. Putting Mary in that role would sexualize her in a way that would scandalize most Catholics, I suspect. Nonetheless, there is a great mystery about Mary's relationship to God the Father. Most of the time, Catholics define Mary in terms of her relationship to her son, Jesus, the Son of God. But Mary was also overshadowed by the Holy Spirit (Luke 1:35; overshadowed is an arresting word that protects the privacy of her personal experience of the Spirit) and entered into a relationship with God that is utterly unique in the whole history of the cosmos. Could it be that Mormon boldness about a "Heavenly Mother" might help Catholics to recover the cosmic significance of the Virgin Mary? All Christians believe that Jesus had a mother, and we believe that Jesus is divine, so it should not be shocking to follow logic to the conclusion that God has a mother. Nevertheless, it is shocking, and it should be shocking!

Early Church Fathers drew a parallel between the Ark of the Covenant, which preserved the treasure of the stone tablets upon which were written the Ten Commandments, and Mary's womb, which sustained Jesus.[9] In fact, the same Greek word for overshadowed is used in the Septuagint (the Greek translation of Jewish scriptures) description of the glory of God overshadowing the ark (Exodus 40:35). Just as it is hard to know where a container ends and the thing it contains begins, it is surely hard to draw a sharp line in Mary's womb between the body of Jesus and the body of Mary. She was the first to commune physically with the body of Jesus Christ. All of the strength, beauty, and vulnerability of a woman's body can be found in her, as well as all of the purity and power of the flesh of Jesus Christ himself. She was, and still is, the literal body of grace. Mormons can help us Catholics recover that beautiful truth.

Alonzo

During the Iconoclast controversy of the eighth and ninth centuries, the Eastern Orthodox fought tooth and nail to defend their right to use icons in worship. They insisted that icons were not just acceptable as a means of worshiping God, but were a necessary part of true worship. Icons, according to the Orthodox, safeguard a full and proper doctrine of the incarnation. In other words, icons teach us what Jesus truly was when He dwelt here upon the earth. Icons are earthly matter that draws us to the divine.

At the incarnation Jesus, the Son of God, came down to earth and entered a body made of earthly matter—a body the Virgin Mary made for Him. He inhabited that mortal, material body so as to draw us to the divine. He was, in Orthodox thinking, a divine icon. His purpose was, in many ways, the same as icons: to help us in our effort to inherit a place in God's kingdom. He was an example to which we could look and emulate.

What does this have to do with Mary? Well, in many ways, Roman Catholics see Mary too as an icon. Just as we look upon Jesus to know how to return to God; Mary serves as an exemplar to be emulated in this same process. Jesus certainly sets the example for all. But in a world so saturated in feminism and the rejection of masculine role models for women, Mary is the ultimate and ideal surrogate. Her total submission to God—as described in the *magnificat*—sets an example for all Christians (male or female) to emulate. Her submissiveness to the Father's will is only overshadowed by Christ's submission to God.

For Mormons, through Jesus's example, we learn of what the Father is truly like. Jesus Himself declared: "If ye had known me, ye should have known my Father also: and from henceforth ye know him, and have seen him" (John 14:7). Christ reveals to us what we do not otherwise know. Mary, for Latter-day Saints, does something similar. In so many ways, she typifies Heavenly Mother. As finite beings, she enables us to grasp—even if only ever so slightly—what a divine, godlike woman would be. She points us to the "heavenly feminine" in a way that no other woman ever has. She exemplifies what every faithful woman will be throughout eternity. And this, not of her own volition, but as a calling or vocation from God. She represents well the ideal mother, disciple, wife, confidant, and Christian.

Now, admittedly, Catholics traditionally recoil at the thought of a mother-goddess (aside from some pagan personification). Nevertheless, they do not traditionally find objectionable descriptive titles for Mary, such as "Queen of Heaven," "Mother of God" (*theotokos*), "Mother of the Church," or "Co-Redemptrix"—all epitaphs which cause Protestants to scream "Heresy!" John Paul II certainly saw Mary in ways that Latter-day Saints see Mother in Heaven. He seemed to adore the Virgin even more that most Roman Catholics. And while—with the rise of feminism and women's rights—more liberal Catholics seem to be moving away from many of the Church's traditional teachings and practices, in contemporary society Mary seems the ideal icon for those who wish to be liberated. In the Bible, she is depicted in submission to only one—God! The

Gospels do not portray her as being "ruled over" by Joseph. At the wedding at Cana, she comfortably gives Jesus instructions and counsel. She is never an image of weakness—and yet is ever an image of holiness. Baring those who outright reject the existence of God, Mary seems the perfect icon for any women's movement. And whether one believes that the "heavenly feminine" consists of the mother of our spirits, or simply the mother of Jesus, the symbolic importance in the life Mary's lived seems valuable to all.

4

Revelation

Stephen

The idea that divine revelation continued beyond the period that saw the closing of the New Testament canon of scripture is one of the most fundamental principles of Mormon theology. It is certainly a principle that puts Mormonism at odds with those churches shaped by the Magisterial Reformation (which refers to Protestants who accepted the interdependence of religious and secular authorities in order to maintain order and suppress heresy, in contrast to the Radical Reformers who rejected any secular authority over the Church). Continuing revelation is not a principle, however, that necessarily contradicts Catholic teaching. Indeed, on the question of revelation, we once again find interesting parallels and challenging similarities between the Latter-day Saints and Catholics.[1]

Catholics believe in saints, miracles, religious eccentrics, mystics, prophets, healings, and visions in every possible shape and size. If you tell a Protestant minister that God has spoken to you, you will most likely be told to stick with what God has written in the Bible. If you tell that same thing to a priest, the priest is likely to ask, "What did he say?" For Catholics, God is always acting to reveal himself in the world, and such revelations are not precluded by the fact that God revealed himself definitively in the Bible. When Protestants broke from Rome, they decided that scripture should be their sole and sufficient source of authority. Protestants did not necessarily deny that God acts in miraculous ways outside of the events recorded in the Bible, but they did insist that these miracles do not tell us anything about God that we cannot already find in the Bible. Consequently, miracles were relegated to personal and private significance. Praying for a miracle of healing was acceptable, but drawing theological inferences from miracles was not. At best, miracles were signs that pointed back to the singular miracle of the Bible itself. Post-Biblical miracles, if they happen at all, were stripped of their revelatory significance.

Catholics think that the Bible does not exhaust the Word of God. God spoke the world into being, commissioned the prophets to speak on His behalf, sent His Word to become human flesh, and left us the words of the Bible, but He still has more to say to us, though never in ways that contradict things He has already said. Even in heaven we will continue to be transformed by our deepening knowledge of the divine. Catholics believe that God is infinite, and thus God can never reveal too much of himself. There is always more to know about God than we could ever imagine.

Revelation can be a heavy word, since a revelation from God carries absolute authority, but revelation really means nothing more than how we come to know God by means of God's own actions. Knowing God might seem to be a complete impossibility, given how different God is from us, but we need to keep in mind that God created us so that we might be able to know him. We are creatures designed for this kind of knowledge. For that reason, I want to suggest that knowing God is not all that different from coming to know another person. Somebody that we do not know can introduce herself to us directly, but we can also learn about her from those who know her well. In addition, we can read letters from the person or documents that they have written. The more important the person is, the more we should want to read everything we can about and by them as well as hear from everyone who knew them. The problem is: What sources are most trustworthy?

Protestants acknowledge that God once talked directly to people, but they believe it is best to focus on the records of those revelations, which God inspired and preserved for our sake. Protestants are spiritually content with the Bible and thus understandably suspicious of any claims that God is still speaking to believers. For Catholics, the Bible is indeed the inspired Word of God, but the Bible does not limit God's freedom to speak in whatever way He wants. Indeed, Catholics have long been critical of the way some Protestants make an idol out of the Bible by treating it as a sacred object rather than as the history and testimony that points us to Jesus. Catholics, for example, would argue that it is not strictly true that the Bible is a necessary means for coming to know God since illiterate people can learn about Jesus Christ through other, non-textual media.

Revelation for Catholics is not just a set of propositions to be believed. Instead, it is also a process to be experienced. At the center of that experience, of course, is Jesus Christ. The Bible is precious because He is. The Bible is the Word of God because all of its words are, in one way or another, about Him. Indeed, no human words can do justice to, replace, or encompass the Word of God. If there is a literal Word of God, it is Jesus Christ, not the Bible.

The Catholic Church has a long history of thinking about these matters, and it has developed some terms that are intended to illuminate some subtle but important differences. The basic terms that are relevant for our discussion are public and private revelation. Public revelation refers to those events, messages, and narratives that God wanted humanity as a whole to hear, and the Bible makes this revelation available to everyone. The point of public revelation is to invite people to know God through Jesus Christ. The history of God's engagement with the world, from creation, through the election of the people of Israel, to the incarnation and the beginnings of the Church, is unique, sacred, and unrepeatable. Such revelations ended, according to St. Thomas Aquinas, with the death of St. John the Apostle.

Public revelation is not, however, limited to the exact printed words of the Bible because this category includes traditions that were handed down by the Apostles in oral form. The Church has conceptualized apostolic tradition in different ways over the centuries, with much debate about how to define it. Sometimes oral tradition is treated as a kind of supplement to the written tradition of the Bible. At other times, efforts are made to show how everything in oral tradition can be found in implicit or latent form in Bible. Nobody denies that everything the Apostles taught and practiced is not included in the New Testament, but how did the early Christians sort out what that oral tradition was, and how do we decide about its validity today? Catholics, of course, argue that the fragility of the oral tradition is exactly why the Church needed (and still needs) a centralized papal authority. The papacy assures that oral tradition is publicized so that true teachings can be distinguished from false. Oral tradition also enabled the Church to determine which books should be included in the New Testament.

Catholics call public revelation, both written and oral, the deposit of faith. This deposit is complete in the sense that it includes everything we need to know for our salvation. It is a treasure that can never be completely disbursed since the more it is taught the greater it grows. Public revelation is not complete, however, in the sense that God is done speaking to us. It is also not complete in the sense that the full significance of the Bible has been made known to us. There is much work to be done by church authorities and theologians in presenting, systematizing, and explicating the revealed truths of God.

Catholics believe that the Holy Spirit guided the early Church in its reception and publication of oral tradition and that the Holy Spirit continues to guide the Magisterium of the Church (the teaching authority consisting of the Pope and Bishops) in order to keep it faithful to the unfolding and deepening of the deposit of faith. Still, Catholics readily admit that no church has a monopoly on the works of the Holy Spirit and that the Holy Spirit does not limit divine revelations to a specific time and place.

The freedom of the Spirit can be encountered in what the Church calls private revelation. Private revelation for Catholics does not mean a revelation that is given only to one or two people, out of the public eye, although that might likely be the case. It refers to a revelation that is given outside the sacred history of the Bible. Who knows how many private revelations there have been since the books of the Bible were gathered together and published in one single volume? That is a question that only God can answer, because only God knows who He has spoken to throughout the ages. These revelations, according to Catholic teaching, do not add to or take the place of Christ's life and teaching, but they can help us to live our faith more fully. Typically, they impact official church teachings by expressing popular and sometimes neglected forms of piety, and thus some private revelations end up incorporated into Catholic devotional practices. Their overall purpose is to give us a certainty that we might find lacking in our relationship to the public revelations of the Bible, but they should also lead us back to a better understanding of the Bible.

There is no better warrant for continuing revelation than the Bible itself. The Apostle Paul writes, "Do not quench the Spirit. Do not despise the words of prophets, but test everything" (1 Thessalonians 5:19–21). As that verse suggests, revelation and prophecy are connected in the sense that prophets are people who receive direct communications from God, though not all people to whom God communicates are prophets. (One can receive a private revelation without being called to be a prophet.) Prophecy is sometimes equated in our day and age with an ability to predict the future, but the biblical prophets did much more than that. They interpreted the will of God for people who needed to know what to do in the present. They had a gift to read the "signs of the time." Prophecy in that sense is needed as much today as it ever was, but so is discernment.

The Magisterium of the Catholic Church does not try to judge every private revelation. That would be both presumptuous and impossible. Some private revelations, however, call out for the Church's response. People want to know if they can trust what others have claimed that God has told them, and so the Church steps in to aid in the process of discernment. When the Church accepts a private revelation, it does not require that every Catholic believe it. What it says is that Catholics, exercising their own prudence, may trust in the revelation in they choose to do so. The Church would not be doing its proper work if it did not scrutinize prophecies that gain the attention of the faithful, but even those prophecies that it does not attend to are rarely scorned or abused.

Some of the most important private revelations have occurred in the last century or two, and they concern the Virgin Mary. The Marian apparitions of Lourdes, Guadalupe, and Fatima have impacted the lives of countless people seeking healing and salvation. The Catholic Church tends to interpret these visions as a matter of interior or spiritual perception, not objective and publicly accessible bodily perceptions. The children at Fatima saw Mary with their hearts, not their eyes, yet they really did encounter her and their lives were truly changed. Nonetheless, the Church's own teaching on Mary should warn against a purely subjective interpretation of these visions. Since Mary was assumed into heaven with her soul and body still inseparably united, she did not appear in these visions as a disembodied spirit.

Various saints like Teresa of Avila have also reported hearing God speak to them in the form of an inner voice. Auditory revelations often involve God giving someone advice or guidance about what to do in specific circumstances. The Catholic Church respects all such revelations as long as they cohere with the deposit of faith, include nothing that contradicts scripture, and result in improved and transformed lives. Humility and simplicity are characteristic marks of someone who receives direct communications from God.

Joseph Smith's early visions of God and his subsequent reports of revelations obviously have public and not just private significance, but I think the category of private revelation might be a helpful one for Catholics who wish to ponder Smith's life and teachings. Smith had both visual and auditory experiences of the divine, and the Doctrine and Covenants collects many of his revelations that addressed a wide range of practical, moral, liturgical, and theological issues. Throughout his visions, he demonstrated a humble and simple character. He was not arrogant about these visions, nor did he use them for personal advantage. He did not even draw attention to himself, preferring to let his prophecies speak for themselves. One thing Smith did not have that Catholic tradition recommends is a spiritual advisor to consult about his visions. The Catholic Church is very hierarchical, of course, and clergy who have visions are always advised to have a confessor or director they can go to for help in discerning the validity and purpose of private revelations. Smith did not have a confessor, but he did surround himself with trustworthy men, and he frequently sought their input and advice. His revelations were very much a communal effort, then. They were the revelations of one man, but they were subjected to collective scrutiny and discussion.

One other aspect of Smith's revelations might strike Catholics as noteworthy. In the Catholic tradition, Saints who receive visions are almost always caught up in an unspeakable ecstatic state. Visions, that is, elevate the recipient out of the ordinary world and into a glimpse of something that is beyond our imagination. A soul enraptured by God loses touch with material things and this disconnection from objective reality is experienced as a timeless moment of transcendence. Joseph did not seem to have this kind of ecstatic experience with his visions, but then again, his view of God is different from the Catholic view. Joseph did not think that God is immaterially beyond all that we can experience here and now, so having a vision of God did not mean being uprooted from physical reality. Unity with God did not require a sacrifice of bodily awareness.

To put Joseph's first revelation in a historical context, I offer this selection from George Fox, the founder of Quakerism: "As I had forsaken the priests, so I left the separate preachers also, and those called the most experienced people; for I saw there was none among them all that could speak to my condition. And when all my hopes in them and in all men were gone, so that I had nothing outwardly to help me, nor could tell what to do, then, oh then, I heard a voice which said: 'There is one, even Jesus Christ, that can speak to thy condition' and when I heard it my heart did leap for joy."[2] Fox, like Smith, was in despair over the churches competing for his attention and the low moral state to which much of Christendom had fallen. They both had personal encounters with Jesus that led them to start reform movements that were more open to the Holy Spirit and demanded higher moral standards of their followers. In times of social crisis, in fact, visions, whether visual or auditory (or both), are more common than in times of cultural and religious stability. God seems to speak to individuals, or people seem to be more ready to hear God's speech, when institutions no longer exercise the moral and spiritual leadership that everyone needs.

I cannot speak for the Catholic Church in any official capacity, of course, since I am not ordained, do not teach theology at a Catholic University, and I have only been a Catholic for the better part of a decade. The Catholic Church officially does not accept the revelations of Joseph Smith as a form of private revelation. Nonetheless, I have found no evidence that any Catholic theologian or clergy have ever investigated those revelations with any thoroughness or depth. I personally think that Joseph had true and authentic visions of God, but more important, I think the category of private revelation can help all Catholics who are interested in Mormonism to come to terms with Joseph's remarkable life and legacy. I doubt if the Catholic Church will ever declare Joseph Smith to be a saint! But there is nothing stopping individual Catholics from entering into a prolonged, sympathetic, and serious investigation of how God has worked through Smith to deepen, clarify, and transform the lives of so many faithful Christians.

Alonzo

As a former Greek Orthodox, one of the things which first intrigued me about Mormonism was its fixation with revelation, with modern Prophets and Apostles. Because I so firmly believe in the Bible as the inspired Word of God—and because I believe that men like Moses, Isaiah, Paul, and others were indeed revelators—I was drawn to the notion that there could be individuals walking the earth today who have the power to see God "face to face" (Numbers 14:14), and who authoritatively speak on His behalf in these modern times. Latter-day Saints believe that God gives today revelations of biblical proportions and nature.

Like Roman Catholics, members of The Church of Jesus Christ of Latter-day Saints also distinguish between "public" and "private" revelation. We too believe that both, if legitimate or real, come from God. However, unlike the traditional Catholic view, Mormons do not believe that all public revelations ended with the Bible. In the LDS *Articles of Faith* two statements on revelation appear, each of which seem germane to our discussion. The first is from *Article of Faith* 8, which declares: "We believe the Bible to be the word of God as far as it is translated correctly; we also believe the Book of Mormon to be the word of God." Significantly,

Mormons believe the Bible was a public revelation from God, intended to be normative for followers of Christ. However, as the *Article* suggests, Latter-day Saints also believe the Book of Mormon—an ancient record of God's dealings with prophets and laity in the western hemisphere from the sixth century B.C. until about the fourth century A.D.—is also a public revelation normative for those followers of Christ who know of it. In other words, a faithful Latter-day Saint should not assume that a Roman Catholic who does not know about, understand, or believe in the Book of Mormon—but is faithful to the doctrines and commandments of the Bible—is going to hell. But for those who know of the Book of Mormon, understand its teachings, and have received a witness of its contents, that book constitutes a public revelation of God, which is normative for those specific believers.

In addition to the 8th *Article of Faith*, we find this in the 9th: "We believe all that God has revealed, all that He does now reveal, and we believe that He will yet reveal many great and important things pertaining to the Kingdom of God." This declaration refers to public and private revelations from God. Thus, in addition to the *Bible* and *The Book of Mormon*, Latter-day Saints believe in *The Doctrine and Covenants* (a series of canonized revelations to Joseph Smith and his successors) and *The Pearl of Great Price* (a body of canonized revelations from the Old Testament and New Testament eras, along with other modern revelatory and historical texts canonized by the Church) as part of the public revelations of the Church. But they also acknowledge that there have been many private revelations given—particularly through the modern prophets and apostles who govern the work of the Church but also to faithful, seeking individuals who make up the laity.

LDS Christians would agree with the Roman Catholic position that God has revealed to leaders of the Church who have lived since the biblical era many things for the benefit of the Church and the furtherance of the work. "Tradition," so called, is an undeniable example of private revelations given by God. And while Mormons and Catholics may not always agree upon which teachings have been "inspired traditions" and which have not, something we can agree upon is that such exist, and that during the period after the close of the New Testament and up to today God has inspired with private revelation many sincere individuals who ultimately preserved public revelations, such as the Bible, the doctrine that Jesus is the Christ, teachings regarding baptism and the Eucharist, and so on. As the LDS Doctrine and Covenants states (regarding private revelation): "And whatsoever they shall speak when moved upon by the Holy Ghost shall be scripture, shall be the will of the Lord, shall be the mind of the Lord, shall be the word of the Lord, shall be the voice of the Lord, and the power of God unto salvation" (D&C 68:4).

While many Protestants (and a few Catholics) are prone to cite the Revelation 22:18–19 as evidence that public revelation ended with the writings of John, Latter-day Saints see this as an erroneous reading of the Bible and of history. In the aforementioned verses John wrote: "I warn everyone who hears the words of the prophecy of this book: if anyone adds to them, God will add to that person the plagues described in this book; if anyone takes away from the words of the book of this prophecy, God will take away that person's share in the tree of life and in the holy city, which are described in this book" (*NRSV*). To the minds of many, John is saying that the New Testament is officially closed and that there will be no more scripture or public revelation. Of course, John was not referring to the New Testament in these verses, as it did not exist at the time John penned these words—nor would it in its final form for several hundred years. John was warning individuals who read his apocalypse to not seek to change it; adding to or taking from its teachings, visions, or content. Mormons do not see in the Bible any evidence that public revelation had come to an end—or that God was promising its imminent end. Christians of the second and third centuries used other books, not now in our New Testament, as scripture; as public revelations. For Mormons, the idea of a "closed canon" of "public revelation" implies man has some power to limit God's ability to reveal normatively—simply because man (not God) says "all public revelation has been given." So, while with Catholics we agree that God continues to reveal via private revelations to the Church and the world—including important private revelations to inspired ecclesiastical leaders—Mormons have a large canon of public revelations, and they remain entirely open to the concept that God could give more public revelations if He so chose. Indeed, Latter-day Saints expect such in the future.

Of course, none of this is intended as a "nah-nah nah-nah na na" diatribe. Ultimately, Latter-day Saints and Roman Catholics are very similar on this point—and, in many ways, in disagreement with traditional Protestant views of revelation. But Mormons simply accept a larger body of normative public revelations than do any of their other brothers or sisters in Christ.

Stephen has spoken of the Catholic view of revelations to their saints, and how that usually includes the seer being elevated "out of the ordinary world" wherein the recipient is "enraptured by God" and "loses touch with material things" in a "timeless moment of transcendence." This is exactly the kind of "ecstatic experience" Joseph Smith had during many of his encounters with the divine. Joseph noted: "All things whatsoever God in his infinite wisdom has seen fit and proper to reveal to us, while we are dwelling in mortality . . . are revealed to us in the abstract, and independent of affinity of this mortal tabernacle, but are revealed to our spirits precisely as though we had no bodies at all."[3] Thus, Joseph was very much what Stephen describes as a recipient of the "unspeakable ecstatic state." However, Joseph seemed to have this experience mostly when he was receiving angels or a theophanic vision—and not as much when he simply received revelations of doctrine or general counsel for the Church. But the otherworldly was something Joseph was very familiar with—as were some of his successors, such as Wilford Woodruff: a man who seemed to live the majority of his life with one foot in this world and one foot in the next.

Stephen rightly states that the Catholic Church will never declare Joseph Smith to be a saint. Of course, Catholicism does not canonize any non-Catholics. However, perhaps it should. In the post-Vatican II era when Catholic ecumenism is at its historically strongest point, and when the Church is in communion with most major Christian denominations, why not acknowledged the holiness and saved-state of those outside of the Catholic Church? If *Unitatis Redintegratio* (the "Decree on Ecumenism") can "acknowledge and esteem the truly Christian endowments . . . which are to be found among our separated brethren,"[4] then why not canonize some of those outside of the Church who manifest those endowments? *Lumen Gentium* (the "Dogmatic Constitution on the Church") indicates that "the Saviour wills all men to be saved (cf. 1 Tim. 2:4). Those who, through no fault of their own, do not know the Gospel of Christ or his Church, but who nevertheless seek God with a sincere heart, and, moved by grace, try in their actions to do his will as they know it through the dictates of their conscience—those too may achieve enteral salvation."[5] Again, why not seek out the Gregory of Palamas or Gandhis of the world, and canonize them? I suspect Stephen would agree: holiness is holiness, regardless of denominational boundaries.

Catholics and Mormons each have something to learn from each other when it comes to the principle of revelation. For Catholics, perhaps the message is do not limit God in His giving of public revelation. Perhaps there are other books out there that were given by Him, and which are normative. Early Christians certainly believed in such texts (not now in the Bible). What if the Shepherd of Hermas really was an inspired public revelation? What if the Book of Mormon really is "Another Testament of Jesus Christ?" For Mormons, the lesson might be this: Catholics are pretty open to taking revelation or truth from wherever it comes. Some Mormons still struggle with that, though it is the official position of the Church. Brigham Young once stated:

> For me, the plan of salvation must . . . circumscribe [all of] the knowledge that is upon the face of the earth, or it is not from God. Such a plan incorporates every system of true doctrine on the earth, whether it be ecclesiastical, moral, philosophical, or civil: it incorporates all good laws that have been made from the days of Adam until now; it swallows up the laws of nations, for it exceeds them all in knowledge and purity; it circumscribes the doctrines of the day, and takes from the right and the left, and brings all truth together in one system, and leaves the chaff to be scattered hither and thither.[6]

LDS doctrine declares that if something is true it is part of Mormonism—regardless of the source of that truth, be it Latter-day Saint, Catholic, Muslim, Buddhist, and so forth. While this is our doctrine, I believe a percentage of Mormons are still suspicious about the teachings of other traditions. Perhaps we are not all as open to the universality of truth as we ought to be.

The undeniable beauty of the LDS and Roman Catholic model is simply this: both traditions refuse to limit God to a *sola scriptura* (by scripture alone) voice. If He chooses to speak in the post-New Testament era, Mormons and Catholics want to hear it. And while we do not entirely agree on how He will do that, both traditions seem firm in their conviction that God has and will continue to do so.

Stephen

I love the story of Samuel and Eli in the opening chapters of the first Book of Samuel. Recall that Hannah has been childless, even though she is the favored of the two wives of her husband. Hannah pledges to God at Shiloh that if she should have a son, she would dedicate him to the Lord. Before the Temple at Jerusalem was built, Shiloh was probably the holiest place in Israel. Archeologists have found the remains of a stone altar that just might be the one that Hannah sat next to as she made her vow. True to her pledge, she gave her son over to the priests of Shiloh to be raised as a man of God. Eli was the priest of this altar, but his sons were not very priestly. They rudely and crudely took all the best parts of the meat being sacrificed on the altar for their own. They were, in a word, gluttons! Corruption was in the air (or should I say on the fire), and something needed to change.

So God calls Samuel. When God first talks to him, Samuel says, simply, "Here I am!" Samuel thinks it might be Eli calling him, so he runs to the old man who tells him to go back to sleep. After the third time, God delivered a message to Samuel in a manner that kept the little boy riveted and transfixed. The Bible says that the Lord "came and stood there" (1 Samuel 3:10). We do not know what exactly this means, but evidently Samuel saw, noticed, or felt God's physical presence. God must have had some kind of form in this revelation and was not simply a bodiless voice. Anyway, after God finally tells Samuel what he wants from him, the little boy, unlike the times before, does not go running to Eli. He laid in his room until morning and was hesitant to tell anyone what he had experienced. Eli knows something has happened and calls for Samuel. The important point for me is that Samuel answers him with the same words that he said to God: "Here I am." He was ready and eager to listen to Eli when summoned, just as he was open to hearing from God.

There are several significant lessons to be found in this story. The Bible is full of evidence that God speaks directly to individuals, but this story is a particularly graphic account of how revelation works. God chose a young man (or boy) who was ready and eager to hear him. This boy had faithful parents who had already pledged him to serve the Lord. Finally, he sought out the wisdom of an older man who had spent many years in worshiping God and studying His ways. Samuel was not only open to hearing God but also receptive to the advice of an elder in the faith. Notice that he was not eager to share what God had told him. That is only natural too. Hearing God speak must be such an unusual, amazing, and serious event that keeping God's words private, perhaps for fear of being embarrassed or disbelieved, is surely an understandable response. Yet when his mentor called him, Samuel answered with the same readiness that he showed to God. He was, in a word, obedient.

The young Joseph Smith also came from a devout family, was also obedient to his revelation, and sought the advice of others in how to handle it. Catholic moral theologians teach that you should always follow your conscience. God will never condemn you if you do what you, by your best light, think is right. I believe that Joseph followed his conscience in responding to God's words to him.[7] That does not mean that I believe that everything Joseph said or did, and that all of the theological consequences he drew from his revelations, were right. Those of us who do not have mystical visions of our own must rely on our own consciences to evaluate the visions others have. We also should do what Samuel did, that is, seek the advice of elders in the faith. We should test the spirits of all of those who claim to be moved by the Holy Spirit, but we should do so with a generous and open heart.

Here I have two specific questions for Alonzo. These are meant as genuine queries, not the stuff of debating points, because they could be asked of any representative of any religious tradition. First, Alonzo mentions the fact that Mormon theology abounds with statements about how the truth can be found in other religions and how the Saints should be open to the truth wherever they find it. So how do the Saints evaluate revelation claims in other Christian traditions? What if the Virgin Mary really appeared to three shepherd children in Fatima, Portugal? The Latter-day Saints, after all, base a lot of their theology on the category of trust. They trust the witnesses who saw the golden plates and they trust the integrity of Joseph Smith. On what grounds, then, do they mistrust so many revelations given to Catholic saints throughout the centuries? The Catholic Church is actually very careful about evaluating miracles and vetting saints. Can the Magisterium's procedures be trusted?

Second, I must admit that I find some of the language used to describe Mormonism's understanding of revelation puzzling. Mormons believe in continuing revelation, but do they really believe in an "open canon," and is it really right to put them in the Protestant camp known as "non-creedal" or even "anti-creedal"? These concepts are what I would call relative, not absolute. That is, no religious tradition can have an absolutely open scriptural canon or be absolutely opposed to all creeds. A truly open canon without any creed would lead to spiritual and ecclesial chaos.

True, Mormonism can evolve, adapt, and change because it is led by a President who is also considered by the Saints to be a Prophet in continuity with the prophetic vocation of Joseph Smith. Yet it is unimaginable that the President of the Latter-day Saints would say, teach, or believe anything that would contradict or deny basic Mormon teachings. He might modify some aspect of Mormon doctrines, as when the First Presidency, led by Spencer Kimball, announced a revelation from God in 1978 that cleared all worthy men, "without regard for race or color," to become priests in the LDS Church. Mormons have continuing revelation, but they do not have contradictory revelations, or at least I do not think they would want to say that revelation can contradict itself.

All churches have creeds, even if their creed is simply the statement that they are anti-creedal. I grew up in a church that solemnly proclaimed its commitment to "No creed but Christ." Everyone thought that meant "no creed," forgetting the Christ part. Mormon theology is incredibly complex, and Mormons are, no doubt, ambivalent about formal creeds, even going so far as to blame the corruption of the early Church on the quest for creedal consensus. Nonetheless, Mormons have informal and formal statements of what they believe. There are two such documents, in fact, that serve as informal creeds of the Latter-day Saints. The first is the Articles of Faith, thirteen fundamental beliefs that Joseph Smith composed in 1842. These are included in the LDS scripture known as *The Pearl of Great Price*, and Alonzo quoted from them in the previous section precisely because they carry doctrinal weight. The second is *The Lectures on Faith*, consisting of seven sections that cover not only the nature of faith but also the being, character, and attributes of God. *The Lectures on Faith* were written by a committee and approved by Joseph, and they were included in The Doctrine and Covenants until 1921.[8]

And, of course, Mormons believe that The Book of Mormon (and other documents) is on authoritative par with the Old and New Testaments. Indeed, as much as Mormons draw from apocryphal literature (early Christian texts that were respected by Christians but not included in the New Testament) to make theological arguments, they do not, as far as I know, treat these texts as part of the New Testament, so Mormons have a closed New Testament canon (they do not read the Shepherd of Hermas on Sunday mornings) even though they add to scripture with another testament of Jesus Christ.

All that I am saying is that the Saints are a lot less open about revelation than some of their rhetoric might lead outsiders to suspect. They have a solid set of scriptures that are "closed" to additions for all practical purposes, and they have beliefs that amount to what anyone would call a creed, even if Mormonism is less systematic in expounding its beliefs than most other Christian traditions. These are positive things to my mind, and further evidence that Mormons are closer to Catholics than one might suppose. Mormonism emerged at a time where there was much talk about rejecting creeds, philosophy, and tradition—rejecting anything and everything that added to the New Testament. Mormons stand with Catholics in testifying that more can be and should be said about Jesus than can be found in the pages of the Bible.

Alonzo

Stephen's assessment of the Mormon position on scripture, revelation, and creeds is largely accurate and would probably frustrate most Latter-day Saints. Although I know he is not being critical, he does bring up a few points that could be leveled as criticisms against us.

He asks how Latter-day Saints evaluate revelation claims in other Christian traditions. My short answer would be "inadequately." By that I mean the average Mormon does not think much about the claims to revelation made in other traditions. When they do hear about them, I think most Mormons are simply suspicious of them—largely doubtful of their authenticity.[9] To my mind that directly contradicts what the LDS Prophets and Apostles have taught their members they should do in the face of claims of revelation. The hierarchy of The Church of Jesus Christ of Latter-day Saints has taught that people in other religious traditions—Christian and non-Christian alike—have received revelations, public and private, which were of God. While that doctrine has been taught, some Mormons feel such a truth somehow threatens the "truthfulness" of their own tradition. In other words, some Saints think: "If they have truth, aren't we just a little less true?" This is probably more of a cultural response rather than a theological one. Nevertheless, it is a nonsensical position—and one contrary to the teachings of the Church. Unfortunately, it is a view that I have encountered on more than one occasion, though it makes no sense to me. If, for example, the heaven-sent voices that spoke to Joan of Arc were real, how does that diminish the truthfulness of Mormonism? I see no threat! Nor, I think, should any Latter-day Saint.

To Stephen's second point, I would challenge the position that Mormonism is "anti-creedal." My friend is correct that Joseph Smith made some comments which are sometimes seen as anti-creedal.[10] However, his concern was less with creeds and more with remaining open to change and further light and knowledge.[11] Joseph worried that formal creeds could be used to "set up stakes, and say [to the believer], 'Hitherto shalt thou come, and no further.'"[12] He was concerned that creeds stood in opposition to the principle of continuing revelation. In other words, if one emphatically subscribes to a creedal belief, one runs the danger of embracing the assumption that everything on the subject is now known. Thus, creeds can imply a finality that Joseph—an ardent believer in continuing, modern revelation—was uncomfortable with. The Prophet was regularly receiving revelations that increased his doctrinal understandings, and added to—or, in some cases, even altered—his previously held doctrinal positions or beliefs. Thus, he did not like the idea of speaking, at that stage of the Restoration, with doctrinal finality. He was concerned that the Church not become so driven by written statements on belief that it became theologically stagnant. Joseph was also uncomfortable with the idea that one person should seek to control the beliefs of another. For Joseph, though all true doctrine comes from God, there is a sanctity to an individual's right to believe or disbelieve what he or she wants. He once remarked: "I never thought it was right to call up a man and try him because he erred in doctrine; it looks too much like Methodism and not like Latter day Saintism. Methodists have creeds which a man must believe or be kicked out of their church. I want the liberty of believing as I please. It feels so good not to be trammeled. It doesn't prove that a man is not a good man, [simply] because he errs in doctrine."[13]

Now, as has been pointed out, Mormonism certainly has its creeds—such as its thirteen *Articles of Faith* (though it may be worth noting that these have evolved in number and content over the years[14]). Having said that, I think Stephen is correct that Mormons are not as much an "open canon" faith as we are a faith with a currently closed canon which is subject to being opened again as more revelation comes. We have regular announcements from the Apostles and Prophets of the Church which Mormons see as "revelations." But, we do not canonize each of these—perhaps because of the cost of inserting those in our bound scriptures each time they come: an unfeasible proposition. But we do see a consistent adding to the corpus of revealed policies or statements. (Catholics would probably see themselves as having something very similar.)

One Roman Catholic friend of mine referred to the Book of Mormon as a "closed" canon—and an "unrepeatable event." In actuality, Joseph Smith only translated a third of the Book of Mormon. Latter-day Saints have consistently taught that at a future time, when they are using as they ought to the one-third they currently have, they will receive the other two-thirds. So, the Book of Mormon is also "currently closed," but subject to being opened again—and Latter-day Saints have every expectation that it will be opened again and more of it will be translated, canonized, and utilized by the faithful members of the Church.

Is the LDS New Testament a "closed canon?" Well, we use the same twenty-seven books of the New Testament that the majority of other Christians use. I am frank to say, because Mormons worry about being accused of "adding to the Bible," we tend to not canonize things we might otherwise. So, for example, LDS scholars regularly cite early Christian texts—not only for their apologetic value but also for the brilliance of the Fathers. I, myself, regularly cite them in books and articles I write. However, Mormons are not going to add to their New Testament Hermas, or Barnabas, or other texts of the era—at least in part because of the perception of going beyond the accepted Christian canon. However, again, if Latter-day Saints believe what their Prophets and Apostles have taught, they must accept truth wherever it is found (even in sources such as the aforementioned texts).

So, what can we conclude? Foremost, that Stephen is right—Latter-day Saints need to do better about being more comfortable with their own doctrine on revelation and truth. To quote Stephen, we need to be as "open about revelation" as our "rhetoric might lead outsiders to" believe we are. As a professor of World Religions, I challenge students on this concept every semester. Most, by the end, embrace their doctrine when they realize the plethora of statements by presiding authorities on the subject. But there are always those who feel that the power and significance of their tradition is somehow reduced by acknowledging God has spoken to others. Instead, we should recognize that if God inspired, for example, the Protestant Reformers, or Mohammed, or Mother Teresa, this only confirms our belief that there is a personal God who is aware of and cares intimately about each of His children. Mormons (speaking generally) do need to be better about embracing truth—come where it may. Post-Vatican II Catholic scholars seem very good about this. A number of LDS leaders and scholars are also. (Perhaps this explains the LDS fixation with C. S. Lewis.) But some of our laity still struggle with this. Hopefully, with time, we will change. We rob ourselves of inspiration and revelation until we do.

Finally, even if one believes in continuing "public revelation" (as Mormons do), both Latter-day Saints and Catholics desperately need to continue to seek for "private" or "personal revelation." In his comments above, Stephen said "you should always follow your conscience. God will never condemn you if you do what you, by your best light, think is right." I could not agree more. Indeed, he asked, "How do you evaluate revelation claims in other traditions?" I think this is the key: follow your conscience. Follow the promptings of the Holy Spirit. Compare all claims to revelation with the previously revealed word, and in that the Spirit will direct you. As the Lord promised, "the Spirit of truth . . . will guide you into all the truth" (*NRSV* John 16:13).

5

Ritual

Stephen

Catholics and Mormons are united by a love of ritual. Not every Catholic
and Mormon, of course. People across the religious spectrum can treat
rituals as little more than thoughtless habits or unnecessary formali-
ties. The Catholic and Mormon traditions, however, are steeped in cer-
emony. As long as Catholics have a Pope and Mormons have Temples,
neither tradition will ever be mistaken for the informal, spontaneous, and
unstructured styles that characterize countless Protestant churches all
across America. So much of American religion is improvisational, reflecting the do-it-yourself mentality of entrepreneurial capitalism and rugged
individualism. That is especially true of Pentecostal churches, which are
growing rapidly due to their ability to adapt to local needs. When it comes
to the Holy Spirit, however, Catholicism and Mormonism let tradition lead
the way.

Even in America, there are rituals for every occasion—indeed, for an
event to be a special occasion, it must be set apart by rituals. A religious
ritual can be defined as a sequence of prescribed actions that establish a
connection between the faithful and the divine. Rituals for Catholics are
a way of connecting to the past and to other Christians around the world
as well as to God. Even the space within which rituals are performed
is important. Everything about a religious ritual should be, in a word,
beautiful.

For Catholics, nearly every public act of worship is expressed in ritualistic form. The Mass is a liturgy (from a Greek word that meant a public
duty, especially a service or work required by the state) that utilizes many
small rituals to compose one coherent rite. That is why everything about

the rituals of the Mass should be thoughtfully organized and carefully expressed, from the manner of their performance to the appearance of the performers. Catholic traditionalists bemoan the loss of the "extraordinary form of the Roman Rite" (also known as the Tridentine Mass), which was celebrated in Latin with women wearing head coverings and laity kneeling to receive communion directly on the tongue, but even the ordinary Mass that developed after Vatican II has enough rituals to make those who like their religion simple and neat profoundly uncomfortable.

Beauty for Catholics is a deeply theological category. The Catholic aesthetic imagination, even more so prior to Vatican II, was steeped in the principle that matter can be shaped by human hands to glorify the divine. Art and worship go together, since art is merely God's way of getting our attention through our senses. Art is not a religiously neutral category or a theologically optional practice. The Church is called to honor God through media that reflect the divine glory. Catholic art says that every object in the world can be put in a religious context and depicted in such a way as to direct our gaze toward the divine. The more art the better, in fact, since physical objects can inspire us to worship God without ever exhausting God's own infinite beauty.

Protestants rebelled against this theology of art because they wanted to streamline the Christian message in order to get back to the Bible. It is not true that, in their rush to reform the church of various moral abuses, Protestants overthrew the religious significance of beauty altogether. The Reformers did, however, challenge the way that beauty traditionally was thought to represent the divine. With their emphasis on the sufficiency of grace in all things, Protestants mistrusted art that draws attention to the artists or the way in which the art object was created. Just as believers should claim nothing for themselves, churches should not go overboard in trying to capture our admiration or imagination. That is why the Reformers set out to discard rituals and traditions that they thought the church had assimilated from pagan sources. Some Protestants went so far as to reject altogether any positive connection between Christianity and art, but most decided that art should be as simple as the language of the New Testament. Otherwise, the works of human hands will distract from the words of the Gospel. Protestants thus built churches that were plain, unadorned, and even austere in comparison to the ornate architecture that Catholics favored. Statues were out, but so were simple gestures like kneeling or crossing yourself, which still function for Catholics as a visceral mode of prayer and a quite natural way of asking for God's blessings.

Protestants valued sincerity and simplicity in their inner lives as well as their liturgical spaces.

Mormons side with Catholics in valuing the beauty of ritual, but they also have a strong Protestant streak when it comes to the aesthetics of Sunday worship. Their churches, which they call meetinghouses or ward houses, are as architecturally simple and functional as their temples are decorative and ornate. Every church has a chapel plus offices, classrooms, and other meeting spaces, but their chapels are not set apart by religious art. Indeed, their chapels have no icons of any kind, not even a crucifix. Crosses are just not a part of the Mormon tradition of sacred art. When questioned about this, Mormons will give several answers, from the fact that crosses were associated with Catholics during the nineteenth century to the idea that the Saints like to keep their focus on the resurrected Christ. Mormons call their Sunday worship a sacrament meeting, and it takes a very practical, informal, and educational form. Consisting of hymns, prayers, and two or three sermons (talks delivered by members selected beforehand by the bishop), communion of bread and water is served to the seated congregation. The sacrament meeting is followed by Sunday School and priesthood meetings. The absence of wine or grape juice will stand out to Catholics even more than the absence of crucifixes. When asked about this, Mormons will note that the Word of Wisdom, a revelation Joseph received in 1833 and included in the Doctrine and Covenants, forbids the use of alcohol. Mormons will also say that it does not matter what is used in communion as long as Jesus and His atoning death is properly remembered (D&C 27:2). For Catholics, by contrast, the expressions of faith in worship should always take aesthetically fitting forms, so that outward appearances correspond to inward intentions. Nothing is so ordinary that it cannot be elevated by a beautiful frame or setting.

Protestant worship is often guided by the principle of "a priesthood of all believers," and the egalitarian nature of LDS worship, coupled with the fact that there are no paid Sunday ministers, can make it seem as if Mormons too abide by this principle. Appearances, however, can be misleading. Whereas Low Church Protestants substitute the believer for the priest, so that the priesthood of all believers means that there is no longer a priesthood at all, Mormons have a complex and highly original account of priesthood nomenclature and rituals. Everyone has a role and a responsibility, but there are a variety of offices and levels of authority. Mormons, I would go so far in saying, find great beauty in authority. They set apart their leaders with titles, rituals, and responsibilities, though not, as in Catholicism, with liturgical garments.

Where Mormons are most un-Protestant is in their temples, which are beautifully constructed and elaborately decorated. They distribute communion very informally on Sunday mornings, but rituals of endowments and sealings, where families can be bound together for eternity and individuals can be baptized as proxies for their ancestors, are carried out in very dramatic and artful ways. I am of two minds about Mormon Temples, which are closed to outsiders but open for a period of time before they are dedicated. First, I would wager that most Mormon temple ceremonies are actually more elaborate and more intentionally designed to be pleasing to the eye than many Catholic rituals, which, since Vatican II, have been made more efficient and thus more similar to Protestant traditions. Second, many of the temple rituals, symbols, and their accompanying art seem to me to be again a case of what I called in chapter 1 "reinventing the wheel." The Saints came of age in a time when Protestant artistic sensibilities were austere and restrained; the richness of Catholic art was illicit and alien. While Mormons exhibit both Protestant and Catholic aesthetic sensibilities, to me their temple practices represent the Catholic substance of their theological outlook. What they hold back in their meetinghouses is given back in abundance in their temples.

Aesthetically as well as theologically, what Mormons and Catholics share is what I would call a "material imagination of the supernatural." The heyday of Catholics collecting and revering the relics of saints as a reminder of their exemplary lives is long over, but the Catholic commitment to finding the divine in physical objects continues. Indeed, the impact of Catholicism on the development of music, painting, sculpture, and other arts in the West goes without saying. The Catholic imagination is grounded in rituals, which are themselves forms of religious art. Rituals use matter to convey spiritual truths. Baths clean the skin, but baptism washes away sin. Kneeling, bowing, or, in some Christian traditions like Eastern Orthodoxy, standing can all be signs of respect that Christians use to enter into a mood of worship. Eating can be a mundane activity, but in communion, a very simple (and admittedly token) meal can take on profound significance as well as elegant presentation. Clothing too can serve ritual functions, as well as objects like candles and incense that can be quite ordinary outside of their ecclesial use.

Mormon baptism for the dead is surely its most controversial ritual, and I cannot help but drawn some parallels between that and the Catholic belief in transubstantiation. Many, perhaps most Protestants find both of these rituals to be problematic at best and, more likely, bothersome and even offensive. It is hard, I think, to deny that some early Christians practiced baptism for the dead (1 Corinthians 15:29). Indeed, it is hard to read through the tortuous logic and creative hermeneutics that many Protestants apply to this verse to deny its obvious meaning. Mormons are literalists, we could say, when it comes to 1 Corinthians 15:29. Catholics are literalists when it comes to Jesus's words "this is my body" (Matthew 26:26, Luke 22:19). Their literalism in these regards is a direct outcome of their material imagination of the supernatural.

Mormons do not accept transubstantiation (the idea that the bread and wine actually become in spiritual substance the body and blood of Jesus) and Catholics do not accept the practice of vicarious baptisms for the dead, but both traditions have their own versions of these rejected rituals. Mormons, for example, believe that matter is eternal, that even God is composed of some kind of matter, and thus matter can be infused with divinity. Mormons, we could say, apply transubstantiation to the entire cosmos. Meanwhile, Catholics believe that we can communicate with the dead in the sense of praying for those who are in purgatory and asking the Saints in heaven to pray for us here and now. Both traditions, then, have the theoretical capacity and practical resources to draw near in understanding, appreciating, and learning from each other in terms of the two rituals that most define their uniqueness.

Unfortunately, there are roadblocks to the potential for mutual understanding. Catholicism, of course, speaks with one voice about fundamental theological issues, and on June 5, 2001, the Office of the Congregation for the Doctrine of Faith, directed by then Cardinal Joseph Ratzinger (who would later become Pope Benedict XVI), issued its only formal statement about Mormonism. The statement was in response to what the Church calls a *dubium*, or an informal inquiry or question that anyone can submit to the Magisterium (the teaching authority of Rome). The *dubium* asked about the validity of baptism conferred by the Latter-day Saints. Pope John Paul II approved of Cardinal Ratzinger's one word response: Negative. While there was no official explanation or elaboration of this response, its significance was clear. Mormons are not to be treated by Catholics as "separated brethren," a term that applies to Protestants who are baptized and believe in Christ. In practical terms, this decision means that any Mormon wanting to join the Catholic Church would have to be baptized (again).

In my opinion, this decision is theologically misguided. Several councils and synods in the early Church affirmed the validity of baptism regardless of who performs it or what the performer believes. Doctrinal errors are not considered sufficient to deny the validity of anyone's baptism. This was made clear in the Donatist controversy in North Africa. The Donatists were a schismatic church party that rejected the baptisms performed by Catholic priests. Their reasoning was that some Catholic priests had betrayed the faith in one of the Roman Empire's violent outbursts of persecution and that this weakness or cowardice invalidated Catholic sacraments. Augustine intervened to argue that it is Christ himself who performs the sacraments. As long as a baptism is performed by a rightly ordained priest, the efficacy of that ritual is not nullified by something the priest has done in the past. In more modern times, the Council of Trent reaffirmed this position by resolving that even a baptism performed by a heretic is valid if it is done in the name of the Father, Son, and Holy Spirit and with the same basic intention as baptisms performed by a Catholic priest.

Up until June 5, 2001, the Catholic Church treated Mormon baptisms in the same way that it treated all Protestant baptisms. That is, the Catholic Church accepted them as valid and did not require rebaptism for Protestant and Mormon converts. What changed? It appears that an investigation by then-Cardinal Ratzinger concluded that deficiencies in the Mormon understanding of the Trinity were enough to invalidate their baptismal practices. There was no contention that the Mormon baptismal formula is heretical or ineffective: "Having been commissioned of Jesus Christ, I baptize you in the name of the Father, and of the Son, and of the Holy Ghost" (D&C 20:73). But the Catholic teaching authority did conclude, evidently, that Mormons worship three gods, or at least that they go too far in distinguishing the divine persons of the Trinity from each other.

The Trinity, it needs to be said, is a mystery, no matter how many great theologians have spent their lives trying to translate it into logical terms and metaphysical concepts. It would not still be the subject of countless books, articles, and discussions if it were not fundamentally mysterious. The Trinity is nowhere spelled out in the Bible, which suggests that God did not intend for humans to have a crystal clear definition of His inner nature. The Trinity is both an idea and a reality, but the idea can never, at least in this life, perfectly capture the reality. God is three and one, but theologians who analyze the Trinity typically start out with a oneness that is hard to imagine as three or end up with three parts that are hard to piece back together into one unity. As an object of worship, the Trinity is clear. It cannot be rationally solved, however, as if it were a really difficult but well-designed puzzle.

At best, churches can set parameters around the kind of language we should use in contemplating the Trinity, which is what the Catholic Church has always done. Those parameters are actually pretty simple: Emphasize God's oneness without denying God's threeness, and talk about each member of the Trinity in a way that does not deny their oneness. That this is not always possible to do is not always forthcoming from traditionally-minded theologians, but most will admit that even Thomas Aquinas, Catholicism's greatest and most logically rigorous thinker, honors the irreducible mystery of the Trinity while trying to hold the three and one together in his mind.

Mormonism was born in America during a time when Protestants were very suspicious of creeds as well as formal, scholarly theology, and those suspicions are still a part of Mormon identity. That makes it hard at times to know exactly what Mormons believe, especially if an outsider is looking for terminological consistency and metaphysical depth on par with Thomas Aquinas. Mormon theology is not systematic and propositional in any obvious way, although it has systematic depths and propositional commitments. To learn what Mormons believe, a holistic and sympathetic approach is required. There is no evidence that the Office of the Congregation for the Doctrine of Faith carried out that kind of investigation of Mormon theology in reaching its judgment about LDS baptism.

What I find especially bothersome about this decision is that the Catholic Church accepts baptisms from various Protestant churches that have either an unclear view of the Trinity (because they have no creeds) or a very low view of the Trinity. Many pastors and theologians in the Disciples of Christ denomination, of which I was a member for nearly twenty years, think of Jesus in more human than divine terms. They also routinely deny original sin, which is the sin that, for Catholics, baptism remits. The Disciples of Christ, however, are a respected, mainline Protestant denomination that has been involved in dialogue with Rome for decades. Could it be that they get a free pass because they are familiar to Roman theologians, while Mormons are still considered exotic and thus subjected to extra (and unfair) scrutiny?

In fact, the official position of the Catholic Church is even worse than I have so far portrayed it. The baptism of heretics, remember, is accepted by Catholics, which means that Mormons, in Rome's eyes, are not even Christian enough to be labeled heretics! I have heard it said that some Catholic theologians think that Mormon baptism is invalid because Mormons claim that baptism is a universal practice that began long before the ministry of Jesus Christ. Mormons, from this reading, deny the newness of baptism. They baptized according to the spirit of John and not Jesus. This is a very weak argument, since Mormons believe that Jesus Christ himself was speaking to people and working through history from the beginning of creation. Thus, all water rituals always pointed toward him, even if that was not fully understood until John baptized Jesus. In any case, John baptized many people before he baptized Jesus. The ritual precedes Jesus's embrace of it.

A final reason sometimes given for Rome's denial of the validity of Mormon baptism is Mormonism's alleged rejection of original sin. Mormons certainly have a more optimistic anthropology than many Protestants, especially those of Calvinist inclinations, but they believe with all Christians that everyone falls short of the glory of God and everyone is in need of God's grace and forgiveness. In fact, their view of the breadth of salvation is very similar to Catholicism: Mormons are hopeful that everyone will be saved, and they speculate that people not saved on earth will have opportunities for salvation in the afterlife. Catholics share that hope. There are great debates among Catholic scholars about which Church Fathers, in addition to Origen, taught the doctrine of universal salvation (the Greek term is *apokatastasis*), but it has become an unofficial article of faith for many Catholic theologians. Moreover, it is generally settled opinion that it is at least acceptable, if not downright commendable, to hope that hell will be empty and to pray that all free creatures will repent and be saved.[1] Catholics tend to base this hope more on the irresistible power of grace (based on the will of the Savior) rather than any optimism regarding how reasonable people can be, but both Catholics and Mormons agree that people must freely choose to be with God. They also agree that holiness is a process and that moral growth will continue in the afterlife. For Catholics, growing closer to God is what heaven is all about, which is why sanctification will continue in purgatory until holiness becomes sufficient for entry into the presence of God. Thus, both Mormons and Catholics repudiate the standard Protestant position that one's spiritual growth comes to an end with death and that God makes

Christians perfectly holy in an instantaneous act at the moment of death (or at the moment of the last judgment).

I would call this situation—where two Christian traditions are so close in their hopes for heaven and in their convictions about the power of grace, yet so far apart in accepting each other's obedience to the simple yet profound ritual of baptism—scandalous except that it seems obvious to me that the theologians who advised Cardinal Ratzinger were not all that well informed about Mormon teachings and practices. Overturning this decision, however, should be one of the primary goals in the dialogue between Catholics and Mormons. Mormon baptism for the dead is a beautiful ritual, and it is biblically grounded. Can Catholics find in it some kind of theological truth?

Alonzo

The mysticism of ritual is a powerful part of the worship experience for nearly two-thirds of modern Christians. Roman Catholicism has ever been a ritually rich tradition (though, as Stephen pointed out, less so today than before Vatican II). Eastern Orthodoxy absolutely holds to a high form of liturgy. High Church Anglicans and Lutherans (of the same persuasion) see the value and beauty of ritual. Contemporary Protestant Christians are the "odd man out" on this front. There is certainly nothing wrong with the way Protestants choose to worship. Indeed, the forms described in the New Testament are largely low on liturgy. However, there seems to be a power in ritual—and even more so if the participant seeks understanding and application of the acts engaged in.

Stephen is correct in saying that Mormon Sunday worship seems quite Protestant (at least very much like Low Church Protestantism). Joseph Smith was reared in a Protestant milieu, and LDS worship forms have unquestionably been influenced by that. It seems that the liturgy in the post-Vatican II era has also been influenced by Protestant forms. For some, that is a blessing. For many old school Catholics, this is a great disappointment and a great loss.

Because of my Greek Orthodox High Church liturgical background, my initial experience of Mormon liturgy left me feeling a bit flat. I very much resonated with the doctrines I was discovering, but I struggled with the Protestant feel on Sundays. In those early days I longed for a High Church experience. When I entered an LDS Temple for the first time all of those longings were satisfied. The ritual was very pronounced there, and it felt as though I was coming home. What is curious to me is that many of those raised LDS are puzzled by their first experience with the high liturgical forms of LDS Temple worship—whereas converts like myself often find it satisfying and familiar. The lack of Sunday ritual leaves some life-long Mormons a bit unprepared for the more liturgically rich Temple experience.

Truth be told, Latter-day Saints have a rather rich liturgical tradition. We have rituals for everything: the Eucharist (known by Mormons simply as "the Sacrament"), blessing a newborn, baptism, confirmation, ordination, marriage, and so on. Some of the forms of these rites are, admittedly, simple—though still laden with symbolism. Others, by contrast, are quite elaborate. But the problem is not that Latter-day Saints are void of ritual. The problem is that we are not a very symbolically literate people. So, often Mormons will engage in rites which are highly symbolic, sacred, and ritualistic, but never notice the emblematic components of what they are doing—or the implications of the same.

As in Catholicism, some LDS rites are open to all while others have rules of limited participation or viewing. So, for example, not every Roman Catholic can view the rites or rituals of a papal conclave. Nor can just any person witness some of the rites of the Knights of Columbus. However, anyone—Catholic or non-Catholic—can attend the baptism of a newborn. Similarly, in The Church of Jesus Christ of Latter-day Saints, anyone can view a child's baptism or the blessing of the Sacrament of the Lord's Supper. However, those rites considered to be our "higher ordinances"— namely those performed in dedicated LDS Temples—are not open to the public. No condescension is implied. In both faiths, there is simply a desire to keep the most sacred rites sacred (and, therefore, private).

One thing that sets Latter-day Saints apart from other Christians is their practice of performing salvific rites for both the living and the deceased. Stephen is correct in his assessment of Mormons and Catholics as literalists. Just as Catholics take quite literally Jesus's declaration that the consecrated host is His "body" (Matthew 26:26), Latter-day Saints take quite literally Paul's words about the existence of a rite in Corinth wherein those who were alive chose to be baptized on behalf of those who died without the opportunity to be baptized (1 Corinthians 15:29). Thus, there is a parallel of sorts between the Catholic doctrine of transubstantiation and the LDS rite of Baptism for the Dead. However, perhaps an even stronger parallel can be found between the Roman Catholic doctrine of supererogation and the LDS rite of vicarious baptisms for the dead. In Catholic belief, acts of supererogation are those which go beyond what God requires for one's salvation, and which are performed (or engaged in) by a faithful practitioner. They are acts which exceed the minimal demands of human morality. In supererogation, one does for another what he/she cannot do for him/herself (e.g., lighting a candle and offering a prayer on behalf of the deceased).[2] Faithful members of the Catholic Church perform acts that bless the dead—shortening their stay in purgatory. Likewise, in Mormonism, through vicarious rites for the deceased, the living do for the dead what they cannot do for themselves and, consequently, shorten their time in spirit prison (the LDS version of purgatory). Even the Catholic concept of godparents has its parallels with the LDS notion of vicarious rites. In Catholicism, the godparent makes vows or covenants on behalf of the infant who is not able to make those himself/herself. However, if the infant (once grown) eventually accepts those vicarious promises (via confirmation), they become his/hers—as though he/she had made them himself/herself. Similarly, in Mormonism the vicarious rites of the Temple are a means of enacting a covenant. If the deceased accepts those vicariously made promises, they become his/hers—as though he/she had made them himself/herself. Thus, the parallels between LDS and Roman Catholic rites run deep.

As it relates to LDS iconography, as Stephen pointed out, there is not much in our Sunday worship services. Mormons use a great deal of art in our Sunday classes and even in our Temples, but in the chapel portion of our buildings—which have been heavily influenced (as we noted) by nineteenth-century Protestant worship forms—we tend to have none. I suppose various reasons for this can be postulated: the desire to avoid any appearance of idolatry; the concern that art could distract some from focusing on the emblems of the Lord's sacrifice; the recognition that some works of art will be inspiring to one and yet provocative of unpleasant emotions for another; perhaps even an intent to avoid promoting a specific artist's works. (Remember: the Latter-day Saints are a young religion and, thus, many of the creators of our most appreciated works of sacred art are still alive and painting.) In short, while the leaders of the Church have never offered a detailed explanation of the policy, the practice of not placing artwork in our chapels—though not always part of our tradition—is firmly in place today.[3]

On a related note, Stephen rightly points out that Latter-day Saints tend to not use crosses or crucifixes in their worship or architecture. He is also correct in stating that, when asked why, Mormons will typically say "this is because we prefer to think of the living Jesus rather than the dead one"[4] (a response that is not far from what Protestants say when asked about why they use the cross instead of the crucifix in their worship). While I have heard Latter-day Saints use this explanation—and I get why it might have some place in the minds of Mormons—I think it is largely inaccurate as an explanation of our primary reason for not utilizing crosses. The most sacred symbols employed in LDS worship (on Sundays and in our Temples) depict Jesus's passion—His suffering. If we were really trying to avoid depictions of the "dead Jesus," then I think we would do away with our most holy liturgical representations of that event. In actual fact, history shows that early Latter-day Saints commonly employed the cross.[5] It appears that the primary reason we did away with its use (in the mid-1950s) was because of bad blood between Catholics and Mormons in the state of Utah. The Church was publically criticized by the Roman Catholic Bishop of Salt Lake, and this got some Latter-day Saints' ire up. Since that time Mormons have largely avoided it as an employed emblem, seeing it as a "Catholic symbol" and, thus, not a Mormon one.[6]

On a separate point, Stephen noted that Catholics and Mormons have not always gotten along like "kissin' cousins" (Sorry Elvis!), and ritual has been partially to blame for that. Prior to the dawn of the twenty-first century, Latter-day Saints were largely treated by the Catholic Magisterium as "separated brethren." However, Joseph Cardinal Ratzinger (as head of the Congregation for the Doctrine of the Faith) apparently had a distaste for Mormons and their theology and, consequently, he threw down the gauntlet. (I suspect this was less Cardinal Ratzinger and more those who served as his advisors; but who am I to say? As Stephen has pointed out, as of June 2001, LDS baptisms have been declared "invalid" by the Roman Catholic Church. Thus, while in the last fifty years they have become more ecumenical than ever in their history, as it relates to Mormons the Catholic Church is more closed-minded than ever (absolutely no offense intended). The Church itself did not elaborate on their reasons for rejecting LDS baptisms. However, the official Vatican newspaper, *L'Osservatore Romano*, suggested the problem was really twofold: (1) Latter-day Saints see the Trinity/Godhead differently than do Catholics, and (2) Mormons have a different view than Catholics of what baptism means. Without taking a defensive posture, both of those reasons seem a bit strained. True, Mormons tend to be semi-subordinationists when it comes to the Trinity, in that we do not hold to the co-equal relationship of the Father and Son.

Rather, we see the Son as fully divine, but subordinate to the Father. (In part, we base this view on biblical texts such as John 5:19, 8:28, and 14:28; Mark 10:17–18; 1 Corinthians 11:3; Philippians 2:6–7.) Yet Mormons are essentially what have been called "social Trinitarians." Curiously, according to *L'Osservatore Romano*, the Catholics reject LDS baptisms for our stance on the Trinity but accept Greek Orthodox baptisms, even though the Orthodox also traditionally describe the Son as subordinate to the Father.[7] Thus, this is a puzzling position for the Catholic Church to take. On the other issue of the meaning of baptism, according to the *Encyclopedia of Catholicism*, the sacrament of baptism has three primary purposes: (1) the baptized person becomes a member of the Christian community, (2) through that sacrament sins are pardoned and the baptized is rescued from the power of darkness, and (3) baptism allows us to become "new creations" and the "sons and daughters of God."[8] All three of these aims are the same reasons as to why Latter-day Saints engage in baptism. Thus, it is not clear what all of the hubbub is about. Placing all of my cards on the table, I have long suspected this was primarily about the high conversion rates of Catholics to Mormonism in Latin America. As noted above, Catholics and Mormons have had great relationships when it comes to humanitarian efforts or joining hands to stand up for some moral cause. This bit of testiness regarding LDS baptisms is, therefore, puzzling and unfortunate. Nevertheless, Latter-day Saints require Catholics to be rebaptized if they convert to Mormonism, so we should not take offense at the Catholic position—even if we are almost the only Christian denomination they have singled out as "unacceptable."

Stephen

I like the idea that some rituals in the LDS Church are closed and private. That takes us back to the way Catholicism used to be in the days of the Roman Empire. A seeker who wanted to know about Christianity would have been taught a few of its basics. The curious could come to church to hear the sermon, but they would be dismissed afterwards and thus not given the opportunity to witness baptisms, the Eucharist, and other rituals. If the visitor wanted to continue preparing for conversion, he or she would be entered into the ranks of the catechumenate. That group was set apart from the merely curious, but even catechumens had to withdraw before the main rituals began. This preserved a sense of the holiness and mystery of Christian rituals. When the Church became the dominant force in the Western world, such secrecy was no longer needed or even possible. Everyone was raised knowing all about every aspect of Christian teaching and practice.

The world we live in today is far from being as oppressive as the Roman Empire, but perhaps a return to a little bit of secrecy would not be such a bad thing. There should be parts of Christian worship that are for Christians only. When non-Mormons complain about Mormon secrecy, especially the custom of not allowing non-Mormons into their Temples, I have to wonder what these same people would think about the practices of the early Church. Mormons used to take vows to keep what happens in the Temple absolutely confidential, and I am glad that there is more openness now about every aspect of Mormon belief and ritual. But I am also glad that Mormons have continued the ancient practice of preserving some of their rituals from the eyes of outsiders.

I also do not mind that various churches have their own way of doing rituals, though this can lead to too much suspicion and even hostility among the various Christian traditions. I regret that the Catholic Church does not treat Mormon baptism like it treats all Protestant baptisms, but here I have a question for Alonzo. Latter-day Saints also take an exclusive approach to baptism. As far as I know, if a baptized Protestant or Catholic converts to Mormonism, they are asked to be rebaptized. In other words, Mormons do not count the baptism of any other church as valid or authentic. This is another reason Mormons baptize the dead. They baptize not only the unbelieving dead but also those among the dead who were baptized and faithful Christians. That seems to be an even more exclusive approach to baptism than the Catholic Church! Catholics accept most baptisms by other churches as valid; Mormons accept none.

I know from personal experience that this is an issue that creates much confusion and resentment for many non-Mormons. I have had many conversations with non-Mormon Christians where I have defended the basic Christian credentials of the Latter-day Saints. Inevitably, someone will say, "But if they are really part of the Christian tradition, why do they require Christian converts to be rebaptized?" The answer, of course, is that Mormons believe that Joseph restored the priestly authority to baptize in the authorized way. The implication is that no baptism performed in the many hundreds of years from the end of the apostolic era to the beginning of the nineteenth century was a valid ritual for the forgiveness of sins. That is a hard pill to swallow.

Perhaps Mormons face a dilemma: if they want to be acknowledged as part of the Christian world, they will have to get used to being treated as just one of many Protestant denominations, yet they do not see themselves as one Christian tradition among many. Can Mormons find respect in the Protestant world without being assimilated as just another Protestant variation? Perhaps one way out of this dilemma is for Mormons to recognize that they are much more like Catholicism than Protestantism. Mormonism claims to be a restoration of the whole grand sweep of Christianity. They can certainly enter into richer conversations and exchanges with every Christian organization, but to remain true to their history, they have to set themselves off a bit from the rest of the Christian world. Mormonism thus finds itself in the same difficult place that Catholicism is in: how to be a universal church in a world full of (very effective and spiritually robust) churches. Catholicism and Mormonism both strive for universality, but they end up expressing that in opposing (inclusive or exclusive) baptismal theologies.

Alonzo

Stephen's challenge of the Mormon position on rebaptism strikes at the heart of the issue. If Latter-day Saints are interested in winning the beauty pageant, they need to shoot for a soft-sale of themselves. In other words, Latter-day Saints do profess their Christianity—and that in the face of opposition from many of their brothers and sisters in Christ. Some will argue that we want our cake and to eat it too. We desire to be considered Christians—and we certainly acknowledge the Christianity of other denominations. However, we do not accept their ordinances as authoritative and, thus, we send a message that we really do not want to be part of the club. There can be no popularity—no "Miss Congeniality" prize—if we continue to say, in so many words, we have got something you do not have; something you will never have unless you join us!

The flip side of the coin is this: Mormons claim to be what Catholics used to—we claim to be the true Christian Church.[9] For centuries Catholics taught that there was no salvation outside of the Catholic Church. Connection to the institution and sacraments (through its priesthood) were seen as requisite for salvation. And while, since Vatican II, that is largely not the message anymore—most older Catholics will remember a time when Roman Catholics took a similar unpopular position as

Mormons. They too taught that, as much as they respect those of other Christian denominations, Catholics were the ones with God's authority, doctrines, organization, sacraments, and so forth. This is not so different from the LDS claim.

So, what is the dilemma Latter-day Saints find themselves in? Simply this: What is more important? To be popular? Or to be authorized? Mormons would like to have both. Ultimately, such is not possible. If we take the position of "restored priesthood authority," then we cannot be popular. If, instead, we seek acceptance by our brothers and sisters in Christ, then we can no longer make claims to special, restored priesthood authority that is different from that which is held by the rest of the world.

Which of these incompatible choices will the Latter-day Saints cling to? Definitely authority! Why not popularity over authority? I suppose two reasons. First, as Stephen pointed out earlier, Mormons are literalists. They believe the biblical witness that prophets speak with and for God. Thus, Latter-day Saints are emphatic in their belief that Joseph Smith spoke with God and angels. Consequently, they cannot toss out authority divinely given. Second, Mormons have learned the lesson of Vatican II. Namely, popularity is not worth the costs. Thus, Roman Catholic authors, Bob O'Gorman and Mary Faulkner, noted some of the fallout since the Second Vatican Council: "Attendance at Mass has dropped and, as the definitions about sin have been softened, people no longer line up outside the confessional on Saturday afternoon, as was once the weekend ritual. Catholicism lost its absolutism, and for many it also lost its certainty."[10] In other words, Christians want certainty in their faith. A religion that teaches relativism will never hold onto its parishioners. Catholics are learning this in the post-Vatican II era. They softened their position on authority, doctrine, commandments, sin, sacraments, and so forth, and the consequence has been fewer and fewer Catholics actually engaging in Catholicism. In many ways, the Council backfired. In the minds of many Roman Catholics, and in the view of many outside observers, it did not strengthen the Catholic Church and it did not succeed in bringing other Christians in under the Catholic umbrella. It actually sent many packing![11] Seeing with hindsight, Latter-day Saints are careful to not make that same mistake—even if that means we have to be the ugly stepdaughter of the Christian tradition.

Perhaps we can take our cue from Jesus and how He responded to Judaism. During His first advent, Jesus did not reject Judaism—but He certainly challenged many of the denominations of His day. Most rejected Him and His authority. They would gladly boot Him and His followers out of the Jewish faith—and, by A.D. 70, successfully did so. But Jesus insisted upon making claims regarding authority or divine authorization for His teachings and, even, baptisms—which the "other Jews" did not like. But He was decidedly less interested in popularity and more interested in pleasing God. Thus, He simply could not toss out His claims to authority, revelation, and divine commission.

Now, this was supposed to be a chapter on ritual—though it seems more about authority. However, for Mormons certain rituals require authority in order to have divine validity. Thus, one cannot say "sacrament" without also meaning "priesthood authority." Consequently, any conversation about ritual must ultimately be a conversation about authorization and authority—otherwise rituals are non-salvific. They may be authorized of men, but they do not (according to LDS belief) have the authorization of God. (This may be a nonissue for protestants, and a fine line for Catholics, but it is paramount in LDS theology—and, thus, must be understood by those who observe Mormonism from the outside. So, how can Mormons and Catholics come together on this issue of rites or rituals? Although we are never going to combine our ordinances or sacraments, we can each take a pro-ritual position that acknowledges the transforming effect of a symbolic liturgy. And we can both hold sacred our individual liturgical traditions—preserving them for future generations and, thereby, preserving ourselves. If we abandon our rites—or relegate them to optional, flexible, or void of divine authority—we shall surely lose the power to retain those whom we seek to save.

6

Matter

Stephen

It seems to me that one of the most important tasks facing modern theology is formulating a new understanding of the relationship between God and matter. By matter, I mean all of the stuff that composes the physical universe. That is a pretty vague definition, but matter is a very slippery thing. In fact, physicists are not sure what matter really is beyond being some kind of stuff. The more they look into it, the weirder matter becomes. There is a lot of dark matter out there, for one thing, as well as dark energy and anti-matter, and nobody knows what those actually are. Even ordinary matter gets stranger the more scientists break it apart. One small unit leads to another only to reveal bizarre particles and even more bizarre relationships among those particles. According to quantum mechanics, for example, subatomic particles are entangled with each other in ways that defy the ordinary laws of causation. Einstein called this phenomenon "spooky," and the deeper physicists dig, the spookier matter becomes.

Most traditional theologians shrug off the religious implications of these perplexities by pointing out that Christians believe in an immaterial God. God created matter, but matter does not tell us anything about the nature of God, except that, whatever matter is, God is not that. Matter decays, for example, and it is spatially located. Matter changes forms, and its most elementary movements are unpredictable. God does not change because God is beyond space and time, and God has no form or shape because God is infinite, and God does not need to move because God is everywhere (or at least anywhere He wants to be). Our understanding of matter can get weirder all it wants to, but God remains beyond anything we can know about the material world.

The idea of God that I have just summarized is commonly called "classical theism," since it brings together the ancient philosophical traditions of Plato and Aristotle with the best thinkers in Christian history. Indeed, theologians, beginning with Justin Martyr and going on to Origen, Augustine, and then climaxing with Aquinas, worked hard to creatively and systematically synthesize the ancient Greek philosophical understanding of God with the Bible. That synthesis is the greatest intellectual achievement of Christianity, and its principle axiom is the simplicity of God. That God is simple means that God has no parts, does not change, and is not bound by space and time. Anything made of matter can be divided, but not God.[1] The simplicity of God has many implications, but one of them is that God is not like anything that is made of matter. God is deeply mysterious, but the one thing we can know for sure about God is that He is immaterial. That is why classical theism, for all of its intellectual ambition in discerning the nature of the divine, ends up by defining God more by what He is not than by what He is. God is not a thing of any kind. God does not exist in any way that we can understand. God is the ground of being, or pure being, or beyond being, or maybe even without being altogether. Perhaps the most that classical theism can say about God is that God is just God.

God is not the only immaterial entity in classical theism. There are also angels and souls, but they occupy an intermediary position between God and everything that is not God. Angels and souls have some kind of form; they are created things. But they are not composed of matter. They are, in a word, spiritual. Grasping what they consist of turns out to be almost as hard as defining the nature of God. God too is spiritual, indeed, God is pure spirit, but what is spirit? In God's case, it is something beyond the spiritual substance of angels and souls, whatever that is, yet classical theists often group together God, angels, and souls in a spiritual realm called heaven. It seems we are forced to say of the spiritual what we said of God: whatever it is, it is not material. Yet, doesn't this definition make the two terms, immaterial and material, correlative and thus mutually dependent on each other. And if our view of the nature of matter changes, then shouldn't that alter our understanding of immateriality? God is certainly not a hard object like a rock. God does not grow weaker over time, like an atom undergoing radioactive decay. But what if matter is nothing more than relationship and energy, potential and pattern? Is God not that?

Defining the immaterial substance of spiritual entities turns out to be as hard as defining what it is that composes the physical stuff of finite objects, and the two definitions are essentially related. What I have raised is an enormously complex set of metaphysical questions that seems to require a mastery of Plato and Einstein as well as the Apostle Paul. Surprisingly, Mormonism has something fundamental to contribute to this discussion. Mormons believe that God has a body, a belief that draws nothing but condescension and commiseration from theologians trained in the logical nuances of classical theism. Is it possible that this belief can help all Christians today rethink the relationship between spirit and matter?

To most if not all non-Mormons, the idea that God is composed of some kind of material substance and that He has a body not unlike our own is so absurd that it puts Mormonism beyond the pale of rational debate. This reaction is shortsighted in the extreme. Mormons do not, as far as I understand their theology, say that God's spiritual substance is the same as the material substance that composes rocks, trees, and human beings. But they do see more commonality than difference between the two kinds of stuff. In Mormonism, there is no absolute metaphysical gap—an unbridgeable no man's land—separating God's reality from the reality of the world. Whatever their relationship, Mormons think it is more true to say that there is one basic kind of stuff in the cosmos than to say that there are two basic kinds of stuff that can never mix, combine, or turn into each other.

The idea that God has a body follows from the idea that there are no immaterial entities. Everything that has a material substance has some kind of form, with the possible exception of the chaos that apparently existed before God created the world ("the earth was a formless void," Genesis 1:2). Even chaos, it would seem, has to take some kind of form, which is why many early theologians rejected the idea that God made the world out of chaos. The only thing that would have no form at all would be an absolute void. Only nothing can be formless, because nothing is immaterial—except for God. God, in classical theism, does not have a form, although God is also not formless. God has no limits because God is infinite and omnipresent, but God is not the equivalent of either chaos or nothingness. God is something that exists in way like nothing else that we know. Indeed, when it comes to knowing God, we might as well try to know nothing, which is why classical theism typically ends up in what is called negative theology.

Negative theology is the idea that we have to negate every image, idea, quality, or attribute that we apply to God in order to make progress in understanding God's nature.[2] Take power, for example. Sure, God is powerful, but God is really beyond power, so we have to negate (eliminate, delete) power in our understanding of the deity. Power involves physical bodies exercising force or pressure on each other, or the human mind solving difficult problems, but God is infinitely beyond both physical bodies and the human mind. Power can be quantified, but God's power cannot be measured in any way. God is not powerless, but He is so far beyond power that power must be negated if we have any hope at all of grasping who God is.

Mormons avoid these paradoxical statements and intellectual gymnastics by attributing matter to the divine. In this one simple but brazen gesture they threaten to bring down the entire edifice of classical theism. I am not so sure that this is a bad thing. Many Catholics (and non-Catholics) tend to think that Thomas Aquinas is the first and last word of Catholic theology plus all the words in between. I know that what I am about to say is the equivalent of heresy to most Catholic theologians, but I think Catholic theology is at its most creative when it is doing more than simply commenting on Aquinas's texts. It took centuries for the rich and complex work of Thomas Aquinas to become distilled into the standard compendium of answers to every Catholic question. Perhaps it will take centuries more for Catholicism to move beyond Aquinas, at least with regard to questions that his thought is not designed to answer. If that were to happen, Mormonism might show Catholics how to become post-Thomistic without losing their theological way.

Although he was pronounced a saint fifty years after his death, during his life Aquinas did not cultivate any scholarly disciples, and his thought only caught on when his fellow Dominicans began defending him from the many controversies his arguments initiated. Indeed, for several centuries after his death the Dominicans battled with the Franciscans (and their theological favorites, Duns Scotus and William of Ockham) for theological supremacy in the Catholic Church. Scholasticism got a bad reputation with the Protestant Reformers, who preferred textual analysis of the Bible to logical analysis of theological ideas, but far from being arid and narrow, scholasticism was very diverse and creative in its metaphysical debates. In reaction to the Reformers, Rome needed to consolidate its theological teachings, and that meant less philosophical diversity and creativity. The Council of Trent (1545–63) enshrined Aquinas's victory over his competitors, but it did not silence other theological options altogether. Aquinas was moved even deeper into the center of Catholic theology after

the French Revolution, when Rome went through a period of retrench-
ment and reaction. Popes and Bishops condemned modern philosophical trends and began preparing a comprehensive Christian philosophical
alternative. It was not until Pope Leo XIII issued his encyclical letter
Aeterni Patris, however, that the work of Thomas Aquinas became the
undisputed intellectual foundation for the Catholic Church. Pope Leo did
not exclude the study of other theologians, but he did make it crystal clear
that the philosophy most useful and best suited to the Christian faith is
that of St. Thomas.

This encyclical sparked a Thomistic revival, but almost as quickly,
Thomism broke into a variety of schools, some of which were only loosely
based on his original writings. There are now so many variations of
Thomism that the most popular Catholic theological movement today
is a return to what the master actually said. The effort to get Aquinas
straight—to figure out what he really said and why he said it—is understandable and commendable. Any great thinker can be profitably studied
again and again, and Aquinas is one of the greatest. With every return to
his writings, theologians come up with something new. But that does not
mean his writings are sacred scripture and his metaphysical views are
unimpeachable.

What if his central axiom, that the divine is simple and therefore immaterial, is wrong? If he is mistaken on this point, it does not mean that
everything else he said must be rejected. There is so much to his thought
that even rejecting this foundational claim is not enough to remove him
from the list of thinkers Christians will always need to cherish and consider. Indeed, if he is wrong about immateriality, then it will take a lot of
intellectual labor for Catholic (and other) theologians to think through
the implications of that mistaken assumption. Even if he was not wrong,
it is important for all Catholic theologians to consider that possibility. At
the very least, reflecting on alternatives to Thomism prevents that philosophical school from becoming an intellectual idol that risks replacing
the revelation of sacred scripture. Moreover, confronting alternatives to
Thomism can result in sharpening the logic and insight of its defenders.

One of the dilemmas that Aquinas spoke to but did not resolve pertains
to the relationship between the categories of nature and grace. By nature,
theologians mean everything that God created, and by grace they mean
everything that God does for us to save us and prepare us for heaven. The
rule that comes out of Thomism is that "grace completes nature." From the
Catholic perspective, Protestants pit grace and nature against each other.

They end up in this dualistic position because, from the Catholic point of view, traditional Protestants tend to overly emphasize the destructive consequences of original sin. If nature is completely fallen and beyond recognition as God's creation, then grace must replace, overwhelm, or reject nature (including human nature) in order to redeem what God created. By contrast, Catholics emphasize a basic continuity between grace and nature. Nature is fallen, but it is still essentially good, full of signs that point to God's own goodness. Grace adds to nature without destroying or abolishing it. Grace completes what nature begins.

To Protestant eyes, this formula—grace completes nature—looks like an example of works righteousness. If grace completes nature, Protestants suspect, then nature can cooperate with grace. If grace completes us, then we must not be all that sinful in the first place. Alonzo and I have already discussed the relationship between grace and works in chapter 2. Here I want to point to another aspect of this formula, and that is its dialectical construction. In Catholic thought, grace does not simply complete nature. The relationship of grace to nature is actually more complicated than that. In fact, far from being a simple statement that is transparently clear, the "grace completes nature" formula has resulted in incessant and interminable debates in Catholic theology, and those debates show no signs of slowing or stopping. Here is the problem: Catholic theology rejects the idea that grace and nature are opposed to each other, but it recognizes that there is a deep and abiding tension between them. Nature resists grace, and grace completes nature only over nature's many objections. If there were no tension between them, why would they need to be reconciled in the first place? That is what I mean by a dialectical construction. Nature says both yes and no to grace.

Nature pulls against grace, but grace will not let it break free. Nature, in a way, is stuck with grace, yet grace takes the form of invitation, not compulsion. Protestants risk breaking that tension when they argue that nature is empty of all indications of divine grace. That makes grace an extrinsic supplement to nature, which hardly does justice to its status as the creation of a good God. True, nature is in a state of rebellion, and one sign of that rebellion is humanity's tendency to ignore, decline, or reject God's love. Nature's rebellion, however, is not an all-out war because nature and grace belong together; they are, so to speak, on the same team, with God still in charge of nature no matter how recalcitrant it has become.

Catholic theology risks reducing the tension between nature and grace when it regards nature as better than it is. When theologians downplay original sin, for example, they can end up arguing that all people, regardless of what they say or do, really love God because everyone has grace whether they know it or not. Some ecological theologies thus depict nature as a part of God or a reflection of the Trinity's peaceful relations, which does not do justice to the ways in which nature is turned against itself and a threat to us as well. By going too far in bringing grace and nature together, grace is rendered redundant, because we already have everything that we need to be saved.

At their best, Catholic theologians try to maintain the tension between nature and grace without separating or conflating them. That dialectical balance is best expressed in paradoxical statements like "humans have a natural desire to know God, but that natural desire gets mixed up with other desires in ways that always lead humanity astray." In other words, we are inherently oriented to the divine but that orientation does not disable our freedom to put our faith in ourselves. God's "yes" to us never drowns out our ability to say "no."

Putting that dialectical balance into spiritual practice is impossible without a strong sense of the Holy Spirit. Unfortunately, many Christian traditions neglect this member of the Trinity. The Catholic Church has been at the forefront of keeping the Holy Spirit on a short leash for fear of the religious chaos and dissension that emotionally based movements can cause. This trend began with the excommunication of Montanus, a late second-century preacher who claimed his prophecies came directly from the Holy Spirit. The Pentecostal and charismatic movements of the twentieth century have put the Holy Spirit back on the theological map, even though prejudices remain about its practical and doctrinal significance. Augustine defined the Holy Spirit as the love shared by the Father and the Son, which seems to deny it any agency of its own. It is not easy to reconcile the Holy Spirit as a divine person, equal to the Father and Son, with Augustine's notion of the Spirit as the mutual love of the Father and Son. Still, I would wager that most Christians today, whatever their denomination, think of the Spirit as an active force in the world, stirring our souls, energizing our wills, and focusing our minds on God. In the modern world, we have many experiences with invisible physical forces, so perhaps it is easier for us to think of the Spirit in terms of energy and power, but given the assumptions of classical theism, the Spirit must be not only invisible but immaterial as well.

Mormons have an easier time with conceptualizing and practicing the Holy Spirit's intermingling of the supernatural and the natural. They do not need to resort to paradox in bringing together grace and nature because they do not locate them in the opposite categories of the immaterial and the material. They also are more forthright about conceptualizing the Holy Spirit in terms of an active, guiding, and illuminating force in the world. Admittedly, the Mormon understanding of the Holy Spirit is not easy to grasp. They believe that God the Father and God the Son have physical bodies, though made of a spiritually refined matter that we can hardly conceive, but that the Holy Spirit does not have the exact same kind of body as the Father and the Son. As Joseph Smith taught, "The Father has a body of flesh and bones as tangible as man's; the Son also; but the Holy Ghost has not a body of flesh and bones, but is a personage of Spirit. Were it not so, the Holy Ghost could not dwell in us" (D&C 130:22). The Holy Spirit communicates to our spirit in a way that carries far more conviction than anything we perceive through our senses. It is has more material reality, we could say, than anything in the purely physical world.

What if Catholics began thinking of the Holy Spirit as something more like a material power or force rather than an immaterial substance that never changes and has nothing in common with finite objects? I was leading a Bible study at a medium security prison on the typical temptations that befall men when the Holy Spirit led me to this verse: "Do you not know that your bodies are members of Christ? Should I therefore take the members of Christ and make them members of a prostitute? Never! Do you not know that whoever is united to a prostitute becomes one body with her?" (1 Corinthians 6:15, 16). These words astonished me. The closer I looked at this passage, the wilder its meaning became. Paul was not saying that you should avoid prostitution because it leads women astray or violates your marriage vows, although he would also agree with that. He did not say that prostitution can degrade your body through various diseases, although he would agree with that. He did not say that giving in to lust leads you to give in to a lot of other sins as well, although he would certainly agree to that. He said that you become one with the prostitute. More than that, he said that you take other believers with you into this shared body when you join a prostitute.

How is that possible? How does one Christian's decision to visit a prostitute jeopardize the whole body of believers? We could say that Christians visiting a prostitute threaten to smear and tarnish the reputation of all Christians, but Paul is not saying that. He seems to think that something ontological happens when two people have sex with each other. There is an alteration in the spirit of each person, so that our shared bodies share our spirits as well. More than share: there is physical intermingling, a mixing that cannot be unmixed. A Christian literally shares in the spirit of Christ's body, and sharing that spirit with a prostitute's body damages the very body of Christ in significant ways.

Today we think of prostitution (or pornography) as a victimless crime. It is hard to persuade young men and women to avoid being loose with their bodies. As long as protection is used and adults consent to whatever is happening, then there will be no long-term consequences. The protection I refer to, of course, pertains to the body. We do not worry about protecting our spirits. Paul has a decidedly social understanding of sin. A single sin has rippling effects. He also had a physical understanding of the spirit.[3] We are spirits (or souls), but those souls have a reality that cannot be grasped by the category of immateriality. Our souls can mix with other souls, and they can be altered by that mixing. When we share our bodies with others, we are doing something that is much more real than just a bodily exchange. We are making a spiritual bond, and that can be very lasting indeed.

If the Holy Spirit is physically real, then it is absolutely true that grace completes nature.

Grace works through nature like other kinds of invisible but materially real forces, and it raises nature to its own supernatural level. It is hard to imagine how this happens in any detail, but then again, it is even harder to imagine how God can be present to us as an entity that is absolutely immaterial. Perhaps it is time to grant that God is the highest form of physical reality rather than another form of reality that is so unique that God is not of this world altogether.

Alonzo

Stephen brings up some very interesting and (I think) valid points about matter, grace, nature, classical deism, and Thomism. And while he has baited me to a degree that I am tempted to dive in, I feel the need to exercise a measure of restraint—if for no other reason than the reality that, as tempting as his descriptions are to the philosopher in me, so much of this (as he has suggested) is a nonissue to Latter-day Saints. We have had our thinkers, even if there is no exact LDS equivalent to the role Thomas Aquinas plays in the Catholic Church, but, truth be told, it seems from the days of Joseph Smith down until today (perhaps even more so today), the

Mormon Magisterium has sought to simplify Christian theology, soteriology, Christology, cosmology, and so on. That is not to say that Aquinas was trying to muddy the waters. But one of the great concerns of the Reformers regarding the scholastic movement was its tendency to focus on the periphery, on the philosophical questions of limited pertinence to salvation (as the reformers saw them). From its inception, Mormonism has also tended to recoil slightly at conversations that where not perceivably central to salvation. Joseph never cared about how many angels could dance on the head of a pin,[4] but he did concern himself over the soul of a man who was fixated on such an enquiry. For Joseph, such questions were not always signs of spiritual shallowness, but they certainly raised a red flag for him when he observed the Saints seriously ruminating on them. Oral tradition attributes this counsel to Joseph: "Don't climb to the extreme branches of the tree, for there is danger of falling: cling close to the trunk."[5] In other words, avoid speculation—particularly about that which has no salvific merit. Cling to the core doctrines of the Church, as revealed in scripture and the teachings of the living prophets, and avoid a focus on ancillary theological matters. In this same vein, Joseph once observed a bunch of the men speculating about the meaning of parts of the Book of Revelation. In response, he simply said: "It is not very essential for the elders to have knowledge in relation to the meaning of beasts, and heads and horns, and other figures made use of in the revelations [of John]. . . . If we get puffed up by thinking that we have much knowledge, we are apt to get a contentious spirit."[6] Joseph was not anti-knowledge, and he was certainly not against asking questions or thinking deeply about profound things. He once said: "The things of God are of deep import; and time, and experience, and careful and ponderous and solemn thoughts can only find them out. Thy mind, O man! if thou wilt lead a soul unto salvation, must stretch as high as the utmost heavens, and search into and contemplate the darkest abyss, and the broad expanse of eternity—thou must commune with God."[7] Joseph exemplified this approach to the questions of life and religion. He was, himself, a deep and ponderous thinker and—as his theology shows—he contemplated some meaty questions. Indeed, when one looks at his teachings in the last few years before his martyrdom, one finds significant profundity and depth. Although, as one scholar on the life and teaching of Joseph pointed out: "Joseph Smith . . . made a distinction between the mysteries of godliness—that is, the deeper things that can only be known by revelation to the soul on the how of a godly life—and the speculative pursuit of matters that are without profit to the soul."[8] Thus, with all of that being said, I will try to keep my response to Stephen's comments on matter largely focused on LDS and Catholic thinking, and how those both intersect and diverge.

In his book, *Crossing the Threshold of Hope*, Pope John Paul II noted that as the Christian Church "entered into Greek culture" it "realized the need for ways of presenting her doctrine which would be adequate and convincing in that cultural context."[9] Much of that "re-presentation" of doctrine consisted of repackaging the Christian message in a way that those from a Hellenistic background would find it appealing. So, for example, though some in the early Church favored a position of creation *ex materia* rather than creation *ex nihilo*, the former (*ex materia*) was jettisoned and the latter (*ex nihilo*) embraced. For many, creation *ex materia* limited God's omnipotence.[10] Creation *ex nihilo*, on the other hand, implied God had no limitations or boundaries. As Stephen has already pointed out, in order to preserve a construct of God as "wholly other," He must not—in any way—be like man or humanity. He cannot have, as all things material do, the ability to die, decay, break, wear out, and so forth.

Of course, while Christians would almost universally agree that we cannot exercise faith in a being that is subject to death, decay, or corruption (of any kind), this does not necessarily require that He be "wholly other" from His creations. As has already been asked, what if humans really are eternal beings? What if we really do not die when our physically bodies cease to function? What if we live forever? If all of those things are true, is it not possible that we are eternal in the other direction also? Is it not possible that we have always existed in some form? If God created all things *ex materia*—and if He is truly omnipotent, then how dare we say that He could not do such if He so chose—is it not possible that the matter from which we were made was eternal? And, therefore, could not you and I be eternal beings too—even if we were not, prior to morality, in the exact material form that we currently are? While I understand that such a proposition can be seen as countercultural or counter-theological, but setting aside our tendency to be theologically eisegetical, isn't it just possible that such is the case? And what reason do we have to emphatically deny our eternal nature? With Stephen I ask, "What if Aquinas simply missed it on this one?"

The Welsh theologian, W. D. Davies, said of LDS doctrine that it can be described as "biblical Christianity separated from Hellenized Christianity."[11] Davies is right! And because of their rather anti-Hellenistic stance, Latter-day Saints do not share the discomfort many other

Christians have with the idea that God could be a material being. Nor do we share the concern that if humans are eternal, we are somehow a threat to God's omnipotence, glory, or "wholly otherness." For Latter-day Saints, all God does and creates is eternal—and that because of His nature. We see a perfect being only creating perfect things. Humans may have the agency to make bad or wrong choices, but that does not suggest that they are necessarily temporary, transitory, or truly finite.

In a May 1843 revelation, Joseph Smith learned: "There is no such thing as immaterial matter. All spirit is matter, but it is more fine or pure, and can only be discerned by purer eyes; We cannot see it; but when our bodies are purified [or resurrected] we shall see that it is all matter" (D&C 131:7–8). Mormons believe that spirit is material; man is material; angels are material; the earth is material; and God is material. While the matter of which He is composed is unquestionably "more fine and pure" than is the matter from which you and I are currently made, nevertheless, that does not negate the possibility that mankind was created in His "image" and "likeness" (Genesis 1:26). And in so being, we may share more of His "being" than we realize. As Christians, we are so prone to allegorize anything in the Bible which suggests a genetic or eternal connection between God and man. He reveals to us that we were created in His "image" and in His "likeness"—and we say, "Shucks! That's just a symbol!" A symbol for what?!? He reveals that we are His "offspring"—and we insist, "Heavens! That is only a metaphor!" A metaphor of what?!? There is an undeniable beauty in God's description of man, not as His "creation" but as His "offspring" and His species. He seems to reach out to us in love, and we seem to push Him away, insisting that we know better than He—and that we are not worthy to be loved by Him or worthy to be literally after His "form," "image," or "likeness." Such a stance, so common among contemporary Christians, denies God's grace, power, ransom, love, and His word!

Curiously, Jesus—whom we each worship as God incarnate—walked the earth in a physical body. Apparently He did not feel that such an act was innately evil or even beneath the divine. (That is itself a testament to how God feels about the material plane.) As a mortal—or a God resident in morality—Jesus interacted with people. He hungered, thirsted, and ate. He embraced, blessed, and loved. And, eventually, He died. But upon His resurrection, and throughout His post-mortal earthly ministry, He retained a material body. One week after His resurrection, He appeared in a closed room to some of His disciples and said: "Look at my hands and my feet; see that it is I myself. Touch me and see; for a ghost (Gk *pneuma*, or spirit) does not have flesh and bones as you see that I have" (*NRSV* Luke 24:39). After each handled Him, He requested some broiled fish and a piece of honeycomb—and again, He ate with them as He had so many times prior to His resurrection. There was a physicality to His resurrected nature. He was a tangible being, a material being. He was embodied, embraceable, located in time and space—all attributes He had when alive; but now of some higher nature and on some higher plane.

According to the Book of Mormon, a short time after His resurrection, Jesus also appeared to some of the inhabitants of the Western Hemisphere and similarly gave them evidence of His post-resurrection materiality—just as He had with His Eastern Hemisphere disciples.

And it came to pass that the Lord spake unto them saying:

> Arise and come forth unto me, that ye may thrust your hands into my side, and also that ye may feel the prints of the nails in my hands and in my feet, that ye may know that I am the God of Israel, and the God of the whole earth, and have been slain for the sins of the world.
>
> And it came to pass that the multitude went forth, and thrust their hands into his side, and did feel the prints of the nails in his hands and in his feet; and this they did do, going forth one by one until they had all gone forth, and did see with their eyes and did feel with their hands, and did know of a surety and did bear record, that it was he, of whom it was written by the prophets, that should come.
>
> And when they had all gone forth and had witnessed for themselves, they did cry out with one accord, saying:
>
> Hosanna! Blessed be the name of the Most High God! And they did fall down at the feet of Jesus, and did worship him. (3 Nephi 11:13–17)

In these two passages (Luke 24 and 3 Nephi 11), Latter-day Saints see God's eternal materiality evidenced. If Jesus sought to help you and me to grasp the resurrection by appearing as He did, either the resurrection from the dead is what the New Testament describes, or Christ has sent the world's most confusing theological message. His post-resurrection appearances suggest that there is a material side to God's nature—and that there will be to the eternal nature of each of us.

While this may not necessarily seem like a salvific point, from the Mormon perspective, to see God as immaterial and incomprehensible is to misunderstand the nature of humankind. Joseph Smith once said: "If men do not comprehend the character of God, they do not comprehend themselves."[12] Latter-day Saints hold that we are (to the extent that we can be as mortals) made in the image and likeness of God. Thus, to think of God in immaterial and wholly non-anthropomorphic terms is to confuse both what we are now (theomorphic humans), and what our divine potential holds (divinized children of the one true God).

In the seventeenth chapter of John we learn: "And this is eternal life, that they may know you, the only true God, and Jesus Christ whom you have sent" (NRSV John 17:3). The Greek suggests that (in some sense) eternal life is intimately connected with achieving a "sure knowledge" of God—an accurate or clear understanding of Him—something, some scholars hold, requires personal revelation akin to that promised in John 14, when Jesus states:

> "They who have my commandments and keep them are those who love me; and those who love me will be loved by my Father, and I will love them and reveal myself to them."
>
> Judas (not Iscariot) said to him, "Lord, how is it that you will reveal yourself to us, and not to the world?"
>
> Jesus answered him, "Those who love me will keep my word, and my Father will love them, and we will come to them and make our home with them." (NRSV John 14:21–23)

Joseph Smith said, "It is the first principle of the Gospel to know for a certainty the Character of God."[13] If eternal life is based on an accurate understanding of the nature of God, as John 17 suggests, then the question of God's materiality is perhaps more germane than most Christians have considered it. Eternal life is necessarily connected to a knowledge of God's nature because one cannot fulfill God's dictate to become like Him if we do not comprehend what kind of a being He is. To the people of the Book of Mormon, Jesus declared: "What manner of men ought ye to be? Verily I say unto you, even as I am" (3 Nephi 27:27). We cannot emulate that which we do not understand. A bust on a pedestal is placed there because it is adored and because it is to be studied—in detail—so that its beauty and nature can be comprehended, as the artist intended. As important as it is for Christians to keep God ensconced on a dais, that does not mean that we must not understand Him or what He is like. Indeed, we must seek to grasp His nature and attributes or we cannot worship Him—for we will be ignorant of His nature, character, being, and so forth.

Now, the issue Latter-day Saints have with "negative theology" is that it seems to fly in the face of John 17:3. It denies God's "know-ability"; and it insists that there is a need for us to be "wholly other" than the divine in order to keep the Divine divine! As nonsensical as that sentence sounds, it is where we are as Christians. We so desperately cling to a negative theology that we throw a tarp over what rests on the pedestal. Our negative theology requires that we deny the beauty of what God has told us about ourselves—and our nature. Negative theology demands that we not believe we are of the "likeness" and "nature" of God. It insists that we reject the claim that we are the offspring of "Our Father which art in Heaven" (*KJV* Matthew 6:9). Suddenly man is the one claiming omniscience, and that seems a dangerous gamble! It erases the beauty of the message of man's eternal nature, as encapsulated in and emulated by God's material nature.[14] I am reminded of the inscription upon the altar at Mars's Hill: "To the unknown God" (*KJV* Acts 17:23). Paul spoke of how those who worshiped this unknown deity did so "ignorantly" (*NIV*), without understanding. To some degree, we have turned the God of Christianity into an "unknown God" whom we love to worship in "ignorance" because we feel it honors Him to be "unknown" and "unknowable." Joseph Smith found this a troubling reality in his day. I think we (Catholics and Mormons alike) should be troubled about it in our own day.

Stephen

Alonzo is right that some in the early Church, when they thought about how God created the world, concluded that God shaped pre-existing matter into its current forms, but I suspect that most Christians in the first few centuries of the church had little if any opinion at all about the status of matter in the doctrine of creation. Even though it took the Church several centuries to develop and affirm creation *ex nihilo*, that does not mean that everyone during that time period believed in creation *ex materia*. And even if they did, what did they think they believed? That is, creation out of matter is itself an ambiguous doctrine that can be interpreted in various ways. Did they believe that matter came into being on its own, or that it was eternal, and if the latter, did they believe it was always formed in some way, or was it a chaotic menace to the sovereignty of God? Even if matter is eternal, it can be related to the eternity of God in a variety of ways (an extension of the divine, part of the divine, equal to the divine, a competitor to the divine, or a god in itself, just to name a few). Some who believed in *ex materia* no doubt thought that God brought matter into existence and then left it there for an undetermined period of time, until He then decided to form a world out of its messy chaos. In other words, the line drawn between *ex materia* and *ex nihilo* was necessarily vague and blurry until all of the implications of these two alternatives could be weighed and evaluated.

If matter is eternal, then it is hard to imagine that it was always a chaotic mess until God intervened to set it right. It must have taken some kind of form even before God formed the world. In fact, this is what Mormons believe. Unfortunately, that is almost as hard to believe as creation out of nothing. What form did matter take before it was molded into the things that we now know and experience in the physical world? Did those forms change even before God changed them? If matter can come up with its own forms, without need of God's creativity, then why did God need play any role at all in the creation of the world? Why couldn't matter evolve into the world without God just as Darwinians think it has? What does God add to matter if it is already eternal and formed?

Alonzo says that "all God does and creates is eternal." While I often agree with my friend, and nearly always learn from him, I just do not know what to think about this statement. Can God create something that is eternal? Surely the definition of eternal is something like "uncreated." Perhaps we are in the realm of those logically impossible questions like, "Can God create a boulder too heavy for Him to lift."

More important, if matter is eternal and God is material, then is not God a product of forces beyond His control? That is, if matter has the capacity within itself not only to take on form but to become intelligent entities, then God is not matter's master, and it follows that God himself must be a product of material forces. If God is secondary to and derivative from matter, then isn't He not only not omnipotent but also not immortal? If He is the product of material processes, then He cannot be eternal and unchanging. In a word, He cannot be God.

One advantage of creation out of nothing is that it cuts through all of these puzzles and speculations. God is God and matter is not. A God who creates out of nothing has no equals, no partners, and no competition. Of course, that also means that there is no drama in the heavens before the world is created. Nothing happens at all in God's inner being, since God exists outside of and prior to space and time. God lives in an "eternal now" that never changes. That takes us back to classical theism, which has its own set of problems, but is the problem less insurmountable than the idea of God being composed of a substance that is as equally old as He is?

Creation out of nothing also has logical advantages, since the eternity of matter is subject to arguments about an infinite regress of causation. Doesn't there have to be a first cause, and if so, doesn't that first cause have to be an entity that is not part of the chain of causation? Many philosophers believe that a cause that stands outside of matter is the only alternative to an infinite regress of material causes. Science seems to concur. Scientists believe that the first cause, in a way, was the big bang, which comports well with the creation out of nothing doctrine. Science can trace causation back to the earliest stirrings (or explosions!) of matter but no farther. They can detect a singular point in time (if not space) when matter burst forth into the void. Science cannot prove that God exists, but the big bang theory is awfully suggestive of the idea that God started it all—and that God stands outside of at least the space and time of the cosmos we live in.

I think where Alonzo and I would agree is that the divine substance is neither matter as we know it nor something that is to be identified with immateriality, whatever that is. In other words, God is not immaterial in the sense of being the opposite of matter. Does that mean that God is material in an immaterial kind of way? That sounds like an oxymoron, or at least a paradox, and perhaps it is only through such awkward locutions that we can get somewhat close to understanding, in this life, the divine nature.

But what does it mean, in the end, to try to transcend the spirit–matter dualism of classical theism? Are we just playing language games by saying that God is neither material nor immaterial? I agree with Alonzo that a lot actually rides on this discussion, from the nature of our resurrected bodies to the value and ultimate destiny of the physical world. Just take the biblical idea that we are made in the image of God. What does that "in" mean? Whatever it means—and prepositions can be notoriously difficult to define and translate from one language to another—it surely points to continuity, not discontinuity. And what does the "image" mean? Most Christians take image to refer to Jesus Christ. We are created in His image. We are created to be like Him. So whatever He is, He must be something distinct from God the Father, and whatever we are, we must be sufficiently similar to Him to be actually and really like Him. Indeed, if Christ is the sum of all creation, and if God will one day be all in all

(1 Corinthians 15:28), then we are literally inside of Him in the sense that He is sufficiently capacious to hold the entire cosmos in His hands. We are joined to Him as a body to its head, as St. Paul writes (Ephesians 5:23, Colossians 1:18).

I have worked out some of the implications of the idea that the nature of matter is grounded in the pre-existence of Jesus Christ in my book, *Jesus Christ, Eternal God: Heavenly Flesh and the Metaphysics of Matter.*[15] For me, putting matter inside of Christ rather than outside of God (either outside of God as a product of the Father's creation or as an equally eternal entity that the Father does not create) is the best way to preserve all of the best features of creation *ex nihilo* and creation *ex materia*.

But there is also a more mundane, less metaphysical issue at stake in this topic, and that is the historical issue that Alonzo highlights of Christianity's relationship to Hellenism, more specifically, to the Greek philosophical tradition represented by Plato and Aristotle. Alonzo quotes a theologian who says that LDS doctrine is "biblical Christianity separated from Hellenized Christianity." That sounds right, but separation does not necessarily mean division or partition. I wonder if we can ever completely detach the New Testament, let alone the formative early years of Christian theology, from its Greek and Roman context. That is a legacy, it seems to me, that is simply part of the genetic make-up of Christian thought. When John the Apostle called Jesus "logos," a Greek word for reason, or when Paul talked about spirit bodies or natural law in terms borrowed from the Stoics, Greek philosophy, for better or worse, entered into the heart of Christian belief. To me, we cannot get rid of the Greek philosophers, no matter how far we can move beyond them. As much as I try in my own work to de-Platonize, so to speak, Christian doctrine, especially Plato's legacy of separating the soul from the material world, I also acknowledge that Plato must have been, in Christian terms, divinely inspired to anticipate so much of Christian thought. Plato and other ancient philosophers will always set the table for theological debates, as much as we might want new dishes to take the place of food that has gone stale! And anyway, rereading Plato, Aristotle, and the Stoics will always be a theological necessity, since these thinkers have depths that we still have not sufficiently plumbed. We are not done with Plato yet, I suspect, just as we have only begun to fathom Joseph Smith's revision of Plato, which leads us back right into the heart of classical theism with the question of how the incarnation can teach us to think about matter in new and marvelous ways.

Alonzo

Evangelical theologian, Reid Ashbaucher, wisely noted: "For one to define and understand the nature of the universe, one must first understand the nature of the force behind its existence."[16] Questions regarding matter necessarily become questions regarding the nature of God, as one clearly cannot separate that which is created from that which creates.

So, is God material? For Mormons, yes! Is the material He is made up of (whatever that may be) the same as that which you and I are currently made up of? Latter-day Saints will typically answer no! Stephen rightly asks, is God the master of the matter, or is the matter the master of Him? LDS doctrine seems insistent that God is in charge—though Mormons would also argue that the laws by which all things are created and governed are eternal. God did not make them up. He and they operate hand-in-hand: co-eternal, as it were! That might be perceived by some as potentially robbing God of true omnipotence. However, for Mormons this proposition does not. Rather than it being a statement about God's limited power, members of the LDS Church see it is a statement about God's nature. The laws by which He operates are eternal—unchanging, as most Christians believe God is. He was not a God who existed outside of eternal law and then invented a law by which He would function. Rather, God is eternal and so is the law which, by nature, is like Him.

Stephen has asked a number of questions regarding matter—most of which I am unsure I can answer. In the case of many of the questions he has posed, I am not sure (for Mormons) that they are truly germane to their theology. But one of the questions he posed in his string of rhetorical queries (heavens, I hope those were intended to be rhetorical!), I find provocative. Stephen said:

> Just take the biblical idea that we are made in the image of God. What does that "in" mean? . . . And what does the "image" mean? Most Christians take image to refer to Jesus Christ. We are created in His image. We are created to be like Him. So whatever He is, He must be something distinct from God the Father, and whatever we are, we must be sufficiently similar to Him to be actually and really like Him.

I find this provocative on many levels. I think it may be the sum of all we are talking about—or all that really matters as it relates to matter!

First, Stephen's suggestion here has consequences for the nature of God. He posits that whatever Jesus is, it must be something distinct from God the Father. That seems to challenge Nicaea's *homoousios*. Can the Father and Son be of the "same substance" and yet be as Stephen has suggested here—distinct? I think they can. Indeed, I think they are! But Stephen's statement certainly will ruffle the feathers of psychological Trinitarians, let alone modalist/sabelianist Trinitarians (who tend to make little or no distinction between the person of the Father and the person of the Son). Regardless, what Stephen has rightly done is to distinguish between the Father and Son—as Jesus repeatedly did in the New Testament, and as most of the Fathers prior to Nicaea consistently did. Stephen's definition, though true to official Roman Catholic and Eastern Orthodoxy definitions of the Trinity is, nevertheless, one often lost within the Church, and, consequently, also the cause of a lack of ecumenism between Mormons and Catholics.

Second, Stephen's claim that we humans are "sufficiently similar" to Jesus as to "be actually and really like Him" also intrigues me. As one who believes Jesus is "fully God," I see Stephen's words as having soteriological implications. I am "actually and really like" Jesus, Stephen says. Christ is, in some way, "like God." (If you accept the Nicene declaration, He is the "same"—rather than "similar" to the Father; at least in substance, but almost certainly in nature too!) Jesus has been resurrected and promises that blessing to me also. As we have already noted, His resurrection included a body that was quite material—one that could be touched and felt; one that ate and breathed; one that was even occasionally embraced and held. Upon resurrection, I too will apparently have a similar body. In this, I will be "actually and really like" Jesus (i.e., the "same as?"). And in this, Jesus (and I) will be "distinct from God" but, it would appear, very much like God. And what, pray tell, are the consequences of all of this? A very material heaven filled with a material Christ, and many, many saved beings who are "actually and really like him." In so being, matter has become deified and has been made eternal. Again I ask, is it different than the earthly matter we initially had? Certainly! But it is, nevertheless, matter, and it is the material make up of all eternal beings!

I cannot answer the mass of Stephen's questions, and I worry about the dangers of our finite logic when speaking of such infinite things. But I think the material and the heavenly cannot be separated. This may make me more like Jesus than it does like God. But owing to the fact that the councils, from the very beginning, declared Jesus as being as much like God as anything can be, I am hesitant to worry. And I wonder if I too might myself someday be able to declare those immortal words: "Handle Me and see, for a spirit does not have flesh and bones as you see I have" (*NKJV* Luke 24:39).

7

Jesus

Stephen

Every Mormon I have ever talked to, and every book of theology written by a Mormon that I have read, confesses to the Lordship of Jesus Christ.[1] In fact, Mormons go much further than most Christians these days by emphasizing the necessity of the cross for our salvation. By His blood we are saved. That resonates with my evangelical upbringing. In the church of my youth, we never tired of singing about the cross, and we ended almost every worship service with that standard hymn of conversion, "Just as I am." I can still hear those words echoing in my mind:

> *Just as I am, without one plea*
> *But that Thy blood was shed for me*
> *And that thou bidst me come to Thee*
> *O Lamb of God, I come, I come.*

We were always being called to repentance by the blood of Christ.

The focus on Christ's blood as the means of atonement also resonates with Catholic tradition. Especially during the Middle Ages, Catholic piety was obsessed with the miraculous efficacy of the bread and wine to convey the physical reality of Christ's presence. Just as the Latter-day Saints, under the leadership of Brigham Young, tried to implement an entire social order on the idea that the shedding of blood is required for social justice, Medieval Catholicism put blood at the center of its social imagination.[2] No two Christian traditions have tried harder to base their theologies in the precious blood of Jesus.

Far from taking the place of the New Testament, The Book of Mormon deepens its witness to Jesus Christ. The Book of Mormon, in fact, could just as easily be called "The Book of Jesus." I would go so far as to assert that, page for page, it is just as focused on Jesus Christ as the New Testament. Whatever one thinks of its historicity, it is hard to deny that it is, as it professes to be in its own words, "another testament" of Jesus, not an alternative or competing testament. Christians have always believed that Jesus Christ fulfills all of the hopes and dreams that are expressed in the story of the Israelites as they sojourn from Egypt to the Promised Land. The Book of Mormon shows how Jesus fulfills all the hopes and dreams of a remnant of those Israelites far removed from those geographical boundaries. It is a narrative about the "other sheep" that Jesus refers to in John 10:16: "I have other sheep that do not belong to that fold. I must bring them also, and they will listen to my voice."

Traditionally, Catholics interpret this passage to be about Gentiles. This interpretation rests on the assumption that Jesus, in His public ministry, reached out only to His fellow Jews. This is a very questionable assumption. His primary mission was to the people of Israel, but He did not preach the good news exclusively to them. Before He went to the cross, for example, He said that the Gospel "will be proclaimed throughout the world" (Matthew 24:14) and Simeon, who was given the promise that he would see the Messiah before he died, called Jesus "a light for revelation to the Gentiles" (Luke 2:32). Moreover, according to tradition, Luke himself was a gentile. Given all of this evidence that even before the cross Jesus was sensitive to the importance of His message for Gentiles, would His audience have identified the "other sheep" with them alone?

Mormons believe that Jesus Christ appeared *before His incarnation* to descendants of the ancient Israelites who had made their way to America. These individuals were given a pristine and powerful testimony to the truth of the Gospel, and after many struggles, battles, and lapses into apostasy, Jesus made a final and decisive appearance in America in all of His resurrected glory. What the people of America saw and heard from Jesus prior to the incarnation was from His pre-mortal spirit body; what they saw in America after Jesus's resurrection was the same body that many witnessed during the forty days between His resurrection and His ascension into heaven.

Whether or not other Christians accept these appearances and revelations, all Christians can agree that the four Gospels are a sacred but not an exhaustive description of Jesus's ministry. Jesus did more and taught more than could ever have been recorded in four short books, as the Bible itself attests (John 21:25)—and that is true just in terms of His lifetime on earth! The same person who was born of the Virgin Mary, died on the cross, and was resurrected on the third day was also, in fact, with God from the very beginning—more simply put, as John says, Jesus "was God" (John 1:1)—so how could His story ever be completely told? It will take an eternity in heaven to do that, and even then there will be more glory to behold. To try to fathom this greatness, the Apostle Paul uses several prepositions, concluding that God created the world through, in, and for him. Jesus Christ is the beginning, climax, and ending of every story, because everything points to him.

Catholicism has treated the identity of Jesus Christ in the most rigorous and scientific manner. The identity of Jesus is usually divided into two categories: the Son's relationship to the Father and the relationship between the divine and the human in the incarnation. Needless to say, reflections on these issues amount to some of the greatest speculations in the history of Western theology and philosophy. Such speculations resulted in a variety of creeds. The two most important, the Nicene and Chalcedonian, established formulations about the identity of Jesus that are still the foundation of Catholic belief (the Son is consubstantial with the Father and His two natures are united without being confused with each other in His one incarnate personhood). Nonetheless, even when a majority of leaders and theologians agreed on a creed, there were always those who disagreed or interpreted the creeds in unacceptable ways. The dissenters were given the label of heresy, and members of these heretical groups often faced severe persecution.

One of the most important developments in Christianity is toleration toward heresy, but there is still resistance among many theologians to revisit some of these ancient creedal debates with a generous and sympathetic attitude toward the dissenters. Every theological option should be evaluated on the basis of its agreement with the Bible, church history, the early apostolic witness, and ongoing standards of rationality as well as the personal experience of salvation. Individual Christians, of course, should not have their relationship to Christ judged by the quality of their philosophical acumen. Nor should so-called heretical traditions be dismissed as stubborn and willful rebellions against the obvious truth of the early creeds. In this area of complexity and mystery, any Christian tradition that puts Christ at the center of its worship and ethics should be welcomed into the Christian family. The Catholic Church for much of its history was zealous in its role of safeguarding the truths of the faith, but its history of persecution against minority Christians is one of the reasons that the Church today is so fragmented. It is time to broaden the theological tent by trusting how people describe what they believe rather than telling them what they really think. If Christians want to judge other Christians, they should do so by their fruits, not their metaphysics.

Since I have written about the role of Jesus in Mormonism in other places, I want to focus on a topic here that is particularly fascinating to me. When I was growing up, we spoke all the time about Jesus being the only-begotten Son of God (John 3:16). Both words in that phrase, *only* and *begotten*, are significant. I was always a bit confused about what "begotten" meant (from the Greek, *monogenes*), but I was certain about what "only" implied. Whatever and however God the Father begat God the Son, Jesus Christ was the only one who was in a position to save us from our sins.

As it turns out, I was not the only Christian confused about begotten. Begotten means to generate or produce and is used mostly with regard to a father's biological relationship to his sons. In Christian theology, begotten and Son of God go hand in hand. If Christ is not begotten, then He is not God's Son. Conversely, if He is God's Son, then He must have been begotten by the Father. Pagans thought of their gods as literally begetting divine children, but standard accounts of church history claim that Christians rejected such crude anthropomorphisms. Actually, it took many years for the leading Christian intellectuals to assimilate Plato's idea of a God who is beyond the categories of our understanding. Origen was the first Christian theologian to argue with any depth that Christians did not believe in a God who looks like us, and he wrote in the first half of the third century. He set out to distinguish Christianity from the vivid mythologies of Gnosticism and to persuade pagans that the Christian faith was as sophisticated as the best of Greek and Roman philosophies.[3]

It is hard to say how many early Christians took begotten in a fairly literal manner, but even if many took it metaphorically, that would still have caused problems. A metaphor is a lively comparison that appeals to the imagination as much as to the understanding. The metaphor of begetting conveys the intimacy the Father and Son share. It also does justice to all of the language in the New Testament about Jesus's filial obedience to God. Nevertheless, as a metaphor it associates an intra-Trinitarian relation with the process of procreation, and Christians, as they came of age in the Roman Empire, worked hard to deny any attribution of sexuality to the divine. Especially after Origen, Christians wanted to show their pagan neighbors that they had a higher concept of God than polytheism permitted. If begotten ever had any metaphorical significance in the Christian imagination, it soon became a dead metaphor, emptied of any particular imagery. The majority of theologians involved in the centuries-long debate about the doctrine of the Trinity came to the conclusion that there are no significant differences between God the Father and God the Son. The pre-existent Jesus Christ was and is as eternal as God. It follows that the Father did not produce the Son in any way, whether sexual or not. There is a relationship between the two, so a term is needed to label it, but that relationship is essentially mysterious. Begotten gets at the intimacy of that relationship as long as it is not taken literally or metaphorically. Jesus is truly the Son, the early Church taught, but begotten is just a place holder for their unity, rather than a metaphor or a concept. Begotten lost not only its literal and metaphorical meaning but also any meaning whatsoever.

Christians continued to insist that God is Father and Son (and Holy Ghost too, of course), but God is a father in terms of His paternal care, not in terms of how He came to be a father to a son. Of course, if God is not really a father, then the Son is not really a son either. Just as Christ, which is Greek for Messiah, has become for many people the equivalent of Jesus's last name, "Son of God" has become a title that is completely taken for granted. For most traditionally minded Christians today, calling Jesus the Son of God simply means that Jesus is divine. More than that, as the Son of God Jesus is God. But if that is true, why make a distinction between God the Father and God the Son, and why conceptualize their relationship as one of begetting? Traditional Christian theology answers that question in a totally negative way. It takes its bearings from the Nicene Creed, which gives begetting only one meaning. The creed states that Jesus is "begotten, not made." The Son of God cannot be made because He is eternal. He cannot come into being in any way that suggests a temporal order or sequence of events. In fact, He does not "come to be at all," since He is as eternal as the Father. Therefore, begotten does not mean anything other than "not made." This powerful metaphor ends up serving merely to negate or reject heretical views of Jesus Christ.

The Nicene Creed was written in part as a response to (and condemnation of) the heresy of Arianism. Arius, in the eyes of his theological enemies, committed the error of subordinating the Son to the Father. Arius, we could say, took the idea that the Father begot the Son literally. If the Father begot the Son, then there must have been a time when the

Son did not exist and, therefore, God was not (yet) a Father. Against Arius, theologians like Athanasius defined God as a being who is immutable (never changing). If any being is truly God, then that being must have been God forever. Athanasius accused Arius of portraying the Son of God as a mere creature and not divine. Arius got on the losing side of this issue, but he was not motivated by a desire to insult Jesus. On the contrary, he thought that only if Jesus Christ came to be God can believers hope to become like God themselves. Christ, for Arius, is the firstborn of all creation (Colossians 1:15), the one who comes from God in order to lead the way for the rest of us back to God. He is divine, for Arius, but He is a separate person from the Father. He is, indeed, the Father's Son.

Mormons are often accused of having an Arian Christology. The point of this accusation is to hang the label of subordinationism on their treatment of the Son. For orthodox theologians, the Son is equal to God in glory and shares in every single one of the Father's attributes. The problem with accusing Mormons of being a "return of Arianism" is that they have a dynamic view of the divine, so the charge does not really stick. If God the Father is evolving, then saying that God the Son evolves does not necessarily subordinate the Son to the Father. They can evolve together and thus share the attribute of "growing in perfection." The charge of Arianism would only makes sense if Mormonism preserved a Platonic view of the Father (immutable, eternal) combined with a modern, dynamic view of the Son. They do not do that.

Nonetheless, there is something to the Arian charge in the sense that Mormons can be construed as revivifying the metaphor of begotten. For Mormons, God does not create the world out of nothing. God shapes the world from pre-existing material, so God is a maker, not a creator. Regarding our spirits (or souls), Mormons tend to think of God's production of them along the lines of begetting. Every human being is thus produced or begotten in heaven by God long before our souls are joined with our bodies on earth. Heaven is structured like a family, and that goes for the Father and Son too. The process by which God forms our souls is most similar to the process whereby parents produce children. It is an intimate act that is fittingly called begetting. Far from being an exception to this rule, the Father's relationship to the Son is the highest exemplification of it. Jesus Christ truly is the Son of God.

With this view, Mormons restore a real meaning to the label "Son of God." Indeed, the Saints raise the family structure to the highest possible level by suggesting that God himself can be defined according to the patterns of family unity. God has always been part of a family, and heaven will be a matter of expanding our family connections, not transcending them. The love that a family shares is a direct reflection of and thus an immediate means of participating in the love of God. I know of no Christian tradition that values family so highly. The Catholic Church, with its emphasis on a celibate clergy and its defense of the monastic ideal, goes in a different direction by implying that personal holiness and family life are distinct, though certainly not incompatible.

There is another connection between Mormonism and Arianism. If I am right about Arius, he was concerned to keep Christ as a model for our spiritual journeys by closing the gap between Him and us. Christ is perfect in a way that we never will be, but His perfection is the goal toward which we should strive. Mormons too emphasize divinization as the point of salvation. Salvation is a process of becoming a part of God's family. The Saints thus do abundant justice to this passage from the Gospel of John: "But to all who receive him, who believed in his name, he gave power to become children of God, who were born not of blood or of the will of the flesh or of the will of man, but of God" (1:12–13). Jesus Christ is the Son of God, but all believers are children of God and are called to claim their rightful place in the Father's family.

There is much to be said of this view of the divine, but there are questions as well. Does God the Father have a father, and how far back does that go? Does God the Father have a divine wife? I think these questions demonstrate the limits of taking the begotten metaphor too literally. If Catholic Christians have gone too far in erasing the meaning of begotten from theological discourse altogether, Mormons go too far in the other direction. Perhaps Catholics and Mormons can meet somewhere in the middle to rehabilitate the language of begetting and to reaffirm the foundational importance of family by recovering the marvel that God the Father has a Son, and His name is Jesus Christ.

Alonzo

Latter-day Saints and Roman Catholics each have metaphors for conveying the Christian message. Some we share, like baptism as a symbol for Christ's death, burial and resurrection; and as a representation of the death of the old, sinful man and the birth of the new Christian (Romans 6:4). Yet, there are a number of scriptural or creedal metaphors which we do not share—interpreting literally what our brothers see as metaphorical; and perceiving as symbolic that which our brothers see as actual. The sacrament of the Lord's Supper is a curious example of this Catholic/ Mormon paradox. What in the New Testament seemed to Latter-day Saints quite obviously metaphorical is for Catholics, instead, quite literal. At the Last Supper Jesus said to His apostles (after blessing and breaking the bread): "Take, eat; this is my body" (*NRSV* Matthew 26:26). Likewise, after giving God thanks, He passed the cup of wine, saying: "Drink from it, all of you; for this is my blood of the covenant, which is poured out for many for the forgiveness of sins" (*NRSV* Matthew 26:27–28). Jesus said this as He sat at meat with His closest, most intimate disciples. Mormons believe that they could not have misunderstood Jesus to mean these words literally. Whereas Roman Catholics see in the Last Supper the first recorded account of Transubstantiation, Mormon's see Jesus creating a symbol—a powerful metaphor—by which His disciples would remember Him, His passion, and the historic event we call the Last Supper. For many Catholics this has to be literal, this has to be an example of Transubstantiation. Jesus did not say: "Eat this as a symbol of my body" or "Drink this as a metaphor of my spilt blood." Rather, He said: "Eat this—it *is* my body!" "Drink this—it *is* my blood!" For Latter-day Saints, on the other hand, the argument could be made that such a radical doctrine—if Jesus really meant it—would have to have been defined and explained to this group of fishermen and tax collectors. The leap would have been more than any of these theologically illiterate men could possibly have been expected to make. Indeed, the assumption that the bread, once blessed or consecrated, was literally Jesus's body—when He sat there fully embodied before them—would have been confusing indeed; and in ways it is not for us today when we talk of Transubstantiation.

Now, our subject in this chapter is not Transubstantiation. However, the example makes an important point. Mormons take a number of biblical declarations quite literally, and Catholics take a number of them rather symbolically. Is one faith's practice more logical than the other's is? If it were, I suspect there would be some pretty dramatic conversions taking place. Christology is one such doctrine where Catholics read the Bible metaphorically and Mormons read it more literally.

Stephen speaks of Latter-day Saints as Arian Christians. In many ways that makes me uncomfortable. Of course, much of what we know about Arius's teachings we get from his antagonists who sought to paint him in the worst possible light. But there are some doctrines historians traditionally attribute to Arius—and we will assume those are accurate. For example, Arius believed that Jesus received the title "Son" as a reward for being obedient to the Father's will during the time that Jesus was a mortal upon the earth. Mormonism, on the other hand, holds that Jesus was God's "Son" in His preexistent state. Indeed, for Latter-day Saints, Jesus was a member of the Trinity or Godhead in that preexistent state. He was God—and part of the Godhead or Trinity–long before He was born as Mary's son. Arianism, on the other hand, sees Jesus as so subordinate to the Father that He is but an archangel—eternally suspended half way between God and halfway between humankind. Arius apparently held that Jesus was not an eternal being. However, as Stephen has already pointed out, Latter-day Saints are emphatic that Jesus is eternal. Thus, while Arius would say: "There was when Jesus was not," Mormons might argue: "There was when Jesus was not a member of the Godhead, but there was not a time when Jesus was not." So, in many ways, LDS Christians are decidedly different from Arians.

For Mormons, Arius's mistake was not that He subordinated Jesus to the Father. Heavens, the vast majority of the Fathers of the Church prior to Nicaea were subordinationists. Justin Martyr, Origen, Ignatius, Irenaeus, Tertullian, and others each held a subordinationist view of the Trinity.[4] Jesus Himself described His relationship with the Father in subordinationist terms when He said: "The Father is greater than I" (*NIV* John 14:28). When called "Good Teacher" by a man, the Lord responded: "Why do you call me good? No one is good but God alone" (*NRSV* Mark 10:17–18; see also Luke 18:18–19; Matthew 19:16–17). The apostle Paul informs us that "God is the head *over* Christ" (*CEV* 1 Corinthians 11:3, emphasis added). Jesus told the Jews that "the Son can do nothing by himself; he can only do what he sees his Father doing" (*NIV* John 5:19), and "I don't do anything on my own. I say only what my Father taught me" (*CEV* John 8:28). In his letter to the Philippians, Paul noted that Jesus, "being in very nature God, did not consider equality with God something to be grasped, but made himself nothing, taking the very nature of a servant" (*NIV* Philippians 2:6–7). Although these are but a sampling of the many subordinationist Christological teachings present in the New Testament, they do establish a pattern of belief in the Bible and early Christianity. Namely, Jesus held Himself to be in some way subordinate to the Father.

Thus, for Latter-day Saints, Arius's "error" was not subordinating the Son to the Father. Rather, his real mistake seemed to be relegating the Son to a status of demi-god or archangel. That was his great heresy! Jesus, in Arius's eyes, might be called a god (with a lower case "g"), but He was certainly not fully God (with a capital "G"). That was heretical then, and it is now!

One of the most controversial parts of LDS Christology is to be found in our interpretation of the title "Only Begotten of the Father." With Stephen, I would agree; whatever "begotten" means, since Jesus is the "only" one to have been such, it must be different for Him than it is for each of us. Thus, I totally get why Catholics see this differently than do Mormons. In LDS theology, however, Jesus is not simply the "Only Begotten of the Father." Rather, Jesus is the "Only Begotten" of the Father *"in the Flesh."*[5] In other words, for Latter-day Saints, we are all "begotten" of God. We are all His sons and daughters. In the words of the Apostle Paul, "Since we are God's offspring, we ought not to think that the deity is like gold, or silver, or stone, an image formed by the art and imagination of mortals" (*NRSV* Acts 17:29). Mormons see each of us as "begotten" of God; each are His "offspring" (to use Paul's language). However, Jesus is His "only" offspring to be "begotten in the flesh." Thus, in LDS belief this means that each of us were spiritually created by God, but Jesus is the only of God's children—His creations or offspring—which He fathered spiritually and physically. God is the source of Jesus's pre-mortal spirit. He is also the Father of Jesus's mortal tabernacle. Hence, Gabriel informed Mary that "the Most High will overshadow you; therefore the child to be born will be holy; he will be called Son of God" (*NRSV* Luke 1:35). Jesus is the only of God's children, the only of His creations, to have God as His mortal Father.[6] In that way, Jesus is the "Only Begotten of the Father in the flesh." In that way, Jesus's begotten nature is different than ours.

This certainly does not imply that the only difference between Jesus and us is the fact that He was begotten by the Father both spiritually and physically. Jesus is divine—and fully so. He is a member of the Godhead or Trinity. He is God—not an archangel. He is greater than us all—and will eternally be so. But we do share something in common with Him. We each have a divine origin; a divine parentage. Stephen noted that Arius felt that Jesus had come to show us how to become like God. By this we assume he understood a doctrine of theosis, divinization or deification.[7] The Orthodox Church has taught this for centuries. The Fathers of the Church were obsessed with it. Roman Catholic scholars, particularly since Vatican II, seem rather enamored with the doctrine. If we can rightly attribute to Arius a belief that Jesus came to teach us how to become like God, then Latter-day Saints are

definitely Arian in this regard (though I would question any other parallels). While early Christians chaffed at the pagan tendency to attribute
to God any anthropomorphic attributes, the Bible certainly attributes
them to Him. Of course, again, one might argue these are metaphors.
But perhaps they are not. Perhaps God does have form and emotions
akin to those attributed to Him in the very books He revealed. Perhaps
we are just what Paul claimed we are—God's offspring. If so, then "we
ought not to think that the deity is like gold, or silver, or stone" (NRSV
Acts 17:29) or some mystic, incomprehensible force or being that is void
of body, parts, or passions. Maybe the problem lies in seeing God as
anthropomorphic instead of seeing us—His creations or offspring—as
theomorphic. Perhaps is it less heretical or blasphemous if we say not,
"God is like us" but, rather, "we are like God." Thus, the anthropomorphic attributes the Bible often attributes to Him are really theomorphic
attributes we have because humankind was created in God's "image"
and after His "likeness" (Genesis 1:26).

So what is the essence of LDS Christology? Jesus is a fully divine being
who is literally God's Son. He is the firstborn of the Father's spirit children. He is the Only Begotten of the Father in the flesh. He received divinity from the Father and mortality from Mary. Because each of us is God's
"offspring," Jesus is ultimately our elder Brother and certainly our ultimate exemplar. He is an eternal being who was given by the Father a place
in the Godhead and, thus, was God from the "beginning" of this Holy
Plan of Salvation instituted by the Father. He is God, but subordinate to
the Father, as He is dependent upon the Father for His existence. Because
of His perfection, obedience, and flawless passion, salvation comes in and
through His atoning blood, and in no other way. That is the essence of
LDS Christology.

Stephen

"Take, eat; this is my body." Those are indeed, at least for Catholics, the
most important words of the Bible—and also the most mysterious! The
Bible is full of miracles, but many Christians today doubt not only that miracles can take place in the modern world but also that miracles took place
in biblical times. How much of this decline in belief in miracles is due to
the widespread skepticism, beginning with the Protestant Reformation,
toward transubstantiation? For Catholics, the transformation of bread and
wine into the body and blood of Jesus is the foundation and model of all

miracles. Without that understanding of the Eucharist, matter is mere matter, dead and unable to be vivified by the power of the Holy Spirit.

Those words—"Take, eat; this is my body"—are probably the most disputed passage in the Bible, even though they are also among the clearest. Hear what St. Ambrose, the fourth-century Bishop of Milan, said:

> We see that grace can accomplish more than nature, yet so far we have been considering instances of what grace can do through a prophet's blessing. If the blessing of a human being had power even to change nature, what do we say of God's action in the consecration itself, in which the very words of the Lord and Savior are effective? If the words of Elijah had power even to bring down fire from heaven, will not the words of Christ have power to change the natures of the elements? You have read that in the creation of the whole world *he spoke and they came to be; he commanded and they were created.* If Christ could by speaking create out of nothing what did not yet exist, can we say that his words are unable to change existing things into something they previously were not? It is no lesser feat to create new natures for things than to change their existing natures. What need is there for argumentation?[8]

After all, Christ's body was born in a miraculous manner, and in the Gospel of John He identifies himself with the bread several years before the Last Supper. His teaching in the sixth chapter of that Gospel, after the miracle of the feeding of the five thousand and after He walked on water, is extremely clear. "Do not work for the food that perishes, but for the food that endures for eternal life, which the Son of Man will give to you" (6:27). When the crowd presses Him for a sign and people bring up the story of their ancestors receiving manna in the wilderness, Jesus tells them that the Father gave them bread from heaven. They reply, "Sir, give us this bread always" (6:34). He responds with the great teaching that He is the bread of life. He specifically identifies himself with the manna! They keep pressing Him to explain what He means. This dialogue, which takes place in the synagogue at Capernaum, is so important that it needs to be read again and again. After they repeatedly ask for an explanation, He finally gives them one: "Very truly, I tell you, unless you eat the flesh of the Son of Man and drink his blood, you have no life in you. Those who eat my flesh and drink my blood have eternal life, and I will raise them up on the last day, for my flesh is true food and my blood is true drink. Those who eat my flesh and drink my blood abide in me, and I in them" (6:53–56).

That is a lot of scripture to treat in a metaphorical manner. Nonetheless, many biblical historians today think that these passages were written after the early Church had already established its ritual of the Eucharist. The only good reason for their skepticism is that they cannot imagine that Jesus would have spoken so directly and plainly about a ritual—the Lord's Supper—that had not yet taken place. The skeptics at least have the virtue of making the issue clear. Either Jesus knew the future and could instruct His hearers in what was to come, or He did not know the future, and so this passage was added to the Gospel of John as an apology (a rationalization) for the practices of the early Church. Here is where I think Mormons are not on the side of modern historicist reconstructions of the Bible, since the Book of Mormon is full of stories about Jesus Christ instructing people in the ancient America's about rituals, like baptism and yes, the Lord's Supper, that are still centuries in the future.

If transubstantiation is not true (and I think there are many ways to understand transubstantiation, which is, after all, the single greatest mystery in Catholic liturgical practices), then communion is little more than a token gesture of stimulating the memory. A friend once asked me to visit her Unitarian church with her, and on that Sunday morning, they talked about communion. To give the children a taste of what this ritual is like (which they did not practice in this church at all, so it would not have been familiar to the kids), they invited the children forward, said the words of consecration, and gave them cookies and apple juice. I was deeply offended, but why? If this ritual is only a memorial, then what is served does not matter. If it is a memorial, then the same memory can be recalled through a variety of foods.

Flannery O'Connor, the great Southern Catholic writer, told the story of being invited to a dinner party by poets and intellectuals in New York City. Someone put her on the spot to defend transubstantiation, but somebody else came to her aid by saying that communion was a perfectly good symbol. She was more disturbed by the person who was trying to help her than the one who was challenging her. According to her own report, she said, in a very shaky voice, "Well, if it's a symbol, to hell with it." She goes on to note: "That was all the defense I was capable of but I realize now that this is all I will ever be able to say about it, outside of a story, except that it is the center of existence for me; all the rest is expendable."[9]

Having said all of this about transubstantiation, I want to wholeheartedly agree with Alonzo's brilliant insight that Christian traditions frequently have their most substantial differences over how they distinguish between literal and metaphorical truth. This is probably true of religious dialogue between any religions. It is a hypothesis well worth another book to test and explore!

Mormons teach that Jesus is the only-begotten son in the flesh but that all people, in terms of their spiritual bodies, are begotten of God the Father long before they have entered into this world of flesh, bones, and blood. We will have to return to this issue in the chapter on the soul, because Mormons teach that not only do our souls pre-exist our bodies but also that they are, in some sense, begotten by God. To say the least, the idea that all people are begotten, in their pre-mortal state, by God the Father is an astonishing and provocative thought. It is astonishing because it redefines what we mean by the "human family." It is provocative to traditional Christians because it appears to make Jesus Christ one of us rather than one with God.

The Mormon theology of begetting also leads to a unique perspective on the virgin birth of Jesus. Mormons attribute that birth to the activity of God the Father, not the Holy Spirit. Catholics and Protestants both point to the passages in the Gospels that give the Holy Spirit this role (Matthew 1:19, Luke 1:35). Of course, most Catholics and Protestants argue that the three persons of the Trinity work in such concert that what one of them does the others do as well. Thus, it can be said the Father too was involved in the conception of Jesus. Attributing the virgin birth specifically to the Father, however, especially when combined with Mormonism's materialistic metaphysics, strips some of the mystery from that event. For Mormons, the virgin birth is a unique event but not a violation of the laws of nature, since those laws cover both the spiritual and physical dimensions of existence. Thus, Mormons, it seems to me, tend to have a literal view of God the Father operating in Mary to bring forth Jesus in her womb, at least in the sense that something of God the Father's body was passed into Mary's body. That makes sense given the Mormon insistence that God has a body. Catholics believe that God created the world out of nothing and thus God can create a body for Jesus in Mary's womb without needing to put anything of himself there. Both positions make sense given their starting points. Which one is harder to imagine? Which one is more biblical? Which one makes more sense today? Those questions are too big for this book but are well worth pursuing.

Finally, I want to agree with Alonzo that Mormons do not have an adoptionist Christology. Adoptionists typically view Jesus's baptism as the moment when the human being named Jesus of Nazareth was turned into the Son of God. A voice came from heaven during His baptism and proclaimed, "You are my Son, the beloved" (Mark 1:11). Most Christians interpret this voice as revealing of Jesus's divinity rather than constituting it, and that includes both Mormons and Catholics. Mormons have a very cosmological understanding of Jesus Christ. His life and activities go back as far as time itself can go, which is to say, forever. That cosmology is different from the standard cosmology of classical theism because Mormons do not believe that eternity is timeless. That is, they think that eternity is infinite duration, not a time beyond all time. Given their understanding of time and their cosmology, they pay Jesus Christ the greatest compliments that can be paid, and they put Him at the center of this universe, even though they open up the possibility that there are other universes with their own cosmologies and thus their own distinct forms of salvation.

Mormon theology thus shares interesting similarities to an approach to Christology that can be called the Cosmic Christ, the Primacy of Christ, or "incarnation anyway" theology. Embodiment is good, for Mormons, not a curse or a corrective. The gift of flesh to souls is an opportunity for spiritual growth and progress. This goes for Jesus Christ too, who is both the creator of the world and the one for whom the world was created. Mormons affirm with the Apostle Paul that the world was made by, through and for Him (Colossians 1:16). The creation of the world, it follows, cannot be separated from God's plan for our salvation. We were created to be united with Jesus. His incarnation was planned from the very beginning, which makes divine embodiment the blueprint for material reality. The plan for salvation might have been altered to adjust God's intentions with the unpredictable ways of the world, but the incarnation would have happened regardless of the specifics of the human fall. The world was created for Him, and the drama of sin has never altered His unique place in the whole universe. He was pre-existent, and so were we. Indeed, our pre-mortal existence follows from His, since we were meant to be His companions from the very beginning.[10]

Alonzo

Because Mormonism looks rather Protestant to most outsiders, one might suspect that Latter-day Saints are not really "into" post-biblical miracles. Truth be told, I think we are fixated on them. Certainly the entire Joseph Smith story is saturated in the miraculous. Angels, visions, prophecies, and the appearance of God! Mormons frequently practice the laying on of hands to heal the sick or afflicted. They receive "patriarchal blessings"— which are prophecies given about their lives by one who has that charism or gift. They speak of personal revelation—and seek it daily on various matters. And they hold that each week when they partake of the Sacrament of the Lord's Supper the most miraculous of all things happens—God sanctifies, cleanses and forgives them of their sins and endows them with the power to overcome more and more of their fallen, human, sinful nature. One can only describe that as miraculous. And while, as an active participant in the Eastern Orthodox tradition, I saw my religion as "mysterious," I have continually found in Mormonism an attachment to the "miraculous."

Thus, the LDS challenge to transubstantiation is not evidence that Mormons reject the miraculous. Indeed, we would argue that for one to *truly* be Christian one must believe in, look for, and experience the miraculous. With Stephen, I acknowledge that Jesus (in His famous "bread of life" discourse of John 6) repeatedly referred to Himself as the "bread of life." If I am reading him correctly, Stephen feels so many references (beyond the Last Supper) to Jesus as "bread" cannot be symbolic. In his words: "That's a lot of scripture to take in a metaphorical manner." For Latter-day Saints, such is not a concern. In the Book of Mormon we are informed that *"all things* which have been given of God from the beginning of the world, unto man, are the typifying of him" (2 Nephi 11:4, emphasis added). Elsewhere in that same text we read: "Behold, I say unto you that *none* of the prophets have written, nor prophesied, save they have spoken concerning this Christ" (Jacob 7:11, emphasis added; see also Mosiah 13:33–34). And in the book of Moses[11] the Lord himself stated, "And behold, *all* things have their likeness, and *all* things are created and made to bear record of me" (Moses 6:63, emphasis added). From these prophetic utterances it appears that (1) all things given by God symbolize or typify Christ; (2) all prophets have prophesied and testified of Christ; and (3) potentially all things can remind us of Christ. Indeed, one late nineteenth–early twentieth-century

Protestant typologist remarked, "The red line of [Christ's] blood runs all through the Old Testament, and . . . thus we are constantly reminded of the shed blood, without which there is not remission."[12] So, for Mormons, Jesus's repeated reference to Himself as "bread" does not necessarily teach transubstantiation any more than the constant reference to Christ as the "Lamb of God"[13] teaches zoology. The typology pointing to Christ and His ransom sacrifice for us is embedded throughout the scriptures. The use of bread or wine as a symbol of Christ's redemption is particularly appropriate because we digest it—and in so doing, our body breaks it down and it becomes part of us. Thus, the food we partake of during the Lord's Supper nourishes us, sustains us, and becomes part of us. If we are to be saved by Christ, we must allow Him to spiritually nourish and sustain us; and we must allow Him to become part of us.

Of course, Stephen has pointed out that not all Catholics understand transubstantiation the same. I have found this to be true. But Stephen's concern seems to be that if this dogma is not "true," then the rite becomes a mere "token gesture." I question that conclusion. For Latter-day Saints, while we do not believe that the bread and wine become literally Jesus's body and blood, we do, nevertheless, believe that real power is conveyed in the ordinance or rite. Thus, Mormons do not believe that blessed or consecrated bread is only powerful if it is literally Jesus's body. If, by God's power or priesthood, it has truly been consecrated, then it is endowed with power; power to remit sins and power to change the recipient from fallen man or woman to holy son or daughter of God. For Mormons, it is the authority used to consecrate the bread (or wine/water) and the sincerity of the heart of the participant that effects the change or conveys the power; not the literal or symbolic meaning of the phrase "this is my body." Whether literal or metaphorical, the bread is the body of Christ because partaking of it represents the partaker's belief that through Christ's laying down of that body the patron can gain remission of sins. That is the truth we each hold in common! Whether the consecrated bread and wine are literally the body and blood of Christ (as the Catholics claim) or power-filled symbols (as the Mormons hold) is not the issue. The faith, belief, and action of the practitioner is the issue. This seems true of all rites, sacraments, or ordinances. Symbols are vehicles which God uses to bring us to Him. Symbolism is God's language. One can hardly deny this if one reads the Bible or engages in the Mass, or any of the sacraments. All covenants are written in the language of symbolism. All rites are symbolically acted out. That does not take away their power. If we understand the symbolism, it endows them with power.

Now, Stephen says that Mormons "attribute [the birth of Christ] to the activity of God the Father, not the Holy Spirit." He notes that, contra the LDS position, the Gospels give the Holy Spirit the role of begetting Jesus. Matthew's description (1:18) is significantly more vague than is Luke's. The physician offers this description of the event: "The Holy Spirit will come on you, and the power of the Most High will overshadow you. So the holy one to be born will be called the Son of God" (*NIV* Luke 1:35). A Latter-day Saint might read this verse as follows:

- Mary received the Holy Spirit (or, as the Greek says, Holy Spirit), thereby being enabled to endure both the presence of the divine and the miraculous act itself.
- At that point the power of the "Highest"—typically referential to the Father—overshadowed her.
- Mary became "pregnant" through/during the "overshadowing" of the Father—and in a way entirely undefined by scripture, though clearly miraculous.
- Because of how this transpired, the child she would give birth to would be called "the Son of God" rather than the "Son of the Holy Spirit."

Stephen notes that "what one person of the Trinity does they all do." While the Cappadocians might worry that this sounds a bit Sabellianistic—blurring the lines between the three persons of the Trinity and their individual roles or responsibilities—nevertheless, I would agree that the Father, Son, and Holy Spirit have one will or mind. In this sense, the will and acts of the Father are fully embraced as the will and acts of the Son or of the Holy Spirit. But in this passage Luke seems to distinguish between the person of the Father and the person of the Holy Spirit. The apostle acknowledges the role of the Holy Spirit in the begetting of Jesus, but he does not attribute the begetting to the Spirit but, rather, to the Highest (i.e., the Father). And that is the LDS position. I have ever been a fan of the prolific Roman Catholic scholar, Raymond E. Brown. Latter-day Saints would traditionally agree with his interpretation of the Gospels on this matter. In his book, *The Birth of the Messiah*, Brown wrote that according to the Greek text,

> the reading "child of the Holy Spirit" gives the false impression that Matthew has said that the Holy Spirit is the father of the child. There is never a suggestion in Matthew or in Luke that the Holy Spirit is the male element in a union with Mary, supplying the

husband's role in begetting [Jesus]. . . . The relationship of the Holy
Spirit to Jesus' divine sonship was articulated first in reference
to the resurrection (Rom 1:4) and then in relation to the ministry
beginning with the baptism (Matt 3:16–17). Thus, an articulation of
this relationship in reference to Jesus' conception came after con-
sideration Christian reflection upon the Spirit of God.[14]

Mormons certainly do not propose to know exactly how God begat Jesus.[15]
But for Latter-day Saints, the most important factor is this: Jesus is the
"Son of God," the "Son of the Highest." If we are worried about taking
metaphorical that which should be taken literally, then I will draw on
Stephen's earlier argument and say there simply are too many references
in the New Testament to Jesus as the "Son of God" (I count 47 references
to that exact phrase) to believe that this is a metaphor for the idea that
Jesus was actually begotten by the Holy Spirit.

It is parenthetic, but I suppose I should add this: for Mormons the
virgin birth is not a "violation of the laws of nature" specifically because
those laws are God's laws. When Christ walked upon the water, and bade
Peter to do the same, neither Christ nor Peter was violating the laws
of nature or the laws of God. Christ simply understood those laws and
used them. What we call miraculous are really events which take place
within God's laws, or in accordance with those laws. They are "miraculous" because we do not fully grasp how those laws work. Thus, we find
such events awe-inspiring. But Latter-day Saints do not believe God creates laws (e.g., laws of nature, science, physics, or whatever you prefer to
call them) and then disobeys those same laws in order to accomplish a
miracle. Rather, He operates within those laws. The miraculous nature
of any event is simply evidence that is of God—and that you and I have
yet to obtain God's mind. But were we with Him, as the angels of heaven
are, though we likely would still be in awe of His power, goodness, love,
mercy, and forethought, we would, nevertheless, see miracles for what
they are: acts of God performed according to His laws and His will. And
the ultimate miracle is this: "God so loved the world that he gave his
only Son, so that everyone who believes in him may not perish but may
have eternal life. Indeed, God did not send the Son into the world to
condemn the world, but in order that the world might be saved through
him." (*NRSV* John 3:16–17).

8

Heaven

Stephen

Heaven is such a vital dimension of Christian belief, yet it is often neglected or dismissed in sermons and theological treatises. There is a great fear, at least among mainstream preachers and theologians, of depicting heaven in overly saccharine and mawkish ways. This fear is an understandable reaction to the Marxist-dominated critique of heaven that was so prominent in the nineteenth and twentieth centuries. Marxists argued that Christians and capitalists conspired to use heaven as a means of recruiting and fooling the masses. In the words of the song written as a parody of the hymn, "In the Sweet By-and-By" by labor activist Joe Hill in 1911, "You will eat, by and by, In the glorious land above the sky, Work and pray, live on hay, You'll get pie in the sky when you die." Heaven promised all of the benefits that justice should have delivered on earth. Because of heaven, the critics said, people were slow to protest against harsh labor conditions and corrupt upper classes. While rejecting heaven above, Marxists wanted to build a heaven on earth, and many Christians agreed with that project. It was better to work for improved social conditions here and now than to encourage people to patiently await their future rewards.

It is hard not to conclude that modern theology has suffered a failure of nerve when it comes to heaven. Part of the problem is that sermons about hell have been virtually eliminated from America's pulpit. We are a cheerful and optimistic people, so hell could never be a permanent fixture in the American character, yet in recent decades, even evangelical and conservative Christians have rushed to separate themselves from stereotypes of fundamentalist fulminations about fire and brimstone. If hell is not real, however, how can the belief in heaven be anything more than a polite way of saying that all people are above spiritual average and good in their own way? Without its opposite number, heaven begins to look pretty irrelevant and even trivial.

If heaven is real, then it is worth trying to imagine it. I would go even further and argue that thinking about heaven is one of the best ways to think about life on earth. Whatever it will be like, heaven will preserve all that we most value in the world, so what a tradition teaches about heaven is a reflection of what that tradition consecrates in everyday life. There is a correlation between heaven and earth that Jesus Himself pointed out in the prayer He taught His followers. "Thy will be done on earth as it is in heaven." Heaven is the way things should be given God's complete and unmitigated authority. It is not another world so much as it is this world brought out of sin and saturated with God's glory. The earth and all that is in it is disordered by disobedience to God's plan, but through grace we can glimpse what it means to walk in righteousness and live in peace and harmony.

Martin Luther, the great Protestant Reformer, once stated, "We know no more about eternal life than children in the womb of their mother know about the world they are about to enter."[1] That is a humbling thought, but it cannot be taken literally. Fetuses cannot think, question, or imagine, but adults can. A fetus cannot reflect on the intimacy it has with its mother and try to infer from that intimacy what life after birth will be like. Christianity claims to know quite a bit about God, and we can infer from that knowledge what eternal life with God will entail. Besides, the Bible tells us a lot about heaven, even giving us a portrait of a heavenly chorus surrounding the throne of God (Revelation 4:6–11).

One problem with trying to revive the importance of heaven in theology is the prevailing prejudice against anthropomorphic conceptions of God. Anthropomorphism means the projection of human characteristics onto God (or onto anything, for that matter, from clouds to dogs).

How can we describe heaven if we do not put fully embodied people there, with all of their joys and concerns? And how can we picture God governing heaven if we do not depict Him with some kind of personhood, intentions, and actions similar to our own?

Thick descriptions of heaven cannot help but be anthropomorphic, yet many Protestant theologians worry that a human-centered heaven looks too much like a reward for moral effort and an affirmation of selfish desires. Heaven, for Protestants, should be pure grace and thus the same for everyone. It should not be overly pleasurable because pleasure is what got humans into trouble in the first place. If Grace contradicts or at least chastises our fallen human nature, then nothing of that nature should be affirmed or celebrated in heaven. Even the language of reward is suspect, since there is nothing we can do to put ourselves in a position to deserve any reward. Heaven thus should be all about God, not us. It should be theocentric, not anthropocentric.

If heaven is not about us and God is absolutely other from what we are, then it is impossible to have even a glimpse of heaven in this life. Catholicism, with its rich development of religious art and its emphasis on sacrifice and its rewards, does not have the same problems as Protestantism in depicting heaven. Nonetheless, Catholicism has its own guardedness regarding the afterlife. Thomas Aquinas, for example, inherited from Aristotle the ultimate priority of contemplation over action, with the result that heaven became for much of the theological elite a fulfillment of intellectual intuition rather than a place for effortless activity. Reinforcing this contemplative ideal, some Catholic theologians and mystics use images of light in order to signal the way in which heaven is beyond all description.[2] Light is one of the most fundamental mysteries of the physical world and has long been a rich symbol in Christian discourse. It usefully belongs to both the material and the mental realms, since thinking can be considered a form of illumination. Light seems instantaneous in its transmission of information, and it reveals objects while remaining hidden from view. Imagining heaven as light can help us think of a dominion where connections are as immediate as the flip of a light switch and where God is so pervasive that He permeates us like a heat lamp. Nevertheless, the metaphor of light does nothing to convey the way in which our identities will continue in the afterlife and the way that God will be an object of worship and not just a vague source of glowing comfort.

Mormons have a graphic view of heaven, and that is where I think they can be very helpful to Catholics and Protestants. A graphic view of heaven, however, is not unique to Mormonism. Many early Christians had a very vivid, concrete picture of heaven, as do many evangelical Christians today. It is the particulars of its graphic view of heaven that distinguishes Mormonism from more traditional versions of the afterlife. If I had to put my finger on the central teaching of heaven in Mormonism that makes it so different, I would say that the saved in the Mormon view are depicted as becoming more individual, more personal, more real the longer they are in heaven. This is in direct contrast to Catholic theology. The emphasis on the oneness of God in Catholicism is so strong that God threatens to take up all the available space in heaven. What I mean is this: If God is infinite, as classical theism states, then God's actuality is the only true reality. God lets the world be the world, but when God's will is finally accomplished and unimpeded, then all things will be subjected to God and God's being will not be limited in any way. When God's will triumphs, there will be no reality outside of God's authority and presence. God will be truly infinite, which means that God's reality will assume, transform, and replace every other reality. It follows that the more we become what God intended us to be in heaven, the more we will become absorbed into the divine. We will become one with God, whose oneness leaves no room for division or separation. Perhaps the best that can be said about where this leaves our individuality is that we will become one of the thoughts of God.

The ancient Greek philosophers held up contemplation as the highest form of human existence. Christians hold up love as the summit of existence. Contemplation is not necessarily passive, although for many people it means finding a quiet, still place in order to become immersed in music, drama, novels, or other kinds of art. We have to clarify our thoughts and overcome all distractions to reach a contemplative state. All of the little things of ordinary life become an impediment or disruption to that state. Love is quite different! Interruptions and distractions are the very point of love! Love means dealing with requests, demands, needs, and intrusions that prevent us from gathering ourselves into a single act of contemplation. Love requires real and unpredictable exchanges between persons who can truly give of themselves to others while being open to receiving what others have to give. Love flourishes in community, but only if that community does not let the individual disappear into momentary flights of transcendence. Love keeps people grounded, and it can do that in heaven as well as earth.

One problem with thinking about heaven as a real community of individuals is that communities are socially stratified. There are, for want of a better word, rankings of individuals according to their degree of participation in what the community offers. These rankings mean that some people will have more authority than others based on their deeper immersion in common activities. Many Protestants instinctively reject any hint that heaven will have rankings, other than Jesus being at the top. They are skeptical of any social arrangements in heaven that fall short of absolute equality in every way. Such views, I am convinced, have more to do with our pride in democracy than in our understanding of the biblical message. Even democracy, however, is not incompatible with hierarchy. Democracies guarantee equality of opportunity, based on shared rights, but not identical outcomes or a sameness of performances.

The Protestant insistence on an absolutely egalitarian heaven also stems from their view of salvation. If we can do nothing whatsoever to earn grace, then nobody is closer to God than anybody else. Due to original sin, we are all equally distant from God in this life and thus we will all be equally close to God in the next. Catholics, with their emphasis on holiness as a process and their reverence for saints as moral exemplars, acknowledge that salvation is a journey and that some of the faithful are farther along the path than others.

Catholics are thus in a better position to appreciate how Mormons view heaven as progressive, not static, creative, not serene, as well as radically individual. Other theological traditions also talk about how the saved will continue to deepen their knowledge of God in heaven, but Mormons think of heavenly progress in terms of the deepening of individual personality, not the absorption of individuals into the mind of God. Even the Trinity, for Mormons, consists of three distinct persons, so there is no single divine substance into which the saved will be assimilated. Consequently, heaven will enhance what makes us distinct from each other as well as what creates communal belonging. The endpoint or goal of individualization in heaven is not just the free expression of personality, however. It is to become more like God by exercising the virtues and attributes that God possesses. Thus, we have the Mormon version of what traditional theologians call divinization, the idea that the destiny of believers is to become, in some sense, gods themselves. I want to turn this topic over to Alonzo, because I am eager to hear what he has to say about it.

Alonzo

In the first book of his *Confessions*, we find Saint Augustine's famous affirmation: "Thou hast formed us for Thyself," O God, "and our hearts are restless till they find rest in Thee." Heaven is the longing of every Christian heart. For some that longing exists in response to a fear of damnation and divine punishment. For others it is evidence of faith in, and love for, the God who gave us life.

The variation in our response to the universal longing to be with God is itself a portent of things to come. While some Christians may be bothered by the suggestion of any inequality in heaven, it seems our conscious choice to respond differently to that innate longing for God is reason enough for God to justifiably distinguish between those who truly loved Him during this life and those who merely feared Him. Thus, I like Stephen's analogy that "salvation is a journey" and "some of the faithful" (e.g., those who have achieved sainthood or those who have lived undeniably holy lives) "are farther along the path than are others." Denominationalism aside, this seems to me an undeniable truth.

There is ample evidence that anciently both Jews and Christians perceived heaven as being a place with numerous degrees or divisions. Indeed, respected biblical scholars—such as Colin Kruse (Anglican), I. Howard Marshal (Evangelical Methodist), and Raymond E. Brown (Catholic), among others—have pointed out that among Paul's contemporaries differing views of heaven were in vogue, commonly professing a belief, not of a singular heaven, but of one with three, five, or seven divisions or locations.[3] Thus, in 2 Corinthians 12:2 the Apostle Paul states, "I know a man in Christ who fourteen years ago was caught up to the third heaven" (NRSV). It is almost universally assumed that Paul, like the Jews of his day, believed that there were varying degrees in heaven—likely because there were varying degrees of holiness and commitment to God here. The psalmist seemed to perceive this truth (see, e.g., Psalms 115:16 and 148:4), as did King Solomon (1 Kings 8:27) and Moses (Deuteronomy 10:14). Similarly, in John 14:2, Jesus announces, "In my Father's house are many mansions . . . I go to prepare a place for you" (KJV). Commenting on this verse, Raymond E. Brown suggested that John appears to be teaching the same idea found in Slavonic Enoch (14:23); namely, that "in the world to come . . . there are many dwelling places prepared for men."[4] Clement of Alexandria (A.D. 153–217), Irenaeus (A.D. 120–202), and Papias (A.D. 70–155) also each taught that there were variant heavens for the variously committed creations of God.[5]

While it is true that salvation comes by the grace of God—and we are all dependent upon that grace—nevertheless, it would be naïve to suggest that all who rely upon the grace of Christ for their salvation are equal in their reliance upon, their faithfulness to, and their love for God. While I am emphatically not preaching salvation by works here, who can honestly say that they have lived a life equal in discipleship and love to, say, Mother Teresa? And who would argue that the life they have lived has shown to God their personal devotion to Him and adoration for Him to a degree equal to the life of that saintly sister? Just as we are unequal in our response to the promptings or urgings of the Holy Spirit and to God's manifestations of grace, there may well be variant rewards contingent upon how we have responded to those manifestations—and contingent upon how we have loved Him and others, as He commanded us. If we love Christ, we will do the things He has asked of us—things so simple that we have little excuse for rejecting them (e.g., exercising faith in Him, repenting of our sins, accepting baptism at the hands of those authorized, receiving His Holy Spirit, and other ordinance where we meet Christ in a special way). If we are unwilling to take those very simple steps as an expression of love for Him, then we show that we desire less from Him and desire less to be with Him. Thus, it is not so much our works that separate us, as it is the degree of love we have for Him and His ways.

It has already been noted that "sermons about hell have been virtually eliminated" from Christian discourse—or the teachings of the Christian church. Of course, "You're going to Hell!" is not a politically correct thing to say to one's neighbor or a member of your congregation. However, as loving as the Lord was, an honest reading of the New Testament leaves one with the distinct impression that Jesus was hardly into political correctness. This banishing of hell, though not universal, is increasingly common among the major branches of the Christian community. Indeed, the *Encyclopedia of Catholicism* states, "While the Church has canonized many saints, affirming that there are human beings in heaven, it has never affirmed that there is, in fact, a single human being in hell."[6] That is certainly a shift from the Church's stance during the ancient and medieval eras. Roman Catholics are no longer united on this point. Some continue to believe in the literal existence of hell, and others—not so much. Mormons believe in a place called hell, but they certainly see Dante's description as metaphor. For Latter-day Saints, those who openly live wicked lives—knowing that the way they are choosing to live is offensive to God—will pay a price for those conscious acts of wickedness. Those who "fight the good fight" (1 Timothy 6:12), on the other hand, will be forgiven for their sins and shortcomings through the passion and grace of Christ—thereby enabling them to escape the consequences of wickedness imposed in "hell." One passage of LDS scripture explains:

Therefore I command you to repent—repent, lest I smite you by the rod of my mouth, and by my wrath, and by my anger, and your sufferings be sore—how sore you know not, how exquisite you know not, yea, how hard to bear you know not. For behold, I, God, have suffered these things for all, that they might not suffer if they would repent; But if they would not repent they must suffer even as I; Which suffering caused myself, even God, the greatest of all, to tremble because of pain, and to bleed at every pore, and to suffer both body and spirit—and would that I might not drink the bitter cup, and shrink—Nevertheless, glory be to the Father, and I partook and finished my preparations unto the children of men. Wherefore, I command you again to repent, lest I humble you with my almighty power; and that you confess your sins, lest you suffer these punishments of which I have spoken, of which in the smallest, yea, even in the least degree you have tasted at the time I withdrew my Spirit. (D&C 19:15–20)

Thus, for Latter-day Saints, hell does exist. But it is temporary; and it is reserved for those who willfully live lives of wickedness, rather than for those who seek holiness—but simply fall short of perfection, as all of us do. Consequently, hell serves a purpose (in LDS soteriology), as does heaven.

When heaven is mentioned, I think many Christians envision Raphael Santi's Sistine Madonna. At the base of the famous painting, one finds the most popular and commercialized aspect of Santi's famous work: two naked, winged cherubs contemplating the greatness of Madonna and Child. But is that what heaven will be? Will we throughout eternity have naught to do but lay upon fluffy clouds contemplating the holy ones? Or is it something more? Stephen rightly notes that some Christians struggle with a heaven that has any purpose central to the creature. It is, for many, totally about the Creator. Certainly, God must be extoled—and will be by each of us throughout eternity! However, a heaven that is entirely about the Creator seems to depict Him in rather narcissistic terms. How does a God so thoroughly associated in scripture with love come out only loving Himself in heaven? It makes absolutely no sense! If God is love, then He must have that which He loves—or His love is wasted because it cannot exist aside from its recipients. Thus, for His creations, heaven will be a time to express immeasurable gratitude for His gifts freely given. But it will also be a time for Him to love that which He has created and which, through His love, He has redeemed.

Mormons would resonate with Stephen's suggestion that "heaven will preserve all that we most value in the world." And what do true Christians value? God, Christ, the Holy Spirit, family, service and love. Thus, for Mormons, what is heaven? It certainly is not naked winged cherubs reclining on clouds. It is the presence of God, and the continuation of the family unit. It is love eternally: for God, family, grace, and goodness. It is the good of earth-life minus the bad! And it is not a loss of individuality. Rather, it is a perfecting of individuality through the accrual of God's attributes.

Now, when one hears how some Christians describe heaven, one cannot but help wonder: Are they talking about heaven or Nirvana? For Mormons the notion of becoming "absorbed into the divine" thereby becoming solely one of the "thoughts of God"—and losing all individuality—seems puzzling, at best. Contra this, the LDS view has been described by Stephen as making the inheritor more individual, more personal, or more real. The description of heaven as a place where "God is the only true reality" makes no sense to Mormons. We are drawn to the words of John, where (in reference to Christ's Second Advent) he informs us: "See what great love the Father has lavished on us, that we should be called children of God! And that is what we are! The reason the world does not know us is that it did not know him. Dear friends, now we are children of God, and what we will be has not yet been made known. But we know that *when he appears, we shall be like him*, for we shall see him as he is. Everyone who has this hope in him purifies himself, just as he is pure" (*NIV* 1 John 3:2–3, emphasis added). If God is love, then there must be objects of His love. As we have suggested above, the cessation of our individual existence seems to rob God of the loving relationship He desires and seeks to establish with and through each of us.

Consequently, like so many of the Church Fathers, the Eastern Orthodox, and many post-Vatican II Catholics, Latter-day Saints believe in a doctrine of deification. The number of references to this teaching in the writings of the Church Fathers is overwhelming. We will cite but a few. Clement of Alexandria, for example, indicated: "After we are freed from all punishment and penalty which we undergo, in consequence of our sins, those who have become perfect are called by the appellation of gods, being destined to sit on thrones with the other gods that have been first put in their places by the Savior."[7] Similarly, from Saint Augustine we learn: "Our Lord Jesus Christ then is the 'God of gods;' But then who are those gods, or where are they, of whom God is the true God? He hath called men gods, that are deified of His Grace."[8] And Saint Thomas Aquinas taught: "The Only-begotten Son of God, wanting us to be partakers of his divinity, assumed our human nature so that, having become man, he might make men gods."⁹ The key to understanding this doctrine is to be found in the emphasis on grace present in the teachings of these and other Fathers of the Church. Mormons do not believe they can earn god-hood. Nor do they believe that they, once deified, will replace God. But they do believe that God—who is the ultimate manifestation of love—is self-emptying. He wishes to reveal Himself to us here, and He wishes to make us "joint-heirs with Christ" there (*NRSV* Romans 8:17). The pleth-ora of statements by the Fathers regarding this doctrine leads us to dis-miss any claim that we will lose our identity, individuality, or agency once we enter heaven. Rather, through His grace we shall be deified—thereby changing our corrupt nature into a divine nature (2 Peter 1:4). But that deification is a gift—a manifestation of God's love for us. And, as Stephen has implied above, love puts the individual in a real community that does not let you disappear into yourself, or into God, for that matter.

Stephen

I love the Mormon view of heaven. Alonzo's descriptions of it are concise and elegant and much needed in contemporary theology. If anything, he understates the robustness and specificity of the Mormon afterlife. And he is right to chastise theologians who have tried to merge heaven with the Greek ideal of intellectual contemplation (which does indeed, as he points out, sound a lot like the Buddhist vision of nirvana).

One of the most startling passages in the Gospels is from John 14. Alonzo quoted the first part of it, that in the Father's house there are many mansions. A little later in this same discourse, Jesus says, "Very truly, I tell you, the one who believes in me will also do the works that I do and, in fact, will do greater works than these, because I am going to the Father" (John 14:12). Obviously, the apostles who listened to that message did not do greater works than Jesus. They were inspired to perform miracles, but they did not raise others (or themselves) from the dead. Because this verse seems so obviously wrong, many interpreters have suggested that the works Jesus is talking about have to do with preaching the gospel. In other words, Jesus was a preacher, and after His ascent into heaven, the apostles would have to take over that job and preach to even more people than Jesus did. The problem with that inter-pretation is that Jesus was hardly a professional preacher in the sense of what preachers are like today. He was a divine being whose works seamlessly integrated the miraculous with words of wisdom, prophecies about the future, inside knowledge about the Father, and all sorts of revelations about every theological topic under the sun. How is it that the Apostles could do greater works than that?

The only answer, it seems to me, is if Jesus is here referring to their heavenly existence, not their earthly lives. If we believe in Him, then we will be with Him one day in heaven, and there we will do greater works than He did on earth. We will not do greater works than what Jesus does in heaven. Nobody can surpass Him in any way. But what He did in His earthly state was limited by the materials He was working with and the lessons He was teaching. In heaven, reality will still be material and real in some way, but we will all have the power to transform and transcend that materiality in ways that we could never have dreamed of on earth. We will not be able to match Jesus's power. Indeed, our power will be a mere reflection of His, and it will be on loan to us, as it were, like a gift. But we will exercise power that goes far beyond what anyone has seen accomplished on earth. That seems to be the clear implication of this passage.

I know of no Christian tradition that does justice to this passage like the Latter-day Saints. Nonetheless, caution is always essential when it comes to thinking about heaven. It is so easy to project onto the next life all of the desires and dreams that go unfulfilled in this one. It is so easy to think that God must be preparing a place for us that will meet our every expectation for happiness and flourishing. It is so easy to think that we deserve only the best as a reward for our efforts here and now. The Catholic Church has unleashed the artistic imagination to soar into the heights of heaven, but at the same time, it has insisted that we do not really know that much right now about what heaven will be like.

Has the Catholic Church gone too far with caution, especially in the modern era? I think so. I have written a lot about the role of pets in peoples' lives, and I get a common question: Will my dog (or cat or whatever) be in heaven?[10] Aquinas thought not, because heaven is only for those who can rationally appreciate it. Animals do not have a rational soul, he argued, and so there would be no point for them to be there. Even here and now, we have no direct duties to animals because they do not share our rational nature. We should be kind to them, but only because abusing them might lead us to abuse other people. Our duties to animals are thus really duties to other human beings. Being kind to animals is good practice for being kind when it really counts.

This line of analysis appears to contradict the Apostle Paul, when he wrote that the whole creation is groaning in labor pains as it waits to be set free from its bondage to corruption and decay (Romans 8:18–23). From that perspective, heaven will be more like a new earth than an immaterial state of unwavering bliss. Things will happen. We will have stuff to do. It just seems obvious to me that, if we are active in heaven, then we will have to share in the power that God exercises over the earth. We will not have powers of our own, but we will be given a share in God's glory.

Will those shares be unequally distributed? I think so, though it is hard enough to get a picture of heaven in one's mind without trying to figure out what its political structure will be. I say political because that is the word that best names what it means to distribute goods and services in any community or polity. While it would be nice to think that there will be no politics at all in heaven, it is probably wiser to imagine that politics, like every other aspect of human life, will be transcended and transformed rather than obliterated altogether. There will be a politics without competition, a distribution of rewards without envy or resentment, an inequality without regret or recrimination. That is because there will be a ruler without dissent, an authority so perfectly good and wise that doubt and rebellion will be rendered meaningless. That is a political settlement we can only dream about here on earth.

Finally, the Catholic emphasis on the mystery of the divine does have a place in views of heaven. If it is true that we will never grow tired of becoming more like God, then there is something to be said for acknowledging just how different God is from us. People can get to know each other fairly well. Married couples often finish each other's sentences and read each other's minds. God surely is more mysterious, complex, and infinitely deep than this. We could think about God forever and still have more to learn from Him and about Him. I think the Catholic claim that God is infinite can be tweaked a little bit to bring it into sync with the Mormon insistence that God is a real person. God is infinitely real, which does not have to mean that God is immaterial, pure spirit, and without any form whatsoever. God's infinity has to do with depth not extension, we could say. God contains all knowledge within Himself, and His capacity to love knows no limits. There is an intensity or denseness there that defies our understanding. We will be able to move into that density for all of eternity without getting any closer to its heart or its core. That is what a dialogue with Mormonism has suggested to me about the classical idea of God's infinity.

Alonzo

Stephen rightly notes the tendency of humans to project onto the next life all of the desires and dreams that go unfulfilled in this one. Indeed, I have long been struck by the fact that the typical Christian perception of heaven is mansions and gold-paved streets. Don't get me wrong, I know there is scriptural support for such models. The Book of Revelation certainly references the streets of gold in the Celestial City (Revelation 21:21). And Jesus spoke of the "many mansions" in His Father's house—and how He would prepare one for us! (John 14:2). But what strikes me as most significant is this: In the West, where we have so much of the "stuff" affluence can provide, we perceive the ideal heaven as being filled with "stuff"—lots of stuff! In Eastern religions, such as Hinduism—where there are, for many practitioners, so little of the comforts and pleasures of life—heaven is perceived as the cessation of suffering. In both cases we project on heaven what our earthly lives are about. For Westerners, life is about consuming—so heaven is a consumer's paradise. For Hindus, life (in rural India) is largely about seeking to acquire enough food and clean water to make it through another day—so heaven is about an absence of pain, want, and suffering. Who is more accurate? Perhaps both! Certainly a beneficent and loving God would want heaven to be a place where those who have had to suffer no longer do. But, I suspect, He would also design it to be a place where all needs are met, along with a number of wants too. What seems most important, however, is that heaven cannot ever be about the "stuff." It must remain about God, holiness, and love, or it is nothing more than one more consumable—and God would be but a peddler of shiny, enticing trinkets. Heaven must be understood to be the abode of the holy, not because it is of itself holy, but because all those who achieve it—all those who dwell there—have become holy. Its inhabitants (God in particular) make it holy! Not the other way around!

Although tangential, Steven's excursus on animals in heaven was intriguing to me. While I hate to take issue with Aquinas (again), I wonder if he did not miss the mark on this one too. His reasoning for forbidding animals to dwell in heaven was that they are not rational beings and, thus, could not appreciate it. However, in the Book of Revelation we are shown a heaven in which dwells lions, calves, eagles, and men—each of which are found giving "glory and honor and thanks to the one who is seated on the throne, who lives forever and ever" (*NRSV* Revelation 4:6 and 9). This certainly implies a degree of rationality. Indeed, John informs us: "I heard every creature in heaven and on earth and under the earth and in the sea, and all that is in them, singing, 'To the one seated on the throne and to the Lamb be blessing and honor and glory and might forever and ever!'" (*NRSV* Revelation 5:13). John describes each of the beasts he saw in heaven—the lions, cattle, fowls, and so on—speaking and worshiping God (Revelation 7:11–12). Metaphor? Perhaps! Although John does not suggest that such is necessarily the case. Joseph Smith once taught:

> I suppose John saw beings there of a thousand forms, that had been saved from ten thousand times ten thousand earths like this,—strange beasts of which we have no conception: all might be seen in heaven. The grand secret was to show John what there was in heaven. John learned that God glorified Himself by saving all that His hands had made, whether beasts, fowls, fishes or men; and He will glorify Himself with them.
>
> Says one, "I cannot believe in the salvation of beasts." Any man who would tell you that this could not be, would tell you that the revelations are not true. John heard the words of the beasts giving glory to God, and understood them. God who made the beasts could understand every language spoken by them.[11]

Latter-day Saints generally hold that God will save all of His creations—not just humans. One twentieth-century leader of the Mormon Church suggested: "The Lord intends to save not only the earth and the heavens, not only man who dwells upon the earth, but all things which he has created. The animals, the fishes of the sea, the fowls of the air, as well as man."[12] Curiously, this view finds support in a number of ancient texts. For example, in the book of Second Enoch we read: "And just as every human soul is according to number, so also it is with animal souls. And not a single soul which the Lord has created will perish until the great judgment. And every kind of animal soul will accuse the human beings who have fed them badly" (2 Enoch 58:6). In Jubilees, we learn that Adam's fall caused the beasts of the garden to lose their ability to speak—an endowment they apparently enjoyed in Eden. "On that day" when Adam went out from the garden "the mouth of all the beasts and cattle and birds and whatever walked or moved was stopped from speaking because all of them used to speak with one another with one speech and one language" (Jubilees 3:28). Perhaps heaven does have residents other than humans. Frankly, it seems a bit narcissistic to hold that we are the only of God's creations worthy of being saved. In addition, to my mind a heaven void of God's many other creations would be an imperfect abode. Isaiah's description of the millennial day seems also a fitting description of what the ideal heaven would be like:

> The wolf shall live with the lamb, the leopard shall lie down with the kid, the calf and the lion and the fatling together, and a little child shall lead them. The cow and the bear shall graze, their young shall lie down together; and the lion shall eat straw like the ox. The nursing child shall play over the hole of the asp, and the weaned child shall put its hand on the adder's den. They will not hurt or destroy on all my holy mountain; for the earth will be full of the knowledge of the Lord as the waters cover the sea. (*NRSV* Isaiah 11:6–9).

Maybe, just maybe, it is not just all about us humans!

One final point should suffice. In any theological discussion one of the great weaknesses of humankind is the tendency to see everything—God and grace, heaven and holiness, punishment and paradise—through human lenses. In one sense I agree with Stephen that God is significantly different than you and I. In another sense I acknowledge that He has endowed us with the potential (through grace) to become much more like Him than we currently are. As I have noted, our tendency to downplay God's graciousness, and to ascribe to Him an almost selfish nature which seeks to oppress and withhold blessings and gifts in the hereafter, strikes me as shameful, at best, and blasphemous, at worst. God is the epitome of holiness and love. I find it sad that Christians—in every tradition—somehow take comfort in a model of heaven that has God holding back from His creations. Too many think that it can only be heaven if you and I are in some way consigned for eternity to dwell with God while not being allowed to engage with God. We too often envision our eternal relationship with the divine as being like that of a bad friend who allows us to walk along side of him while he eats an ice-cream cone, though he shares none with us. In that warped "relationship"—if it can be called one—we are just supposed to be thankful that we are allowed to be in our "friend's" presence. The LDS view, on the other hand, is one of shared blessings. God is the source of all, but He generously scoops up ice cream (or blessings) for all who dwell with Him because He finds joy in sharing with us and blessing us—His creations, His children. So, though I cannot conceive in the least what great things God has in store, nevertheless, because I know the proprietor, I know the party is going to be good!

9

History

Stephen

For many Protestants, history is a problem. If you try to believe and practice only what you read in the Bible, then you end up skipping over the theological wisdom of centuries of church history. The lives and testimonies of so many faithful Christians become stones to be stepped over on the way back to the Bible. The only people who count are the ones who wrote or appear in sacred scripture. History becomes little more than one long illustration of how people inevitably fail to please God. Everyone has a story, but from the Protestant perspective, every story throughout Christian history amounts to the same repetitive plot: even at their spiritual best, humans are inherently idolatrous. However much we try to be good and to do good things, we fall infinitely short of the glory of God. History is useful because it is littered with the spiritual failures of those who tried too hard to please God. By definition, post-biblical history can tell us nothing essential or significant about our faith. History, in other words, does not have revelatory power. Only the Bible has that.

For Catholics, by contrast, history is a source of truths that complement, enhance, and reinforce the Bible. While Protestants try to get back to the beginnings of the faith, Catholics believe that even the beginning is intrinsically historical. The Gospels start a story that continues in the Acts of the Apostles, with various letters filling in the gaps and pointing toward new developments. Being a Christian means becoming part of that story, and such participation requires a thorough confidence in God's providential ordering of historical events. Christianity, in other words, is history all the way through, no matter how literally you take the Bible.

The lives of past Christians are not just useful as pedagogical tools. The stories of the dead are not just informative or interesting. The dead are very much still a part of the body of Christ. They are still a part of the Christian team, even if their efforts on our behalf are not visible. In fact, they are captains of the team, because they have already finished the race and are now in closer than ever to the team's owner!

The roots of the Christian veneration of the dead go deep. Early Christians who hid in the catacombs worshipped God in the midst of an underground city of the dead. When tombs serve as altars, you do not need to be reminded to give thanks for those who have come before you. Stories about martyrs became one of the most important means of spreading the young faith, and the bodies of those martyrs became associated with miracles of healing. Sometimes those bodies themselves became miraculous when they did not show any signs of decomposition. It was important for Christians to try to preserve some of the personal belongings of the martyrs, or even their bones, in order to keep them a part of the community. Christians prayed to the dead and asked for their prayers, a practice that had biblical precedent (Rev. 5:8 and 8:3–4). The Church was a family, and the dead were living ancestors in the faith.

The importance of venerating ancestors did not really strike me until I spent some time in Asia a few years ago. So much of Asian spirituality is focused on cherishing family connections that extend into the distant past. From Temple remembrances to family shrines, the Asian attitude toward the dead made me ashamed of the way we in America rarely make time to do something as simple as visit a cemetery. We are quick to forget out dead. Isn't that one of the reasons we are becoming an increasingly secular society?

Veneration for the dead did not become a part of my life, however, until I became a Roman Catholic. Like most converts, I joined the Catholic Church at the Easter Vigil, which is celebrated on Holy Saturday. One of the highlights of that Mass is the use of the prayer known as the Litany of the Saints. Recited or sung, it is a very long appeal to many of the Church's greatest saints for guidance and protection. After calling upon the Lord (and expressly the Holy Trinity), the list of saints begins with Holy Mary, moves through the angels, turns to John the Baptist and Joseph, calls to the patriarchs and prophets, names all of the disciples, and then goes through the names of many traditional saints. It subsequently appeals to all holy men and women to intercede for us by helping us to avoid temptation and to protect us from Satan and all the enemies of the Church. I do not know how long it actually lasts, but I heard it while lying prostrate before the altar, and it seemed to last for an eternity. I was not prepared for how powerful it was. It seemed to me that the Church was making available to me a who's who of spiritual warriors and assigning them as my personal bodyguards. This was my new team, and it did not matter that I would be a benchwarmer compared to these superior supernatural athletes. I was home.

Of course, like any custom or ritual, venerating the dead can be easily abused. In the late Middle Ages, for example, collecting relics got out of hand, and there is no doubt that the Protestant Reformers were right to criticize superstitious practices associated with them, although their criticisms often took a turn toward uncharitable ridicule. Still, when you think about the way so many people today collect anything that has been touched by a celebrity, you wonder if the desire for relics is not hardwired into the human brain. Where is the Protestant critique of relics today when it is so needed to combat the idolatry permeating American culture? Medieval Catholic practices were often abused and exploited, but it seems like the vacuum left by the decimation of Christian relics has been filled with practices that have no positive meaning whatsoever.

The Reformers were gradualists on some issues, but on the topic of praying to or for the dead, most of them were hard-liners. They were, in fact, revolutionaries. They reacted to the intercession of the saints by drawing a thick, bold, and impenetrable line between the living and the dead. Christianity henceforth was supposed to be about the living, not the dead.

I tell this story about veneration for the dead because I think it opens up some common ground that is significant for Mormon–Catholic dialogue. Mormons love their history, and they should! Mormon history is replete with heroic tales of perseverance and triumph as well as tragic narratives of persecution and rejection. The Mormon story is an epic that, as many people have pointed out, repeats some of the basic plot structure of the Old Testament. Mormons are a people called to be separate from the world, and in response to that call they sought a promised land to settle and practice their faith in peace and freedom. Other Americans would not let them alone, however, and they were forced into various exoduses that did not end until they reached Utah. Just as the Book of Mormon reads like a retelling of some aspects of the Old Testament in the New World of the Americas, Mormon history from the nineteenth century to the present day can seem like a condensed form of the biblical story as a whole, almost as if twenty-one centuries of Christian history has been squeezed into about two hundred years of modern chronology. History carries much of the identity of the Mormon people, and Mormons treat their history with reverence. Talk to a Mormon for more than a few minutes and you often end up talking about where their ancestors came from, who was the first in their family to become a Latter-day Saint, and what part their family played in Mormonism's key events.

History has revelatory power for Mormons, just as it does for Catholics. Catholics too tell stories about their spiritual heroes (whom they call saints), although after Vatican II, the role of saints in the Church has been minimized and diluted. Catholics too remember the victims of anti-Christian prejudice, those martyred for their faith. Most important, just as Mormons preserve and treasure the teachings and revelations of Joseph Smith that occurred after the Book of Mormon, Catholics draw from the documents of the great church councils and teachings of the popes and theologians after the closing of the New Testament canon. Both churches look to historical developments that occurred after the death of the apostles in order to find clarifications, expansions, and affirmations of revealed doctrine. In other words, the religious meaningfulness of history for Mormons and Catholics does not end with the New Testament.

This commonality might be surprising since, from the perspective of the doctrine of providence, Mormons and Catholics have an absolutely opposite way of looking at history! Mormons see the Holy Spirit's guidance of Christianity as beginning with a great fire of revelations but quickly burning out until the time of Joseph Smith. Mormons call the falling away of the faithful the Great Apostasy, and indeed apostasy is one of the main themes of the Book of Mormon.[1] That book teaches its readers to expect apostasy as a regular and habitual condition of even the most passionate Christian generations. Mormons thus view history as full of fractures, disruptions, interruptions, and catastrophes, while Catholics have a much more developmental view of the past. For Catholics, continuity, as it is established by the Holy Spirit, overcomes even the most scurrilous human attempts to derail the plan of God.

What I find a bit frustrating about the Mormon view of history is how its interpretation of Apostasy goes by the wayside when it comes to the Mormon view of its own history. When Mormons look back over the last two hundred years, they see continuity in much the same way that Catholics find continuity over two thousand years. That seems to me to be a case of a double standard. When Mormons look at Catholicism they see apostasy, but when they look at their own past they see steadfastness and fidelity, even when their own history is full of splits, rebellions, accusations, and a splintering of Smith's teachings (for just one example, notice the way Smith's own family broke from those Mormons who followed Brigham Young to Utah). Here I have one suggestion about what a theological dialogue could achieve: Perhaps Catholics need to be more aware of apostasy in their own tradition and Mormons need to be more aware of continuity in Catholicism!

Alonzo

The twelfth president of the LDS Church, Spencer W. Kimball, taught the Saints that the word "remember" is the most important word in the entire English language.[2] Likewise, the Spanish poet and philosopher, George Santayana, reminded us: "Those who cannot remember the past are condemned to repeat it."[3] Remembrance is a powerful tool in educating our conscience but also in increasing our devotion to God and His Church.

The principle of filial piety (i.e., the veneration of ancestors) so prevalent in Asian religions can teach Westerners some powerful lessons regarding the importance and power of remembering the past. While Roman Catholics do not necessarily have the devotion to ancestors that many Asian practitioners do, nevertheless, they do have a fixation regarding Saints (not Mormons, but holy Christians of the past!). LDS practice mirrors in significant ways the principle of filial piety. We do not worship our ancestors, but we do reverence them. We are a bit fixated on family history work—collecting memories, genealogies, and tributes to the deceased in our own families. And LDS Temples allow faithful practitioners to enter and perform rites on behalf of the deceased. This is one area in which Mormons are passionate. You often hear the LDS mantra: "Families are Forever!" For Latter-day Saints, this can only be a reality if we "remember" our ancestors and our covenants with God. Temple worship is a central component in all of this for practicing Mormons.

Stephen is correct in saying that reverence for ancestors is largely lost in Western culture. In the Greek Orthodox home in which I was reared the patriarch and matriarch of the family were central, doted upon, and revered. My great-grand parents lived with my grandparents until they died. My grandparents then lived with my parents. The expectation is that my parents, when they are no longer able to take care of themselves, will live with one of their children. While my great-grandparents received

Social Security benefits, they did not need them because their needs were entirely taken care of by the family. While this approach to family life and filial piety was common among many of the first, second, and even third generations of European families who immigrated to the United States, it is a rarity today—even among the descendants of those immigrants. Unfortunately in the United States today, the elderly get a nursing home rather than their children's home. And, though they took care of their children when they were helpless, the elderly do not expect their children to reciprocate when the parents become helpless themselves. In the West we have become a people who want to forget—forget the past and forget our responsibility to those who have gone before us. In this we are sorely lacking in our Christianity!

Now, Mormonism has a rather short history. Full, but short! In our two hundred year story, we have had our martyrs and visionaries; our saints and our sinners. Indeed, as Stephen has pointed out, in many ways our history replicates events in Catholic history, only in a very condensed time frame. Like Catholics, Latter-day Saints have their places of pilgrimage (e.g., Carthage, Nauvoo, the Sacred Grove, etc.), we have our relics (e.g., the death mask of the prophet Joseph, the bullet pierced watch of John Taylor, etc.), and we have our venerated people (e.g., Jesus, Joseph, and the various prophets and apostles of this dispensation). I suppose some Latter-day Saints do not like to think of themselves as being similar to Catholics but, truth be told, we have some pretty similar components in our worship and history—if we are willing to remember and contemplate them.

In this chapter Stephen has leveled a criticism against Mormons that, as much as I hate to admit it, is an accurate one. Many Latter-day Saints are prone to see Catholicism as an "apostate" version of Christianity. They are prone to forget that the Catholics preserved for the world (including for the Latter-day Saints) the Holy Bible, ordinances such as the Lord's Supper or baptism, doctrines like Jesus's messianic role and His act of ransom. Too many Latter-day Saints forget that Joseph Smith walked into the Sacred Grove and had his first vision (wherein he saw God) because of the provocation provided by the Bible (which Catholics canonized and preserved). Certainly the Protestants had some influence upon Joseph also. For example, it was a Methodist minister who preached the sermon on James 1:5 ("If any of you lack wisdom, let him ask of God"), which sent Joseph to the Bible, and from the Bible to the grove. So, for all of the doctrinal and liturgical differences Latter-day Saints have with their non-LDS Christian brothers and sisters, we do need to be better about remembering that LDS history did not begin in 1820 when Joseph saw God, or in 1830 when the prophet officially organized the Church. Christian history is LDS history, and Catholic history is LDS history. And, were it not for Roman Catholics, Joseph Smith would likely have been born outside of the umbrella of Christianity and in a nation that was largely heathen.

One aspect of history Catholics are good at—and all other denominations of Christianity could learn from—is having a sense of the symbolically sacred. I am, myself, a bit of a symbologist—having written a few books on the subject.[4] Because of my Orthodox background I find liturgy and symbolism powerful and purposeful. One aspect of Catholicism that seemed to rub some of the reformers wrong was the Catholic tendency to adore saints and symbols. Protestant liturgy is traditionally low, and most (setting aside the occasional Anglican or High Church Lutheran) tend to see little value in the vernation of relics. However, it is important for all denominations to realize that relics are symbols—and they ground us in our religious history. They preserve historical memories so that we do not forget the past and what it symbolizes for those of our day. So, for example, archeologists note that the tomb of Christ that serves as a pilgrimage site for Christians dates way too late to actually be the place where Jesus was buried.[5] However, as the faithful flock to that symbol of Christ's resurrection—an empty tomb—they feel the Spirit of the Lord testifying to their souls that Jesus lived, taught, suffered, and died as God's Only Begotten Son, and as the Savior of the world. It matters little where the actual tomb is located, or where the actual cross was raised. What matters is what those symbolize to us. And thus, for the faithful such relics act as conveyers of God's Spirit and as preservers of divine truth. Similarly, I was recently in Belgium and had an opportunity to be in the Basilica of the Precious Blood during the veneration of the relic—a glass container of Jesus's blood, said to have been collected by Joseph of Arimathea when he received the body of Christ for its burial. Is the blood displayed in that Church actually the blood of Jesus? No one can say for certain—though I have my doubts. But what I cannot deny is that, as I looked upon the relic and contemplated what it symbolized, the sacred history of the Christian Church flooded into my mind and heart. Whoever's blood is in that glass container, it functions for thousands upon thousands who have viewed and venerated it as a symbol of a historic reality—"That for me, a sinner, He suffered, He bled and died."[6] Relics are a reminder of history—even if they are not, themselves, actually historic. They are symbols which provoke thoughts of the sacred and, thus, holiness in the life of the viewer.

Each of us needs this aspect of religion. Whether our pilgrimage is to the Sacred Grove or the Church of the Holy Sepulcher; whether the relic which provokes us is the death mask of the prophet or the remains of a martyr; whether the statue we gaze upon is Thorvaldsen's Christus or Michelangelo's Pietà does not matter. What is important is that these symbols of our history—Christian history—are preserved and partaken of; and that you and I contemplate what they stand for. As we do so, we allow the sacred events of history to change us because the Spirit of God will wash over us.

Stephen

Symbols and families: I wonder if the reason why many Christians of whatever tradition do not have a very strong grasp of the value of symbols is because we have let our family ties weaken and dissipate. Let me explain. Families are held together by symbols. Four of my most precious possessions have to do with my family. I will inherit someday a picture of my great-great-great grandfather and his father in their Civil War uniforms as well as some of the papers relating to their enlistment and discharge. I sit on the same rocking chair that my grandmother sat on for hours every day. She lived to be 99, and sometimes I wonder if the great amount of time she spent rocking on that chair didn't contribute to her longevity by keeping her blood flowing and her muscles working. I also have my dad's coin collection, which he has given me to enjoy while he is still living. Finally, I have a painting my mother made while she was still in high school. It might look ordinary to others, but it looks beautiful to me, which is why it is hanging in our entryway. We all have similar stories if we are blessed to have been given something preserved from our distant (or not so distant) past. These gifts, or relics, whatever you want to call them, carry symbolic rather than monetary meaning. They are, in a word, sacred. They sew together the vast stretches of time and make the past part of the present, turning time's fragmented moments into a smooth flow of moving pictures.

Alonzo has spoken eloquently about the ways in which our society does not expect us to take care of our parents and grandparents. If we do not cherish our own history, especially the ancestors who made our lives possible, then how can we have any strong ties to the past in any of its forms? So many people today grow up in fragmented families where the lines to the past have been broken and blurred. Our society emphasizes the new, to the extent that a constant turnover in goods and possessions is the norm. Our houses keep getting bigger, but our hearts are too full of worries about the future to give any thought to how we got to where we are. Symbols are the language that lets the past speak to the present. The cross, for example, is a symbol that can immediately bridge thousands of years by making the atonement visibly real right before our eyes. Christians cannot afford to become a people who do not know how to preserve, interpret, and pass on the symbols that connect us to the past.

I like to think that history is the debt we pay to the past. I learned that lesson from the great French philosopher Paul Ricoeur, who was one of my professors in graduate school and has continued to exercise great influence on my thought ever since.[7] Ricoeur was an original thinker, one of the best minds, I think, of the twentieth century, but in everything he wrote and said, he acknowledged his dependence on previous philosophers and philosophical traditions. He was always careful to locate what he thought in lines of discourse that can be traced deep into the past. This was not just a matter of cautious scholarship. He was paying his moral debt to his teachers. That debt, I want to suggest, involves treating the dead as real people with ongoing agency and significance in our lives. Only if the dead are still with us in some way, still able to participate in our lives, and only if we can have some influence on their ongoing existence, do we have an obligation to remember their lives faithfully and to respond to their memories with patience and care.

If the dead are simply dead, then we owe them nothing. They are gone, and their stories are nothing more than fodder for the stories we want to tell about ourselves. Much of secular history is the product of an atheistic view of the dead. For the atheist, there is only the present. The past has life only in our current memory of it, and even that is ever fleeting and changing. Without ontological substance in its own right, the past is what we make of it. It is useful as a means for reflecting on the future, but it has no reality of its own. It is useful really only in terms of how we choose to manipulate it and create it anew. The past lives only inside of our own minds, and even there, it has no existence outside of our self-interests.

If the past is dead, why do we feel compelled to tell the stories of our ancestors? If they have nothing to say to us, why should we work so hard to discover the records of their lives? Historians today do have a motive behind their labors. They tell stories about the past in order to illustrate how superior the modern world is. Secularists and progressives think we are better than our ancestors on every fundamental moral issue, and thus they turn to the past to prove how wrong people once were. History thus functions as a way of demonstrating how important it is to continue to make progress on social issues like gender, sexuality, and poverty. The past is important because it shows how far we have come and thus how far we still have to go. But does that give the dead the dignity that is, as human beings, their due? I doubt it. If the dead have no dignity, then we can turn their stories into testimonies in favor of our own modern prejudices. We can make them say whatever is convenient for our own purposes. In practice, this means we convict our ancestors of all the moral crimes which we think we have overcome. The dead give us examples of what to avoid—we study them in order to end up feeling better about ourselves.

I think my ancestors were better people than me. They went through greater hardships and more serious challenges than I have ever faced. They exercised more care over the Christian faith and struggled to build a world where they could pass on that faith to their children and grandchildren. They exercised more restraint over their desires, sacrificing for the future in ways that make most of us today look like moral brats. I know that this is the way Mormons view their history too. They openly acknowledge and celebrate the heroic deeds of their spiritual ancestors. That is refreshing and encouraging. I hope that as Mormonism continues to grow that they never lose their intimate dependence on their faithfully departed.

Families are sacred, but they can also become idols. I do not think Mormons treat their families as idols any more than anybody else does, but it is worth remembering this truth when talking about how important families are in the LDS tradition. For some people, hearing that "families are forever" is daunting, perhaps even terrifying, not consoling. If you grow up in an abusive family, you need some distance from the abusers, even if you also need to eventually reconcile with your loved ones, no matter how much they have not loved you. Families fail, but that failure should not be permitted to last forever. The family in the Catholic Church is treated with great reverence, but clerical celibacy is a reminder that Christians belong to the family of God, beginning with the brothers and sisters in the faith but extending to include all human beings, past, present, and future.

In fact, Christianity's impact on family structures in its early years is complex and mixed. People who converted to Christianity often had to leave their pagan relatives behind. The Church was a new association that transcended the boundaries of tribe, clan, and blood ties. In the ancient world, you were defined by your family. Who your father was determined everything about you. If your family made a mistake, all of its members paid the price. In Christianity, you were defined by the blood of Jesus, not the blood of your ancestors. That is a revolutionary change in family life. It does not mean that families are not important. It means that families are the foundation for adding relations onto our lives, not keeping others out. Families should be welcoming to strangers, widows, orphans, guests, and they should give children the love they need to be the kind of people who extend family connections outward, in increasingly inclusive circles of care. It is a tricky balance—loving your children but teaching them that love is meant to be shared beyond the family and not kept within it—but Christ on the cross gives us an example of how to do it well. One of the last things he said concerned his mother. "When Jesus saw his mother and the disciple whom he loved standing beside her, he said to his mother, 'Woman, here is your son.' Then he said to the disciple, 'Here is your mother.' And from that hour the disciple took her into his own home" (John 19: 26–27). At the hour of his death, when he was giving himself to the whole world, he remembered his family.

Alonzo

Our conversation about history has taken us from biblical history, to reformation history, to modern history, and now to family history. We are not rambling—though it may seem to some as though we are. But, as Stephen has pointed out, these aspects of history are all interrelated (or, at least, should be, if we are as grounded as we ought to be).

Families can be a source of tremendous blessings and also a source of great pain—as can, frankly, religion. For example, conversion away from the faith of one's youth and to a new religion can bring separation from family and friends. Even if one's immediate family is accepting of the conversion, since it is virtually impossible to bring all of one's extended family into the new faith, some kind of religious separation is inevitable. I speak from experience when I say that the tears and heartache that follow such division, especially when it occurs in one's immediate family, are incalculable.[8] My conversion from the ultra-conservative Greek Orthodox faith to The Church of Jesus Christ of Latter-day Saints was tremendously difficult for my family and me. It strained our relationship—and that strain remained for a couple of decades. My parents were hurt by the conversion, which most certainly implied to them that I felt the things they had taught me throughout my youth were false. For me, being rejected (in the numerous ways that I felt that I had been) was rather traumatic. Denomination was placed before family (by both sides), when the family of God should have been placed before denominations. If Christianity teaches us anything, it should be (to paraphrase Paul) that Christians should love their family as Christ loved the Church and gave Himself for it (Ephesians 5:25). We cannot afford to act in an unChristlike way toward those we love, or even toward those we do not. My own history has taught me the dangers of this as it relates to immediate family; Christian history teaches us this as it relates to those who hate us.

Author David McCullough wisely noted: "There is no such creature as a self-made man or woman. We love that expression, we Americans. But everyone who's ever lived has been affected, changed, shaped, helped, hindered by other people. . . . The laws we live by, the freedoms we enjoy, the institutions that we take for granted—[and] we should never take [things] for granted—are all the work of other people who went before us. And to be indifferent to that isn't just to be ignorant, it's to be rude. And ingratitude is a shabby failing. How can we not want to know about the people who have made it possible for us to live as we live?"⁹ It is a universal failing, but McCullough is right. How dare we?! Stephen reminded us that the past is important because it serves as a reminder of the dignity we owe those who went before us. I suppose this is one reason why Mormons are so fixated on the Church of the New Testament. While we acknowledge a living, breathing Church will evolve—heavens, that is why we are so big on having modern prophets and apostles—nevertheless, in the same breath we tend to get huffy about placing the modern Church over the Church of the New Testament (as doing so almost suggests "We've come up with a version better than what Jesus did!"). Thus, Latter-day Saints really focus on the importance of connecting themselves to the ancient Christian tradition more than the modern one. And I suppose this same need to be grateful is also behind our honor and veneration of our pioneer ancestors.

One common thread which binds Mormons and Catholics together (though it is seldom acknowledged) has to do with the dead. Stephen remarked, "Only if the dead are still with us in some way, still able to participate in our lives, and only if we can have some influence on their ongoing existence, do we have an obligation to remember their lives faithfully and to respond to their memories with patience and care."

His is a plea for a greater degree of vigilance to our history, to those who have gone before us and who have made it possible for us to move forward in faith. No love is lost by Catholics and Mormons on each other's divine manifestations. Latter-day Saints doubt the various appearances of the Virgin Mary to Roman Catholics. And Catholics have a very strong suspicion about the claims Mormons make about visions had by the Prophet Joseph. That being said, Catholics do believe that Mary has appeared, and this helps to ground them, both to the historic Church and also to the reality that there is a God. Latter-day Saints, on the other hand, do believe in the visions of Joseph (and his successors), and these help to ground us in our belief in the restoration of the historic Church and also to the reality that there is a God. Additionally, just as various Catholics have had experiences with Mary or other angels, a significant number of Latter-day Saints have professed similar experiences with deceased ancestors—particularly in relation to Temple work. Why we are so prone to doubt each other's experience, but so firm in our belief of our own—particularly when they have some strong similarities—will ever be a mystery! It certainly is not productive when we point a finger of doubt and scorn. We should each be grateful for whatever experiences our brothers and sisters of other faiths are having which cause them to be more committed to the cause of Christ.

Like Stephen, it is hard for me to not think of those who went before me—the famed Mormon pioneers, or my Greek Orthodox priest great-great grandfather—as being better than me; better in their spirituality and in their spirit of sacrifice for the sacred cause which they so firmly believed in. Although we live in a time of ease and luxury, and Stephen and I have been very blessed in how we have been privileged to live in this modern era, yet all of that is a call—a call to do something with our history and with sacred history. It is clearly a call to use the blessings of the modern era (technology, time, talents, and temporal wealth) to move God's cause and kingdom forward in a way our ancestors could not, simply because of the era in which they lived. I think the best way to pay back those whom we owe so much to—our God, our Savior, the Prophets, our ancestors, and even those we know not—is to make our page in the sacred history of this world a holy one, a contributing one, a sacrificial one, a Christian one!

Soul

Stephen

The soul is immortal. This is the refrain of poets, theologians, and philosophers throughout the centuries. But most Christians do not really
believe that the soul is immortal if that word is taken to mean eternal.
They believe that the soul cannot be destroyed or annihilated (except, perhaps, by God), but they do not believe that souls have always existed. Most
Christians believe that souls last forever but they have a definite starting
point in time. Like everything else that exists, they are created out of nothing. Moreover, we can pinpoint the exact time that God created each soul,
which makes them unique in the whole cosmos. We do not know when,
exactly, God created the world, but we know that God created our soul and
joined it to our body at the time of our conception (or soon thereafter).
Your soul does not exist until you do.

What most Christians do not know, however, is that the early Church
was open to a variety of views about the origin of the soul. Indeed,
before St. Augustine jumped with all of his theological weight into this
complicated topic, many Christians believed that souls existed long
before bodies. This idea is called the preexistence of souls, and it is an
idea that Mormons, almost alone of Christian churches today, affirm
and defend.

Rarely in the history of ideas can you witness the exact moment when
one version of a concept replaces another. Ideas change, of course, but
most intellectual development evolves at a glacier pace, which is why historians have to develop long and complex narratives covering centuries in
order to depict the factors involved in even the most dramatic philosophical and theological shifts. Augustine of Hippo, however, had a mind that

was never at rest, and everything he thought left theology dramatically changed in one way or another.

Before Augustine, there were at least four theories, with varying degrees of theological pedigree, about when souls were created.[1] The first, traducianism, argued that souls were passed down from ancestors through procreation. Adam's soul was created, but the rest of our souls were inherited from him. This theory was eventually given up for a variety of reasons, the primary one being that it seemed to depict the soul as a material substance. The second theory is known as creationism (not to be confused with creationist views of the origin of life, in opposition to Darwinism). Creationism is the view most Christians hold today. Souls are created from nothing only when they are needed (when someone is conceived). The third theory is that souls exist in heaven and are sent to bodies when they are needed. Souls are created by God, but they are created at some point before God created human beings. The fourth theory is a variation of the third, because it argues that souls existed in heaven but "fell" into the world when they rebelled against God (or in some variants, they were punished by being forced into physical bodies). The fourth view denies the goodness of material existence (physical bodies are seen as punishment for the mistakes souls made in heaven), and so was not taken too seriously by most orthodox theologians. But what about the other three?

Tertullian, the first theologian with systematic philosophical ambition in the West, was influenced by the Stoic conception of matter.[2] Theologians who shared this influence thought that matter exists on a continuum of degrees of perfection, and that even God is composed of some kind of material substance. They sided with traducianism because they did not think of the spiritual as immaterial. They also thought traducianism did a good job of explaining original sin. When Adam sinned, his action results in a deformation of his soul, and everyone ever since has inherited a soul inclined toward disobedience and disorder. Platonic metaphysics, which drew a bold line between the material and the spiritual, gained in influence by the third and fourth centuries and eclipsed this view of the soul. Given Plato's identification of matter with death and decay, theologians who followed Plato had no choice but to put the soul on the side of God and angels in terms of its immateriality. But how far could Christians go in identifying souls with the divine? Were souls with God from the very beginning, as the Neo-Platonists assumed? Are they eternal? Do they have a history that precedes the moment when God conjoins them to bodies?

Plato thought that souls were eternal because that explains how humans can have intuitive insights into conceptual truths. How do we instinctively grasp the law of non-contradiction, and how is it that young children, once shown a logical proof or a mathematical principle, understand it immediately? Plato decided that our rationality must not be limited to the physical senses, which are subjected to the changing world of appearances. Anything true is true for everyone and at all times, so to know a truth is to participate in that eternal realm. Our capacity for knowledge is what makes us kindred to the divine.

Neo-Platonists took Plato in an even more theistic direction. We must have been with God in the beginning, the Neo-Platonists argued, since we are mired in the world of multiplicity and change and yet feel a desire to return to the oneness and stillness of the divine. The route that desire takes is intellectual cognition, which puts us in touch with the transcendent truths that our embodied state prevents us from grasping. Knowledge is thus a kind of remembering. When the light bulb goes off and we get some idea, what we experience is more like remembering something we have forgotten than discovering something brand new.

Augustine converted to Christianity in part because of his reading of the Neo-Platonists, especially the leading figure of that school, Plotinus. In his earliest writings, he agreed with the following propositions drawn from Plato: truth is eternal, to know something is to become one with it, and only like can know like. Add these up and you get the conclusion that the soul must be eternal in order to grasp eternal truths. As he puts it in a syllogism in *The Soliloquies*, one of his earliest books, "If a thing, A, existing in another thing, B, lasts forever, B must last forever. Therefore, if learning is eternal, the mind also must be eternal."[3] By the time he wrote *On Free Will* (around 395), however, he was not so sure. For one thing, he was changing his view of knowledge. He decided that knowledge comes from within, which means that an inner voice or interior state must be the source of eternal truths, and that inner source is none other than Jesus Christ. If we know eternal truths by an inward illumination, we do not need Plato's theory of remembrance. This sets the stage for a fascinating and revealing discussion of the soul.

After discussing the relative merits and drawbacks of the four options that I summarized above, he still tends to favor the preexistence of souls but decides that "none of these views may be rashly affirmed."[4] The issue is just too obscure and perplexing, and scripture does not show us which view is true. He notes that Christians should feel free to decide for themselves which view to accept. "There is no danger if we hold a wrong opinion about the creature, provided we do not hold it as if it were assured knowledge."[5] In other words, it is important to be certain about what we believe about God, but when it comes to the constituent parts of human nature, like the soul and its relation to the body, we have some leeway. In fact, we are stuck in the position of having competing theories, none of which are clearly better than the others, and none of which are resolved by biblical revelation.

In later works, especially in the *Retractions*, written to set the record straight by correcting his early works, he decides in favor of the position that the soul is created out of nothing. That shift had a formative impact on all subsequent theology. Still, Augustine clearly did not think that the origin of the soul, even in his later writings, could be theorized with a high degree of certainty. After Augustine, however, subsequent theologians took his late position for granted. The immortality of the soul now came to refer to its end and not its beginning. The soul is resistant to destruction, but it is most certainly capable of being born.

Once a topic of great theological curiosity and diversity of opinion, the creation of the soul became a settled doctrine after Augustine, and the Catholic Church forgot the pluralism of beliefs that it once tolerated on this issue. What happened? In the debates about the Son's relationship to the Father that were triggered by Arius and other heretics, theologians increasingly divided the existence of all things into two completely separate camps (well, three actually). There is the world of created things and the realm of the divine. The former is material and thus temporary and the latter immaterial and thus eternal. Only God, who exists in a category all to himself, is both eternal and immaterial. Souls and angels exist in a third, intermediary camp, since they have an immaterial status but not an eternal nature. They are created, but they have a status that sets them apart from the order of the physical cosmos. In the case of angels, they are created before the world while in the case of souls, they are created after the world is created. Angels and souls are not to be put in the same category as the divine, because that would take away from his uniqueness and thus his divinity, but they are also not to be put in the category of matter, since they are spiritual entities.

Our souls are a bridge of sorts between the natural world and our supernatural destiny. They explain why we are part ape and part angel, why we can act like beasts and yet have Jesus tell us to be perfect like our heavenly Father (Matthew 5:48). God gave us rational souls, which makes us different from other animals. Thanks to our souls, our minds are not simply reducible to our bodies. But souls do more than elevate our neural circuitry into the spiritual realm of freedom and responsibility. Each soul is unique and thus brings more to the body than the capacity for rational reflection. Souls function to confer identity as well as provide our capacity to reason. Although they are simple, immaterial entities, they must contain the basic elements of who we are, elements that act like seeds, which we then nourish and cultivate to make a life.

Souls answer the question of where our personal identity originates. Clearly, we are born with many of the signs and indications of what our personality will come to be. Babies and toddlers express their own unique characteristics long before they are old enough to act in free and thoughtful ways. True, we change as we grow, and we are free to create new habits as well as change old ones, but there seems to be a core or kernel to our identities that we do not create. The more we think about ourselves, the more we come to the conclusion that our personalities are a given, a gift rather than achievement. Even our freedom is something we learn to accept as an essential part of that legacy. We are free to do our best with what we have been given, but we are not free to give ourselves a totally new identity. Our freedom is not absolute (it is not absolutely free); it is shaped by our character, our bodies, and the relationships we are born into.

Here we run into the central problem with the traditional Christian account of the soul. If souls confer identity, and they were made by God, doesn't that mean that God is the source of our identity? Can't we then blame God, rather than our genes or our free choices, for at least the basic outlines of our character, including the tendencies toward sin that make our personalities so flawed? True, we are free, but if our souls are made by God, then our freedom is restricted by God's eternal plan. We are free to choose what to do in the world but we are not free to be anything we want to be. How we go about making our decisions is a product of the kind of person God has decided we will be. That conclusion puts more responsibility for sin on God than most traditional theologians want, which is why the preexistence of souls can be a plausible hypothesis. If our souls have a history, then it is that history, not God's fiat, which shapes our ongoing identities. God made us, but God did not make the ways in which we fail to live up to God's original design.

So far I have suggested that we exercise our freedom in a context that comes to us from outside of our control. Our choices are limited by the many factors that constitute the parameters of our identity. If that is true, how far back does our personality go? "Deep" is an overused word, but human uniqueness means that every individual personality is infinitely rich. You can reflect on your own history of choices and actions, for example, without ever feeling like you have exhausted all of the meaning of your identity. That is because we are more than the sum of our parts, which is another way of saying that we are free. If our personalities go way down, do they also go way back? If we are infinitely deep, then are we also infinitely old? In other words, just as personalities have a depth that has no discernible bottom, do we also have a past that has no apparent beginning? That seems quite possible to me, especially since the Bible suggests that God thought about us before the world was even created (Ephesians 1:4). Catholic theologians steeped in Plato's theory of the forms can agree that we existed in the mind of God from eternity, but what kind of existence was that? When did God start thinking about us, and when were we able to start thinking for ourselves?

Mormons not only grant souls a preexistence (an existence prior to our mortal lives on earth) but also imagine that our souls had a full preexistence with the same kinds of actions and consequences that we have today.[6] That is, our souls were free in the pre-mortal life just as they are free in this one. They developed their identity conferring properties through their freedom to make decisions and learn from their mistakes, which is the same way we develop our personalities today. If that is true, then it seems to suggest that freedom is the foundation of personality no matter where you locate the origin of the soul. But if we are absolutely free (what philosophers call libertarian freedom), and our personality originates in our free will, then we mortal, embodied beings do not need a preexistent soul to illuminate the mystery of our personalities. All we need is freedom here and now. Indeed, if we are free to do and become whatever we want, then an existence prior to this one cannot have much if any influence over our lives. Thus, the hypothesis of a preexistence soul seems an unnecessary obfuscation of a topic that is already overfull with mystery.

The preexistence of souls helps to explain our personalities better when we do not assume that freedom is absolute. If we are the sum of many forces and conditions in addition to our free choices, then the idea that we had a long life behind us before we were born can help make sense of how freedom is always contextualized and mitigated by wider circumstances. But here it is important to point out that Mormon theology seems to posit not only the preexistence of souls but also their eternity. From a Catholic perspective, this is a grievous theological error. If souls are eternal, then they must be uncreated. What, then, would make them any different from God? But let us return to our discussion of the identity conferring function of souls. The eternity of our souls seems to me to put so much weight on our preexistence that it makes our use of freedom in the brief time that is allotted to us in this earthly life nearly inconsequential for our personal development. That is, if we were developing our personalities from eternity, wouldn't they already be strongly settled before we were born? An eternity of decisions and actions would eclipse any other factor in shaping our earthly identities. If I find it hard to change habits that I developed when I was a little kid, how could I ever possibly hope to change habits that I developed from the depths of time?

Mormons do have a fairly simple solution to this problem. They can side with Plato (perhaps this is the only issue Mormons side with Plato on!) by envisaging that souls, fully individual before birth on earth, simply forget their preexistent lives when they enter their bodies. If that is the case, can we try to remember those lives here and now? To try to do that seems to mix Christianity with various aspects of the occult (or spiritualism) and with New Age ideas about past lives. Yet if we cannot remember past lives, what difference does it make to believe in them? Moreover, I am left with this nagging question: If my soul is eternal, then isn't my personality also eternal? That means there is no explanation for why I am the way that I am. At this point it seems like the amazing mystery of the soul is becoming mystifying in ways that might not be so good.

To make matters even more complicated, since Mormon theology denies the immateriality of God, it also denies the immateriality of souls. This move, I think, actually helps to make the identity conferring power of souls more plausible, even as it risks turning souls into divinities. Today, the role of the soul in explaining the mystery of personality has been replaced by genetics. Many scientists portray our genetic make-up as a nearly invisible army controlling everything we do. We are puppets, and our DNA is both the strings and whatever it is that is pulling the strings. I doubt if that many people really think they are nothing but genes, tempting as it is to blame what goes wrong in our lives on microscopic physical entities over which we have no control. Christians certainly do not think that human behavior can be exhaustively explained by reference to material causes. Our personalities are too rich, complex, and mysterious to be the product of a strictly physical chain of causes. We are spiritual, not merely material creatures. Yet it is hard to conceive of how an immaterial soul can have such causal power over the world. Perhaps the way DNA works to shape our character provides an analogy for how souls do the same thing. If DNA takes the place of souls in the modern mind, then it might be useful to think of souls along the lines of DNA.

There is surely room for such speculations, and a genuine need for them, but I am left with the hunch that the preexistence of the soul merely pushes the problem of personality back in time rather than solving it altogether. Say we are born with souls that already have had a life before this one. Our souls, in their pre-embodied form, have made decisions, had relationships with other souls, and have come to our bodies if not fully developed then at least with the basics of our emerging personalities. That is a helpful way of thinking about personality, because it explains why we think of ourselves as beings who are not the product of our own thoughts. Still, if our souls are the origin of our personalities in this life, how did they get their personalities in the life prior to this one? In other words, why did we act the way we did before we were born? Souls can explain human personality, but what explains the personality of souls? Where did the personality of my soul come from before my soul gave me the personality that I now have? The simplest answer to that question is that God created my soul even if he did so long before he created the rest of me, but if God is the origin of my soul's preexistent personality, what advantage is there in thinking that my soul preexists my body? The discussion of souls has to end somewhere, and surely it is best to end it with God.

Alonzo

Which came first, the chicken or the egg? Although seemingly unrelated, the core of this enduring question is actually at the heart of Christian queries regarding the soul. Paraphrased, we ask: Which came first, the person or the personality? As Stephen has pointed out, though the ancient Church had a number of theories regarding this, nevertheless, the majority of Christians today believe the two likely began at the same instant.

Latter-day Saints are unique among Christian denominations, in that they hold that each of us existed as spirits which dwelt in God's presence prior to being born into mortality. We are creations of God—but that creation (according to LDS thinking) did not take place at our conception, but long before it, during what some have referred to as the "preexistence" or "pre-mortal existence" of the soul. Mormons hold that each of us (as spirits) dwelt with God for millions, if not billions of years, prior to being born as mortals here upon the earth.[7] There we learned, developed, grew, and gained an understanding of God, His great plan of salvation, and the role Jesus would play in the salvation of all of God's creations. It was a time of schooling and growth. Thus, as one passage of LDS scripture explains: "Even before they were born, they"—meaning you and I, God's spirit children—"received their first lessons in the world of spirits and were prepared to come forth in the due time of the Lord to labor in his vineyard for the salvation of the souls of men" (D&C 138:56).

In addition to believing that our origins did not begin with our earthly conception, Mormons also believe that our creation was not *ex nihilo* but, instead, *ex materia*. Thus, though Latter-day Saints acknowledge that there was a time when God "created" or "organized" each of us, ultimately we are eternal beings, as we were organized by Him *ex materia*. That from which we were created or organized preexisted our beginnings as spirits. For some, this is an unattractive proposition, as it somehow suggests that we are co-eternal with God. Mormons, however, do not see this as somehow harming or lessening God's divinity or omnipotence. While it may suggest that you and I have a spark of divinity within each of us, ultimately it still places God as the great cause of our existence and the source of all that is alive and good.

Mormons hold firmly to the proposition that agency—or the right to make choices and experience the consequences of those choices—is eternal. While here in mortality we have been endowed with this right by God Himself. However, Latter-day Saints believe that we enjoyed that same privilege in our pre-mortal state, when we were but spirits dwelling with God. Agency is crucial, in LDS thinking, because it allows us to truly be agents unto ourselves. It allows God to hold us accountable for our choices *because* they are truly ours. In Mormon theology, it was during this pre-mortal period that Lucifer fell from God's grace, rebelling against His plan and thereby becoming the devil. The oft quoted passage from Isaiah comes to mind: "How art thou fallen from heaven, O Lucifer, son of the morning!" (*KJV* Isaiah 14:12).[8] Mormons hold that Lucifer rebelled and, in so doing, was cast out of God's presence—becoming the devil, thereby providing opposition to God's plan through tempting mankind. As the Book of Mormon explains: "For it must needs be, that there is an opposition in all things. If not so . . . righteousness could not be brought to pass, neither wickedness, neither holiness nor misery, neither good nor bad. Wherefore, all things must needs be a compound in one" (2 Nephi

2:11). In other words, opposition allows for agency or the opportunity to make choices. If we were not endowed with the power to choose—to rebel, if we so elected—then we could not be truly free. We could not truly be accountable. We could not bring to pass righteousness or wickedness because we would not have the ability to choose the one and reject the other. Thus, in LDS thinking, agency must eternally be a part of God's plan for each of us. Lucifer chose, and in so doing became the devil. You and I are endowed from our pre-mortal existence, throughout our mortal sojourn, and during the vast expanse of eternity, with the gift of agency or choice. Thus, we are ever agents unto ourselves. And therefore, God will hold us responsible for the choices we make and will bless us for the good we select to do.

Mormons hold that when our spirits are born into mortality we have a veil of forgetting, per se, placed over our minds—enabling us to walk by faith and to exercise a trust in God. If we had a bright recollection of our pre-mortal world we could not walk by faith—as our knowledge of God's existence, life's purpose, and our role in that would be crystal clear. Our knowledge would be sure and, thus, our faith nonexistent. One need not exercise faith in what he knows for sure. Thus, God has shrouded us in a veil of forgetting so that our growth might be real and our faith developed.

Perhaps one of the most important passages attesting to the presence of this belief in the preexistence of the soul among those of the early Church is found in the Gospel of John. "As he went along, he saw a man blind from birth. His disciples asked him, 'Rabbi, who sinned, this man or his parents, that he was born blind?' 'Neither this man nor his parents sinned,' said Jesus, 'but this happened so that the work of God might be displayed in his life'" (*NIV* John 9:1–3). The disciples of Jesus took for granted that this man could have committed sins in a pre-mortal state which would have brought this condition of blindness upon him at birth. A number of commentators on this passage have suggested that the pre–New Testament Jewish belief in the preexistence of the soul may be behind the question posed by Jesus's disciples.[9] There definitely was an ancient belief in the soul as preexistent—and in one's ability to sin in the preexistent state. Such a concept appears in rabbinical writings and in early Christian texts. Some will argue that Jesus repudiated the possibility of the preexistence of the human spirit when He responded to the disciples' question, saying: "His blindness has nothing to do with his sin or his parents' sins. He is blind so that God's power might be seen at work in him" (*GNB* John 9:3). It should be noted, however, that in His retort Jesus did not say "there is no such thing as the preexistence of the spirit." Rather, Jesus simply stated "that's not why this man was born blind." In other words, Jesus does not condemn the doctrine of the preexistence of the soul. He simply says such a doctrine does not explain why this man was born blind. The exchange between Jesus and his disciples is clearly reliant upon a premise of the soul's individualized pre-mortal existence.

Is the Mormon model of the soul's preexistence somehow superior to the view of other Christians? Well, perhaps the word "superior" is the wrong one to employ, but the LDS view does explain the disparities in life. If we believe that our spirits or souls did not exist prior to coming to mortality—if we hold that they began at the instant our bodies were conceived—then we must assume that the disparities in life are caused, not by our choices, but potentially by God's seemingly random desire to endow some with trials and others with a life of ease. As an example, my friend Harrison was born with only one arm. If there was no preexistence of Harrison's spirit, then he certainly did not agree to traverse mortality with such a condition, nor can it be claimed that he is somehow respon- sible for it. He is simply a victim of God's decision to make him "bro- ken" or less than "perfect" (whatever that means). However, if Harrison's spirit did preexist, then it is feasible that God did not randomly victim- ize Harrison by sending him into mortality with a missing arm. Rather, it is conceivable that Harrison's disability was something he understood (in the preexistence) that he would be given in mortality to allow him to have the experiences and growth necessary to develop him into the man and Christian God desired him to be. In the LDS view, Harrison may well have embraced this trial in the preexistence, knowing that though this would make his mortal experience hard, ultimately it would be for his personal good and betterment. This same reasoning could apply to health or physical challenges, financial challenges, or even challenges of nationality and place of birth. These are all randomly given us at the point of conception, or they are challenges and opportunities from God, given us as gifts, for the purpose of our growth and development. If such things are decided at conception, then those who conceive us (or simple genetics) are potentially more empowered in these decisions than is God. However, if there is indeed a preexistence of the soul, then ultimately such things may have been decided based upon God's foreknowledge of our needs, in concert with our agency, and with a greater view to what we would need in order to become like the Father and Son.[10]

Stephen

It seems a bit ironic to me that Mormons reject the traditional Christian belief that souls can exist without bodies while traditional Christians reject the Mormon belief that souls existed before bodies. Both have a mystery on their hands! Traditional Christians believe that the soul is immortal but not eternal, while Mormons believe that the soul is eternal yet always (in some way) material and thus not really immortal. If souls can exist without bodies, then why, for traditional Christians, do we need the resurrection of the body? And if souls are eternally developing, growing, and changing, then why, for Mormons, do they need to become embodied on earth?

Traditionally, all Christians believed in the resurrection of the body, but Christians influenced by Plato, which means pretty much all Christians outside of the Latter-day Saints, also believed that souls can still function even without their material bodies. That is, Christians believed in the immortality of the soul and the resurrection of the body. These two beliefs are not so much contradictory as they render each other redundant. If the soul is immortal (that is, it cannot die, although for Augustine it can change; it is not immutable), then why does it need the body in the afterlife? The immortality of the soul turns the resurrection of the body into an afterthought. If the body will be resurrected in the end, then why believe in the immortality of the soul at all? The resurrection of the body seems to affirm the body as the source of our identity and its resurrection as a necessary means of perpetuating that identity in heaven. If that is so, then what does the soul contribute to our glorified bodies in heaven?

If traditional Christianity connected our identity (what makes each of us unique) with the way in which we are both bodies and souls, Mormons connect it to the preexistent soul, which lives and thrives and makes decisions without our bodies. They prefer to call this soul a spirit, and, of course, they do not think of it as immaterial. For Mormons, our spirit is a kind of body-before-embodiment, the way in which we existed with God (for billions of years or eternity?) before God made earthly bodies for us. As Alonzo emphasizes, this means that agency is at the heart of Mormon anthropology, so much so that he calls agency "eternal." That is a pretty heavy statement. Exercising freedom wisely and prudently is hard enough in this life, which makes it daunting to think about being responsible for one's actions forever. Most Christians, I suspect, think of heaven as the place where freedom begins to recede while grace increasingly takes over.

The saved will no longer have to make difficult decisions because they have made the one decision that really matters (to accept Jesus). Mormons have a theology of freedom that never stops, just as it never begins. While the Catholic view of heaven sometimes portrays it as a place of bliss that liberates us from the weight and responsibilities of our freedom, Mormonism teaches that we always have been and always will be free, whether we like it or not.

That is not only a lot of freedom, it is a lot of history too. If I am shaped by decisions that I made for billions of years prior to my birth, then how could my fifty-three years spent mostly in Indiana add to my character in any significant way? Perhaps given the complexity of these issues, many Catholics will want to return to Augustine's own tortured uncertainties on this topic!

What I do like about this portrait of pre-mortal drama, however, is that Mormonism tries to be as concrete about the pre-life as it is about the afterlife. By putting so much flesh, so to speak, on our pre-mortal souls, Mormon theology opens up the floodgates to speculations about what happened in the heavens before the creation of the world. It is easy to think that the drama of salvation begins with the fall, while everything prior to that, whether in Eden or heaven, was without any incidents worth noting. For Mormons, drama is eternal. Even before the creation of the world, there were spirits making decisions and, presumably, seeking (or resisting) God. Eternity is not timeless and static. The most dramatic pre-mortal event of all, of course, is the fall of Satan, an event that Roman Catholics also affirm. This cosmic cataclysm, however, is hardly central to the Catholic faith and has fallen out of favor in recent Catholic theological circles for its mythological form, even though it is still taught in the catechism. Given the Catholic definition of angels as immaterial beings created without any of the weaknesses of the flesh and filled with an immediate knowledge of God, it is hard to comprehend how there could have been so much rebellion in their ranks.

Even in early Christianity, there were reasons why theologians and church leaders did not go into too much detail about the fall of Satan. Gnostic Christians (heretical groups that were part Gnostic and part Christian, accepting the divinity of Jesus but rejecting the goodness of this world) argued that salvation consists of escaping this planet and traveling through multiple layers of outer space in order to reach our heavenly home. Each level of the cosmos is defended by various principalities and powers, and the job of the Church is to give those who seek true knowledge the tools to navigate their way through the astral maze. Christians worked hard to distinguish themselves from Gnostics, their chief competitors in the ancient world, and one way they did so was to take most of the drama out of eternity. Angels were created before the world, but they did not do much except praise God, and souls were not created until they were needed for the bodies they invigorated. True, Satan fell from heaven, but it was thought best not to dwell on this in any significant detail. That was the one event—Satan's fall—that marred an otherwise perfectly peaceful and uneventful heavenly abode.

Mormons go for eternal drama in a big way. That is in accordance with the Bible, which talks about various crises and commotions going on in heaven. In Job 1:6, many heavenly beings along with Satan meet before the Lord, an event that appears to have been a regular occurrence. And the Apostle Paul writes, "For our struggle is not against enemies of blood and flesh, but against the rulers, against the authorities, against the cosmic powers of this present darkness, against the spiritual forces of evil in the heavenly places" (Ephesians 6:12). Clearly, Paul thought the heavens were busy with spiritual warfare, much of it taking place beyond our knowledge. I have already pointed out that Mormons can teach other Christians to be more daring in their imagination of heaven. They can also teach other Christians to be more imaginative in their understanding of what went on before the creation of the world. If Satan is a fallen angel, then obviously, lots of stuff was happening long before the world came into being.

There is great spiritual wisdom to be found in the idea that we did not begin our lives on earth but with Jesus in heaven. It gives our narratives a cosmic arc that is satisfying and inspiring. The pre-mortal life was not, after all, random or chaotic. It was ordered to Christ. This is actually as strong a case as can be made for the eternal validity of Christian truth claims! Theology never changes—only our limited grasp of it changes. For Mormons, the more we understand the truth of Christianity, the more we will understand the truth of everything. I would prefer, perhaps, that more emphasis be put on the eternity of Jesus Christ than the eternity of spirits and their hidden worlds and forgotten activities, but I think Mormons are on the right track. Jesus is the one who has always been with God, and we too have always been with God in the sense that God has always determined that we should be his followers and friends. That is as far as I can go, I think, in understanding this set of teachings of Joseph Smith on the soul. Perhaps, however, that is not such a bad way to end our final chapter. A little disagreement leaves the door open for a lot more conversation to come.

Alonzo

As we conclude our conversation—not just about the soul, but about our similarities and differences—I freely acknowledge Stephen's point that some aspects of Mormon theology appear radical to those not raised in the tradition. The LDS doctrine of the eternal nature of the soul is one of those. Existing from birth and on into eternity somehow makes sense to most Christians. Existing eternally before one's birth, however, is hard to fathom. I am reminded of another incomprehensible idea foundational to Mormonism, and yet incomprehensible—even to many members of the LDS Church. In one of Joseph Smith's revelations, we are informed that "past, present, and future . . . are continually before the Lord" (D&C 130:7). In other words, God lives outside of time. He has the past, present, and future before Him at any given moment. While you and I are currently (*present*) residing upon this earth, God knows whether we will be saved or damned (*future*)—not because He has pre-destined it, but because the *future* is before Him while we are living in the *present*. Humans, because we live in a seemingly linear existence, struggle to grasp the notion that (for God) the future has already happened because He is not bound by time as we are. Just as that doctrine seems so mind-blowing—so incomprehensible—I freely acknowledge that the idea that you and I have ever existed (in some stage of development or another) is also difficult to grasp. Understanding the purpose of that pre-mortal existence is, in some ways, helpful in comprehending the concept. Stephen has raised a few questions regarding it that I will briefly address.

Latter-day Saints certainly do not believe in reincarnation.[11] So, though we talk of a previous existence, or preexistence, that should not be confused with reincarnation or the transmigration of souls. And when I refer to our eternal existence "in some stage of development or other," I certainly do not mean we have progressed from a lower life-form to a higher one. As Stephen has suggested, Mormons use the term "soul" in a slightly different way than do most other Christians. For Latter-day Saints, each of us progresses through stages of development from what we were, to what we are, to what we will become. In an attempt to not make this terribly complex, I will run the risk of oversimplifying the doctrine. But the basics of LDS thinking are as follows:

- Each of us has existed eternally as pure matter or "intelligence." As I noted earlier in this book, one of Joseph Smith's revelations explained: "Man was also in the beginning with God. Intelligence, or the light of truth, was not created or made, neither indeed can be" (D&C 93:29).
- At some point in the preexistence, God began the creative process. Part of that process was to organize this "light," "intelligence," or "matter" into spirit entities—with personalities, gender, and many of those attributes we associate with individualism. At this point, we became "spirit" children of God the Father. We were in His image. We were endowed with agency. We learned, developed, grew, and were tutored by Him. Although we were spirits, we were material. Again, through Joseph we learn: "There is no such thing as immaterial matter. All spirit is matter, but it is more fine or pure, and can only be discerned by purer eyes" (D&C 131:7).
- As spirits, there were many things for us to learn—but, ultimately, a number of things we could not learn or experience while not having a mortal body, and while not having a "veil of forgetting," per se, between us and God. Thus, mortality was provided as a learning and growing experience. We would gain physical bodies which would teach us a number of things that we could not learn as spirits—such as developing faithful endurance because of the natural trials of aging and the mortal experience. The veil associated with this body would also allow us to learn to walk by faith—something largely incapable of being learned when we dwelt in God's presence with no veil to separate us and with a clear understanding of His will and plan. But mortality, being exactly the opposite, would stretch us both in our willingness to obey God's promptings and in our ability to exercise faith (particularly in what St. John of the Cross termed "the dark night of the soul").
- Upon death each of us loses the mortal body we briefly had, but we do not forget the experiences and lessons of life. We are, at death, once again but spirits—albeit more educated or experienced spirits. We temporarily dwell in a place Latter-day Saints refer to as the Spirit World; a place where the Gospel continues to be taught and where those who knew not Christ in morality can learn of Him and embrace His truths and redeeming acts. Indeed, all who go there will learn of things they

misunderstood in morality, and each will have access to truths God expects them to embrace.

• During the resurrection our spirits will be reunited with our bodies (which will at that point be in a state of absolute perfection and glory). For Mormons, this uniting of the spirit and the body constitutes a soul (i.e., spirit + body = soul). Paul's words to the saints at Thessalonica seem helpful: "May the God of peace himself sanctify you entirely; and may your spirit and soul and body be kept sound and blameless at the coming of our Lord Jesus Christ" (*NRSV* 1 Thessalonians 5:23). Like Latter-day Saints, Paul seems to distinguish between the spirit, body, and soul. The spirit and soul are not, for him, synonymous. Similarly, in the LDS Doctrine and Covenants we find this: "And the spirit and the body are the soul of man" (D&C 88:15). Please know, I am not trying to prove the LDS view here; only to demonstrate the concept that for Latter-day Saints the "spirit" is not the "soul"—but the soul is the combination of one's spirit and one's resurrected body—eternally united, never to be separated, and (through the grace of God and Christ) filled with glory, light, beauty, bloom, power, and so on.

• In the end, Latter-day Saints hold that the final state of existence, in which we will be for eternity, is as a glorious, resurrected soul. We will then be like God, eternally subordinate to Him, but like Him in nature and being.

Now, briefly, to a couple of Stephen's enquiries. He asked a question which I think most non-Mormons would also be curious to understand: "If souls are eternally developing, growing, and changing, then why, for Mormons, do they need to become embodied on earth?" As I suggested above, God created mortality as a gift to us to give us experiences we could not fully have as unembodied spirits. In God's presence we could not fully walk by faith, for we had a sure knowledge and the ever present reality of God's existence. In our preexistent state as spirits we were not subject to sickness, death, or a variety of tragedies so common in mortality. Thus, by our experience here we learn a form of patience, compassion, and, again, faith that could not be fully lived or developed there. Each of these experiences (if we responded as God would have us) develop in our nature certain divine qualities that make us like Him, so that we can dwell with Him throughout all eternity.

Stephen also posed this question which, admittedly, is slightly harder to parse: "If the soul is immortal . . . then why does it need the body in the afterlife?" According to LDS theology, the goal of God in creating this earth and giving us this mortal experience was to eventually make us like Him. God is, for Latter-day Saints, a being who does have a body, parts, and holy passions. We take quite literally the biblical claim that we were "made in God's image." And Mormons perceive God as the ultimate Father who wants for His child all that He has and more. Thus, this mortal experience—and the promise of resurrected bodies—are all gifts from a good and gracious God who seeks to make us as He is, and who seeks to bless us beyond measure. A resurrected body (as Jesus's demonstrated) apparently allows us to do things a mortal could not do, in addition to things a spirit could not do. Thus, to be like God and to have the powers Jesus suggested the Father has, we need a resurrected body. But the extent and exact nature of those powers are something, I suspect, only a resurrected being can fully grasp.

Perhaps one last point should be made regarding Stephen's thoughts on the soul. I think he hit the nail on the head when he said: "There is great spiritual wisdom to be found in the idea that we did not begin our lives on earth but with Jesus in heaven. It gives our narratives a cosmic arc that is satisfying and inspiring. The pre-mortal life was not, after all, random or chaotic. It was ordered to Christ. This is actually as strong a case as can be made for the eternal validity of Christian truth claims! Theology never changes—only our limited grasp of it changes. For Mormons, the more we understand the truth of Christianity, the more we will understand the truth of everything." Latter-day Saints do believe that truth—including the truth which is Christianity—existed from the very beginning. During my graduate school days at Notre Dame one of my professors (a rather famed theologian) shot down a comment made by one of the students in class. This Bible-believing student had made a comment that the paschal lamb of the book of Exodus was a typological symbol for Jesus Christ, the Lamb of God, who would be slain for the sins of the world. Our professor, in a tone of condescension, said: "None of the 'prophets' of the Hebrew Bible had any idea about Jesus, His passion, or His messianic role. You're reading the Old Testament through Christian lenses. It was inappropriate when the early disciples of Jesus did it, and it is inappropriate today!" Frankly—and with no condescension intended—while I know that (as Christians) we are sometimes guilty of reading into a verse or two things we should not; nevertheless, I was surprised that a man who considered himself a Christian could also say he thought that the

biblical "prophets" were not prophetic, and that Christianity was largely
something Paul made up years after the death of Jesus. I think Stephen
is right that a doctrine that Christianity is eternal makes Jesus's message normative for salvation. It explains the ultimate message of the
Old Testament prophets. It implies the foreknowledge of God (i.e., He
did not have to scramble when Adam and Eve ate the "forbidden fruit"
because our redemption through Christ was already planned). The eternal nature of Christianity connects Judaism (and the message of the
Hebrew prophets) to Christianity (and the witness of the Apostles) in
a way they might otherwise not be connected. Ultimately, it is a testament that all of this is really about Jesus; from the pre-mortal world,
throughout the Old Testament, including the New Testament, and
down to today. It has all been about Christ! As I noted earlier, the Book
of Mormon teaches that all things typify Christ (2 Nephi 11:4). It also
informs us that "none of the prophets have written, nor prophesied,
save they have spoken concerning this Christ" (Jacob 7:11). And the Lord
himself declared, "all things are created and made to bear record of me"
(Moses 6:63). For all of the differences Catholics and Mormons may
have, one thing we surely are united on is this. And the fact that this is
our foundation, and our firmly shared truth, should give us reason to
continue our conversation, and build on our points of common ground.

Conclusion

WHERE DO WE GO FROM HERE?

MANY EUROPEANS CAME to America for religious freedom, which meant freedom from the restrictions of Old World traditions and institutions, but Mormonism was born out of the dream for more, not less religious authority. Scholars have long observed that the disestablishment of religion in America subjected Christianity to powerful democratizing forces. Without government regulation, a theological free market, if not a spiritual free-for-all, ensued, and Protestant churches were forced to compete for members. During an era when America's democratic sensibility and egalitarian ethos set Protestantism free to splinter into hundreds if not thousands of ecclesial fragments, Mormons wanted to turn back the clock to a time when religion and culture were united in a hierarchical order and social concord. Mormon theology is truly representative of the American innovative spirit, but in terms of providing a religious foundation for every aspect of a believer's life, Mormonism looks like it stepped right out of the Middle Ages.

All of this makes Mormons, to borrow from the title of a book by J. Spencer Fluhman, a very peculiar people.[1] And one of those peculiarities is its resemblances to Roman Catholicism. As Protestantism became ever more diverse, Protestants increasingly found their unity in what they were not, rather than what they shared, and two groups stood out for that purpose. Whatever Protestants were, they definitely were not Catholic or Mormon. It was quite natural then, as Fluhman's book demonstrates, for nineteenth-century Protestants to consider Mormonism to be a species of the Catholic menace. Although it may sound strange, we hope this book demonstrates that these Protestant biases were more insightful than those nineteenth- and twentieth-century Protestants could have known.

Catholics in the nineteenth century did not accept that Mormons were "one of us" but some Catholics did come to the conclusion that Mormons should not be grouped with the Protestant movement. In 1860, Archbishop Karl August von Reisach (1800–1869) contributed an article to an Italian journal on the obscure religious movement in America that few European Catholics knew much about. For apologetic reasons, Reisach was eager to show how Mormonism was the byproduct of Protestant weakness and confusions. His Catholic perspective, however, helped him to see that Mormons brought something ancient to American religion that did not fit into the Protestant framework:

> If one carefully considers the origin and the development of the doctrine of this pseudo-church and the society of the Mormons, one must recognize that their entire social and religious system is a natural consequence of North American Protestantism, since Mormonism is a reaction against the fundamental errors of the Reformation. Therefore . . . this very odd system carries a bright testimony to the truth of the principles of the Catholic Church.[2]

The Archbishop thought that Mormons and Catholics shared an enmity toward Protestantism, especially its rejection of "the Catholic doctrine that the nature and authority of the church is a divine institution." He thus appreciated the way that Mormonism tried to establish "an authoritative and visible church as a mediatory between God and the individual man" and praised Mormons for "giving the church a more inclusive influence on its members and the direction of the members' political society."[3]

Of course, we think we have only scratched the surface of these similarities. Take, for example, the role of magic in the nineteenth century. Protestants, with their focus on scripture and preaching, were suspicious of any religious practices that appeared to make the material world a conduit of the divine. That is why they were committed to erecting a high wall between religion and magic and then adept at employing the category of magic to critique any theological excursions that left the spiritual and the natural too mixed together. When Mormons came on the scene, Fluhman observes, "Antebellum Protestants intuitively connected Mormon magic with Roman Catholic ritual practice and transubstantiation."[4] Mormons and Catholics were thus put in the same boat, given the prophetic visions in Mormonism and revelations from Mary in Catholicism. Mormons and Catholics both have what we can call a "material imagination." This world in all of its ordinary physical properties can partake of the divine. Both traditions also have a sacred geography, with pilgrimages to holy places and a longing for Christ to establish his rule on earth, not just in heaven.

Both are deeply supportive of what we could call "Christendom theology." Christendom is the idea that Christianity, at its Spirit-filled best, can and should provide the cultural substance and social structures for the lives of the faithful. Christendom reached its culmination in the Middle Ages and broke up with the Protestant Reformation, but Catholics still believe that the Catholic Church provides the universal basis for any possible hope for global peace and harmony. And Mormons went to Utah to try to build an earthly kingdom of God in expectation of a very this worldly New Jerusalem. Both of these dreams, one centered in Rome and one in Utah, made many nineteenth-century Americans very nervous as the country was still trying to figure out its own territorial destiny. And both dreams are very much alive, even after Utah became a state and the Papal States were reduced to the limited holdings of the Vatican City.

And both traditions were deeply unsettling to Americans in terms of their teachings on sexuality. Just as Catholics had celibacy, the Saints had polygamy, and both were seen as threats to the Protestant emphasis on nuclear families. Many Protestants found it hard to believe that priests could actually give up sex, so stories about their debauchery abounded. Those same Protestants suspected that polygamy was just a means for Mormon leaders to satisfy their craven desires. Celibacy and polygamy, apparent opposites, subjected Catholics and Mormons to the same suspicions of sexual deviancy.

So much more could be said. Both traditions have strong views on the importance of a bloody atonement for our salvation. Both read the Bible through extra-biblical documents (the creeds or LDS scripture). Both can be very exclusive, claiming to be the only true Church, and also very inclusive, applauding truth wherever it is found and leaving plenty of room in their theologies for the possibility of universal salvation. Both see family as the foundation for social justice. Both have developed their own infrastructure in schooling (Catholic schools are well known but Mormons have their own educational system, including high school "seminaries" and college-level Institutes of Religion). Both have also developed their own charitable infrastructures.

One of the most important differences between the two is that Catholicism has become much more respected in America in the last fifty years, beginning with the Presidency of John F. Kennedy. We hope that this will become in the not-so-distant future yet another similarity these traditions share. That is, we hope that someday Americans will examine Mormonism just as they examine Catholicism or any other branch of the Christian tree—in terms of both its truth claims and the fruits of its faith.

And a final word needs to be said about Protestantism. We do not want to make Protestants the common enemy in order to draw Catholics and Mormons closer together. Because we have emphasized the similarities between Mormonism and Catholicism, we have also pointed out the ways in which both of these traditions are different from Protestantism. We hope that our analysis of Protestantism does justice to the ways in which Catholicism and Mormonism share a pre-Reformation approach to ritual, tradition, and history. And we hope our analysis honors the fact that the Protestant Reformation really was a religious revolution and thus, like any radical critique, deserves to be taken seriously, which means answering its questions but also criticizing its own assumptions and terms of debate.

So where do we go from here? A first step might be to visit each other's churches. The Mass provides a singular education in Catholic theology and piety, and there is no better way to get to know Mormons than to join them for worship. After that, who knows? We invite you to take your own steps and continue the journey we hope that we have begun.

Notes

INTRODUCTION

1. Jim Robbins, "Aggressive Mormons Aim at Latin America," *National Catholic Reporter* 30, no. 13 (January 28, 1994): 8. John Dart, "Catholic Bishops Upset by Conversion of Latinos: Mormons, Adventists and Other Churches Are Accused of Using Unfair Tactics to Gain New Spanish-Speaking Members," *Los Angeles Times*, March 3, 1990, http://www.articles.latimes.com/1990-03-03/entertainment/ca-1528_1_catholic-bishops. Also see Bastien Inzaurralde, "Plan for Mormon Temple Rattles Catholics in a French Suburb," *Christian Science Monitor*, October 28, 2012, http://www.csmonitor.com/World/Europe/2012/1028/Plan-for-Mormon-temple-rattles-Catholics-in-a-French-suburb.

2. Dawn Megli, "Growth of Latino Membership Shows Mormonism's Surprising Diversity," Annenberg Digital News, May 5, 2012, http://www.neontommy.com/news/2012/05/growth-latino-membership-shows-mormonisms-surprising-diversity.

3. Wilfried Decoo, "As Our Two Faiths Have Worked Together—Catholicism and Mormonism on Human Life Ethics and Same-Sex Marriage," *Dialogue: A Journal of Mormon Thought* 46, no. 3 (Fall 2013): 1–44.

4. Craig L. Blomberg and Stephen E. Robinson, *How Wide the Divide? A Mormon and Evangelical in Conversation* (Downers Grove, IL: InterVarsity Press, 1997); Robert L. Millet and Gerald R. McDermott, *Claiming Christ: A Mormon–Evangelical Debate* (Grand Rapids, MI: Brazos Press, 2007); Robert L. Millet and Gregory C. V. Johnson, *Bridging the Divide: The Continuing Conversation between a Mormon and an Evangelical* (Rhinebeck, NY: Monkfish Book Publishing Company, 2007); and Richard Mouw, *Talking with Mormons: An Invitation to Evangelicals* (Grand Rapids, MI: Wm. B. Eerdmans Publishing Co., 2012). See also Richard J. Mouw's *Uncommon Decency: Christian Civility in an Uncivil World*, 2nd edn. (Downers

Grove, IL: InterVarsity Press, 2010). Many of Mouw's examples in this recently updated book are about Latter-day Saints and how Protestant Christians should interact with them.

5. M. Russell Ballard, "The Doctrine of Inclusion," *Ensign*, November 2001, 37–38.

6. *Unitatis Redintegratio*, Chapter 2, Section 9, in Austin Flannery, ed., *Vatican Council II—The Conciliar and Post Conciliar Documents*, Vol. 1, new revised edn. (Northport, NY: Costello Publishing Company, 1992), 461.

7. Barbie Latza Nadeau, "A Mormon St. Peter's in Rome," *The Daily Beast*, posted September 28, 2014, http://www.thedailybeast.com/articles/2014/09/28/a-mormon-st-peter-s-in-rome.html.

CHAPTER 1

1. For another perspective on the end of the Reformation, see Mark Noll and Carolyn Nystrom, *Is the Reformation Over? An Evangelical Assessment of Contemporary Roman Catholicism* (Grand Rapids, MI: Baker Academic, 2008).

2. Bob Dylan, "Gotta Serve Somebody," from *Slow Train Coming* (copyright 1979 by Special Rider Music).

3. For an extensive analysis of the social consequences of the Reformation, see Brad S. Gregory, *The Unintended Reformation: How a Religious Revolution Secularized Society* (Cambridge, MA: Harvard University Press, 2012).

4. These quotations are from "Joseph Smith—History," which he prepared in 1838–39 and was first published in 1842. It is a part of the Mormon scripture called The Pearl of Great Price and can be easily found online at http://www.lds.org.

5. From Doctrine and Covenants 105:35. This is a collection of revelations and inspired declarations mostly received by Joseph Smith and is a standard part of Mormon scripture (along with the Bible, the Book of Mormon, and the Pearl of Great Price). In the rest of this book, references to this document will be included parenthetically in the text as D&C.

6. For an interesting approach to the history of apostolic authority, including discussions of the differences between Catholic, Episcopalian, and Lutheran views, see John J. Burkhard, *Apostolicity Then and Now: An Ecumenical Church in a Postmodern World* (Collegeville, MN: Liturgical Press, 2004). Another very valuable book on religious authority in the history of Christianity is Paul Valliere, *Conciliarism: A History of Decision-Making in the Church* (Cambridge: Cambridge University Church, 2012).

7. See, e.g., Michael Davies, *Liturgical Time Bombs in Vatican II* (Rockford, IL: Tan Books and Publishers, Inc., 2003); Michael Dimond and Peter Dimond, *The Truth about What Really Happened to the Catholic Church after Vatican II* (Fillmore, NY: Most Holy Family Monastery, 2007).

8. Robert P. George, "The Divisions We Must Sustain," *Touchstone: A Journal of Mere Christianity* 16, no. 6 (July/August, 2003): 50.

9. Or, some would prefer, Bishops were the successors to the Apostles and hold today the apostolic office.

10. Elder Orson F. Whitney (1855–1931), of the LDS Quorum of the Twelve Apostles, cited in LeGrand Richards, *A Marvelous Work and a Wonder* (Salt Lake City, UT: Deseret Book, 1950), 3–4.

11. For a good account of the Mormon view of Prophets, see Scott R. Petersen, *Where Have All the Prophets Gone? Revelation and Rebellion in the Old Testament and the Christian World* (Springville, UT: Cedar Fort Publisher, 2005). I have learned much from my conversations about Mormon theology with Scott Petersen.

12. For an interesting examination of the various views of religious authority in a half-dozen Christian traditions, see Robert L. Millet, ed., *By What Authority? The Vital Questions of Religious Authority in Christianity* (Macon, GA: Mercer University Press, 2010).

13. Joseph Smith, in Lucy Mack Smith, *History of Joseph Smith by his Mother*, edited by Preston Nibley (Salt Lake City, UT: Bookcraft, 1956), 233–234 and 237.

14. Joseph Smith, *Teachings of the Prophet Joseph Smith*, compiled by Joseph Fielding Smith (Salt Lake City, UT: Deseret Book, 1976), 256.

15. Perhaps it would be more appropriate to call Joseph the "conduit" through which it was restored. Latter-day Saints certainly do not believe he "invented" Mormonism. But they do believe that, under the direction of God, he restored and organized it.

16. Spencer W. Kimball, N. Eldon Tanner, and Marion G. Romney, cited in Spencer J. Palmer, "World Religions (Non-Christian) and Mormonism," in Daniel H. Ludlow, ed., *Encyclopedia of Mormonism*, 4 vols. (New York: Macmillan, 1992), 4:1589.

17. Palmer, "World Religions (Non-Christian) and Mormonism," 4:1589.

18. Avery Dulles, *The Survival of Dogma* (New York: Crossroad, 1985), 130, 131–132, and 132.

CHAPTER 2

1. Erwin Lutzer, *The Doctrines that Divide: A Fresh Look at the Historic Doctrines that Separate Christians* (Grand Rapids, MI: Kregel Publications, 1998), 83.

2. J. N. D. Kelly, *Early Christian Doctrines*, rev. edn. (San Francisco, CA: Harper San Francisco, 1978), 352.

3. Kelly, *Early Christian Doctrines*, 356.

4. Kelly, *Early Christian Doctrines*, 374.

5. For a rich essay on the ways in which evangelicals misunderstand Mormon discourse on grace, see Robert L. Millet, "The Perils of Grace," *BYU Studies Quarterly* 53, no. 2 (2014): 7–19.

6. For the best English language history of indulgences, see R. N. Swanson, *Indulgences in Late Medieval England: Passports to Paradise?* (Cambridge: Cambridge University Press, 2007).

7. Even some Protestants are rediscovering purgatory. See Jerry L. Walls, *Purgatory: The Logic of Total Transformation* (New York: Oxford University Press, 2011).

8. For an interesting reference to this fact, see Michael H. Hart, *The 100: A Ranking of the Most Influential Persons in History*, rev. edn. (New York: Citadel Press, 2000). Hart, himself a Jew, placed Jesus third on his list (behind Mohammed and Sir Isaac Newton) because, he reasoned, so few Christians actually live what Jesus taught.

9. See Brigham Young, *The Complete Discourses of Brigham Young*, compiled by Richard S. Van Wagoner, 5 vols. (Salt Lake City, UT: The Smith-Pettit Foundation, 2009), 4:2431.

10. See, e.g., Roger Finke and Rodney Stark, *The Churching of America 1776–1990* (New Brunswick, NJ: Rutgers University Press, 1992), who make this very point as a historically demonstrable fact.

CHAPTER 3

1. See, e.g., Charlene Spretnak, *Missing Mary: The Queen of Heaven and her Re-Emergence in the Modern Church* (New York: Palgrave Macmillan, 2004).

2. For this perspective, see Marina Warner, *Alone of All Her Sex: The Myth and the Cult of the Virgin Mary* (New York: Vintage Books, 1983).

3. Karen Jo Torjesen, *When Women Were Priests: Women's Leadership in the Early Church and the Scandal of their Subordination in the Rise of Christianity* (San Francisco, CA: Harper San Francisco, 1993), 265.

4. See Bruce R. McConkie, "Eve and the Fall," in *Woman* (Salt Lake City, UT: Deseret Book, 1979), 59. See also Bruce R. McConkie, *The Mortal Messiah*, 4 vols. (Salt Lake City, UT: Deseret Book, 1980–81), 1:23. See also 1 Nephi 11:18 (in the Book of Mormon).

5. See Robert L. Millet, "The Birth and Childhood of the Messiah," in Kent P. Jackson and Robert L. Millet, eds., *Studies in Scripture*, vol. 5: *The Gospels* (Salt Lake City, UT: Deseret Book, 1986), 142.

6. See McConkie, *The Mortal Messiah*, 1:326–327 n. 4. See also Joseph Fielding McConkie, *Witnesses of the Birth of Christ* (Salt Lake City, UT: Bookcraft, 1998), 61–62.

7. Eliza R. Snow, "O My Father," in *Hymns of The Church of Jesus Christ of Latter-day Saints* (Salt Lake City, UT: Deseret Book, 1985), hymn 292.

8. Elder Milton R. Hunter of the First Council of the Seventy wrote: "Abraham's account (4:26–27) states that the Gods organized man in Their own image and after Their likeness, both male and female. They were created first as spirit beings in the image of their Heavenly Parents and later as mortals in a similar likeness. Thus the males were created in the image and likeness of God the Eternal Father while the females were formed in the image and likeness of God their Eternal Mother. In other words, all the men and women who have ever lived on this earth or who ever [sic] shall live here are literally sons and daughters of Heavenly Parents." See Milton R. Hunter, *Pearl of Great Price Commentary* (Salt Lake City, UT: Stevens & Wallis, Inc., 1951), 104. Similarly, the First Presidency of the Church declared: "All men and women are in the similitude of the universal Father and Mother, and are literally the sons and daughters of Deity." Joseph F. Smith, John R. Winder, and Anthon H. Lund, "The Origin of Man," in James R. Clark, *Messages of the First Presidency of The Church of Jesus Christ of Latter-day Saints*, 6 vols. (Salt Lake City, UT: Bookcraft, 1965–75), 4:203.

9. See the lovely book by John Saward, *Redeemer in the Womb: Jesus Living in Mary* (San Francisco, CA: Ignatius Press, 1993).

CHAPTER 4

1. For a magisterial examination of nineteenth-century debates over the biblical canon, see David F. Holland, *Sacred Borders: Continuing Revelation and Canonical Restraint in Early America* (New York: Oxford University Press, 2011).

2. Douglas V. Steere, *Quaker Spirituality: Selected Writings* (Mahwah, NJ: Paulist Press, 1984), 65.

3. Joseph Smith, *Teachings of the Prophet Joseph Smith*, compiled by Joseph Fielding Smith (Salt Lake City, UT: Deseret Book, 1976), 355.

4. See *Unitatis Redintegratio*, Chapter 1, Section 4, in Austin Flannery, ed., *Vatican Council II—The Conciliar and Post Conciliar Documents*, Vol. 1, new rev. edn. (Northport, NY: Costello Publishing Company, 1992), 458.

5. See *Lumen Gentium*, Chapter 2, Section 16, in Flannery, *Vatican Council II*, 367.

6. Brigham Young, in *The Complete Discourses of Brigham Young*, compiled by Richard S. Van Wagoner, 5 vols. (Salt Lake City, UT: The Smith-Pettit Foundation, 2009), 3:1465.

7. For a very useful book on Joseph's visions, see John W. Welch, ed., *Opening the Heavens: Accounts of Divine Manifestations, 1820–1844* (Salt Lake City, UT: Deseret Book, 2005).

8. Larry E. Dahl and Charles D. Tate Jr., eds., *The Lectures on Faith in Historical Perspective* (Provo, UT: Religious Studies Center, Brigham Young University, 1990).

9. This is just my personal opinion. However, I have come to that conclusion based on a quarter of a century of experience, in which I have been teaching religion courses to Latter-day Saint students (including courses in comparative religions).

10. See, e.g., Joseph Smith, *Teachings of the Prophet Joseph Smith*, compiled by Joseph Fielding Smith (Salt Lake City, UT: Deseret Book, 1976), 327; Joseph Smith, *The Words of Joseph Smith: The Contemporary Accounts of the Nauvoo Discourses of the Prophet Joseph*, compiled and edited by Andrew F. Ehat and Lyndon W. Cook (Provo, UT: BYU Religious Studies Center, 1980), 183–184; Joseph Smith History 1:19 (in the LDS Pearl of Great Price).

11. Joseph's intended definition of the word "creed" may not have been the same as how we use it today. The religious traditions that were influential in his life were mostly Protestant, not Catholic. Thus, the Nicene Creed was likely not what he intended when he spoke of "creeds." Joseph said that he learned (in his very first vision from God) that the "creeds" of those churches he had been affiliating with were an "abomination in the sight of God." Of this, one scholar conjectured: "Of course, it is possible that when Jesus said that 'all their creeds are an abomination,' he was not using the word 'creeds' in a formal sense, but rather simply in reference to 'any system of principles which are believed or professed,' for the word *creed* has this meaning, as well as the formal meaning, in the American language in 1828, according to *Webster's Dictionary of the American Language*." John W. Welch, "'All Their Creeds Were an Abomination': A Brief Look at Creeds as Part of the Apostasy," in *Prelude to the Restoration: From Apostasy to the Restored Church* (Salt Lake City, UT: Deseret Book, 2004), 248 n. 12. Thus, there is reason to be cautious about how we interpret Joseph's use of the word "creed."

12. Smith, *Teachings of the Prophet Joseph Smith*, 327.

13. Smith in Ehat and Cook, *The Words of Joseph Smith*, 183–184. In this same spirit, on May 24, 1844, Joseph rhetorically asked: "Did I ever exercise any compulsion over any man? Did I not give him the liberty of disbelieving any doctrine I have preached, if he saw fit?" Joseph Smith, *The Teachings of Joseph Smith*, compiled by Larry E. Dahl and Donald Q. Cannon (Salt Lake City, UT: Bookcraft, 1998), 135. See also Joseph Smith, *History of the Church of Jesus Christ of Latter-day Saints*, edited by B. H. Roberts, 7 vols. (Salt Lake City, UT: Deseret Book, 1978), 6:273. On April 6, 1844, Joseph stated: "I don't blame any one [sic] for not believing my history. If I had not experienced what I have, I could not have believed it myself." Smith, *Teachings of the Prophet Joseph Smith*, 361. Thus, the Prophet clearly did not wish to coerce or force others to believe as he believed. Did he hope for their conversion? Yes! But did he wish to insist upon it? Never! Joseph did not carry this attitude to the extreme. There are, after all, examples of Joseph excommunicating or censuring those who openly declared beliefs ran counter to the teachings of the Church. Nevertheless, wherever possible, Joseph sought to preserve the sanctity of an individual's right to believe "according to the dictates of [their] own conscience" (*Article of Faith* 11). The position of the contemporary Church is hardly different. Individual liberty to interpret scripture, and individual responsibility toward the formation of one's faith, are

encouraged. However, if that content is misguided and openly expressed with the intent to persuade others, the Church is under obligation to take action to prevent the spread of heresy. Preserving the individual's sanctity to believe how he or she chooses must be balanced against preserving the sanctity and orthodoxy of the Church.

14. For example, an 1834 version employed eight *Articles of Faith*, whereas an 1836 version had only five. One 1840 version used by the Church had eighteen and another that year employed nineteen *Articles of Faith*. In 1842 the Church used a list of sixteen *Articles*, and a version published about three years later had fifteen. In 1849 a version was utilized that contained fourteen *Articles of Faith*. Thus, these have not been stagnant—particularly during the early years. See David J. Whittaker, "Articles of Faith," in Daniel H. Ludlow, ed., *Encyclopedia of Mormonism*, 4 vols. (New York: Macmillan, 1992), 1:68–69; Department of Seminaries and Institutes of Religion, *Introduction to the Pearl of Great Price and Its Teachings: A Guide for Institute Instructors—Religion 327* (Salt Lake City, UT: The Church of Jesus Christ of Latter-day Saints Church Schools, no date), 207. Again, this was in accord with Joseph's sense that the "creeds" needed to be fluid as the doctrinal development and public revelation of the Church demanded it.

CHAPTER 5

1. Avery Cardinal Dulles, "Who Can Be Saved?" *First Things* (February 2008): 17–22.

2. Supererogation is often associated with the application of the "good works" of one person (e.g., Jesus or one of the saints) to the life/"account" of another (e.g., a person who has died and is currently in purgatory). However, Roman Catholics may also view the acts of faithful living practitioners as supererogatory. For example, "the heroic action of a woman who saves a child by throwing it out of the path of a truck, knowingly sacrificing herself in the process, would also be a work of supererogation." See Richard P. McBrien, ed., *HarperCollins Encyclopedia of Catholicism* (San Francisco, CA: Harper San Francisco, 1995), 1232, s.v., "Supererogation, works of." In addition, as suggested previously, supererogatory "acts" may consist of something as simple as saying the Rosary on behalf of a deceased person. Any act that rises above the minimal demands of morality is potentially supererogatory in its nature, merit, and application.

3. The LDS *General Handbook of Instructions* (on par with the Roman Catholic Code of Canon Law) states: "Pictures and other artwork may be placed in appropriate locations in the meetinghouse. However, they may not be placed in the chapel or near the baptismal font. Statues, murals, or mosaics are not authorized. *This policy may not apply to works of art that have been on display for many years in the chapels of existing meetinghouses.*" *Church Handbook of Instructions*,

2 vols. (Salt Lake City, UT: Church of Jesus Christ of Latter-day Saints, 2010), 1:84 (8.4.1), emphasis added.

4. See, e.g., the *Encyclopedia of Mormonism*, which states: "Latter-day Saints . . . like the earliest Christians, are reluctant to display the cross because they view the 'good news' of the gospel as Christ's resurrection more than his crucifixion. . . . The cross, with its focus on the death of Christ, does not symbolize the message of a living, risen, exalted Lord who changes the lives of his followers." Roger R. Keller, "Cross," in Daniel H. Ludlow, ed., *Encyclopedia of Mormonism*, 4 vols. (New York: Macmillan, 1992), 1:344 and 345. Similarly, one LDS general authority stated: "To us, the cross is a symbol of His passion, His agony. Our preference is to remember His resurrection." Robert E. Wells, cited in Daniel C. Peterson and Stephen D. Ricks, *Offenders for a Word* (Provo, UT: The Foundation for Ancient Research and Mormon Studies, 1992), 131–132.

5. See, e.g., Michael G. Reed, *Banishing the Cross: The Emergence of a Mormon Taboo* (Independence, MO: John Whitmer Books, 2012), 67–85. Early Mormons used crosses as jewelry, in our building's architecture (e.g., the stonework and stained glass), on our headstones, on our pulpits, in our funeral floral arrangements, in our early historical markers and monuments—even the Church's original branding iron was in the shape of a cross. "Holy cow!" (quite literally). Even today, LDS chapels are almost without exception built in cruciform shape. So the taboo so common now was not always part of our tradition or practice.

6. See Reed, *Banishing the Cross*, 86–122. While there is no policy stating that a Latter-day Saint cannot wear a cross, this has become somewhat of a social norm in Mormondom. So, the Church does not forbid their use in the private lives of its members, but Latter-day Saints generally feel uncomfortable wearing or displaying them—as most today have grown up during a part of the Church's history wherein they have been in disuse. Institutionally, however, it would be fair to say that, as a policy, we do not use them in our worship services.

7. See Kallistos Ware, *The Orthodox Way*, rev. edn. (Crestwood, NY: St. Vladimir's Seminary Press, 1995), 32; John Anthony McGuckin, ed., *The Encyclopedia of Eastern Orthodox Christianity*, 2 vols. (Malden, MA: Wiley-Blackwell, 2011), 2:706; Thomas Hopko, *The Orthodox Faith*, 4 vols. (Crestwood, NY: St. Vladimir's Seminary Press and the Department of Religious Education—Orthodox Church in America, 1981), 1:57. See also Justin M. Lasser, "Logos Theology," in McGuckin, ed., *Encyclopedia of Eastern Orthodox Christianity*, 1:371.

8. See Anthony Sherman, "Baptism," in McBrien, ed., *HarperCollins Encyclopedia of Catholicism*, 133 and 137.

9. By "true Church" Latter-day Saints traditionally mean the Church that has restored priesthood keys and living Prophets and Apostles. "True Church" does not mean that the Latter-day Saints are the only ones God cares about, inspires, works through, etc. LDS General Authorities have taught many times that God inspires all who draw to Him, regardless of their denominational affiliation.

But Latter-day Saints hold that certain powers, rites, and truths were lost near the close of the New Testament, which have been restored in these latter days. That is what sets Mormons apart from other Christians.

10. Bob O'Gorman and Mary Faulkner, *The Complete Idiot's Guide to Understanding Catholicism*, 2nd edn. (Indianapolis, IN: Alpha Books, 2003), 71. See also Maureen Sullivan, *101 Questions & Answers on Vatican II* (New York: Paulist Press, 2002), 75–76, 82, and 84–86.

11. This is not to suggest that everything that came out of Vatican II was bad. Some much needed "updates" to the Church were the result of the Council. However, the overarching influence has led to an attenuation of many traditional Catholic practices. One friend of mine from Italy has suggested to me that the problem was not the Council, but how the decisions of the Council were interpreted and applied. Perhaps!

CHAPTER 6

1. For one of the best defenses of divine simplicity, see James E. Dolezal, *God Without Parts: Divine Simplicity and the Metaphysics of God's Absoluteness* (Eugene, OR: Pickwick Publications, 2011).

2. For an important critique of negative theology, see Timothy D. Knepper, *Negating Negation: Against the Apophatic Abandonment of the Dionysian Corpus* (Eugene, OR: Cascade Books, 2014).

3. My understanding of the Apostle Paul's relationship to Stoic philosophy is shaped by Troels Engberg-Pedersen, *Cosmology and Self in the Apostle Paul: The Material Spirit* (New York: Oxford University Press, 2010). Also see Ricardo Salles, ed., *God and Cosmos in Stoicism* (New York: Oxford University Press, 2009).

4. Or, as Thomas Aquinas posed the question, can several angels be at the same time in the same place? Can they occupy the same space simultaneously? See Thomas Aquinas, *Summa Theologica*, Part 1, Question 52, Article 3.

5. See Truman G. Madsen, *Joseph Smith, the Prophet* (Salt Lake City, UT: Bookcraft, 1989), 104.

6. Joseph Smith, *Teachings of the Prophet Joseph Smith*, compiled by Joseph Fielding Smith (Salt Lake City, UT: Deseret Book, 1976), 287.

7. Smith, *Teachings of the Prophet Joseph Smith*, 137.

8. See Madsen, *Joseph Smith, the Prophet*, 104–105.

9. John Paul II, *Crossing the Threshold of Hope* (New York: Alfred A. Knopf, 1994), 46.

10. See, e.g., Terryl Givens, *When Souls Had Wings: Pre-Mortal Existence in Western Thought* (New York: Oxford University Press, 2010), 103–104, as well as 84 and 105. Also Robert L. Wilken, *The Christians as the Romans Saw Them* (New Haven, CT: Yale University Press, 1984), xvi; James N. Hubler,

"Creatio ex Nihilo: Matter, Creation, and the Body in Classical and Christian Philosophy through Aquinas" (PhD diss., University of Pennsylvania, 1995), 102 and 107–108; John H. Sailhamer, "Genesis," in Frank E. Gaebelein, ed., *The Expositor's Bible Commentary*, 12 vols. (Grand Rapids, MI: Zondervan, 1976–92), 2:21.

11. See W. D. Davies, cited in Stephen E. Robinson, "LDS Doctrine Compared with Other Christian Doctrines," in Daniel H. Ludlow, ed., *Encyclopedia of Mormonism*, 4 vols. (New York: Macmillan, 1992), 1:399.

12. Smith, *Teachings of the Prophet Joseph Smith*, 343.

13. Smith, *Teachings of the Prophet Joseph Smith*, 345.

14. Of course, for some this argument is moot. Some Latter-day Saints and, I dare say, some Roman Catholics would argue that what really matters in our knowledge of God is (1) that He is personal as Father, Son, and Holy Spirit (however defined in Roman Catholic or LDS terms); and (2) that His character is that of infinite love as seen from the foot of the cross. For some, if a Christian can be like God in those two areas he or she has captured the heart of the revelation of God.

15. Stephen H. Webb, *Jesus Christ, Eternal God: Heavenly Flesh and the Metaphysics of Matter* (New York: Oxford University Press, 2012). Also see Webb, *Mormon Christianity: What Other Christians Can Learn from the Latter-day Saints* (New York: Oxford University Press, 2013). For my critique of *creatio ex nihilo*, see Stephen H. Webb, "*Creatio a Materia ex Christi*," in Thomas Jay Oord, ed., *Theologies of Creation: Creatio Ex Nihilo and its New Rivals* (New York: Routledge, 2015), 69–78.

16. Reid A. Ashbaucher, *Made in the Image of God* (Collierville, TN: Innovo Publishing, 2011), 28.

CHAPTER 7

1. I first wrote about the Mormon view of Jesus in, "Mormonism Obsessed with Christ," *First Things* (February 2012): 21–23, and reply to letters (April 2012).

2. See Caroline Walker Bynum, *Wonderful Blood: Theology and Practice in Late Medieval Northern Germany and Beyond* (Philadelphia: University of Pennsylvania Press, 2007). For Brigham Young's ideas about "blood for blood" justice, see John G. Turner, *Brigham Young: Pioneer Prophet* (Cambridge, MA: Harvard University Press, 2012), chapter 9.

3. David L. Paulsen, "Early Christian Belief in a Corporeal Deity: Origen and Augustine as Reluctant Witnesses," *Harvard Theological Review* 83 (1990): 107–114. Also see Jacob T. Baker, ed., *Mormonism at the Crossroads of Philosophy and Theology: Essays in Honor of David L. Paulsen* (Salt Lake City, UT: Greg Kofford Books, 2002) and Stephen H. Webb, "The New Mormon Ecumenism: Thoughts on *Mormonism at the Crossroads of Philosophy and*

Theology: Essays in Honor of David L. Paulsen," *BYU Studies Quarterly* 52, no. 2 (2013): 177–185.

4. As one historian notes, there is wide consensus that until A.D. 355, everyone accepted subordinationism. See R. P. C. Hanson, *The Search for the Christian Doctrine of God: The Arian Controversy 318–381* (Edinburgh: T & T Clark, 1988), xix, 64, 287. *The Oxford Dictionary of the Christian Church* notes of subordinationism that "it is a characteristic tendency in much of Christian teaching of the first three centuries, and is a marked feature of such . . . Fathers as St. Justin and Origen." Frank L. Cross and Elizabeth A. Livingstone, eds., *The Oxford Dictionary of the Christian Church,* 2nd edn. (New York: Oxford University Press, 1990), 1319. Elsewhere we read: "Christian writers up to the early fourth century had all been subordinationists." David N. Bell, *A Cloud of Witnesses: An Introductory History of the Development of Christian Doctrine* (Kalamazoo, MI: Cistercian Publications, 1989), 55. As examples of the commonality of subordinationist teachings among the mainstream of the early Christian Church, note the following comments from some of the early Fathers of the Church. In the spirit of John 5:19 and 8:28, Ignatius (circa A.D. 35–107/112), Bishop of Antioch, taught the following: "Be subject to the bishop . . . as Jesus Christ [was] subject to the Father," and "See that ye all follow the bishop, even as Jesus Christ does the Father." Ignatius, "Epistle of Ignatius to the Magnesians," Chapters 13 and 8, in Alexander Roberts and James Donaldson, eds., *Ante-Nicene Fathers,* 10 vols. (Peabody, MA: Hendrickson Publishers, 1994), 1:64 and 1:89. Speaking of Jesus's role in God's work, Justin Martyr wrote that there is "another God and Lord subject to the Maker of all things; who . . . announces to men whatsoever the Maker of all things—above whom there is no other God—wishes to announce to them." Justin Martyr, "Dialogues with Trypho," Chapter 56, in Roberts and Donaldson, eds., *Ante-Nicene Fathers,* 1:223. Irenaeus (circa A.D. 135–202), Bishop of Lyons, wrote: "The Father Himself is alone called God, moreover, the Scriptures acknowledge Him alone as God; and . . . the Lord confesses Him alone as His own Father, and knows no other." Irenaeus continues: "For 'the Father,' says [Jesus], 'is greater than I.' [John 14:28] The Father, therefore, has been declared by our Lord to excel with respect to knowledge." Irenaeus, "Against Heresies," Chapter 28, Verses 4 and 8, in Roberts and Donaldson, eds., *Ante-Nicene Fathers,* 1:400, 402. The Carthaginian apologist, Tertullian, wrote this: "Thus the Father is distinct from the Son, being greater than the Son, inasmuch as He who begets is one, and He who is begotten is another." Tertullian, "Against Praxeas," Chapter 9, in Roberts and Donaldson, eds., *Ante-Nicene Fathers,* 3:604. Novatian of Rome (fl. A.D. 235–258) said of Jesus's subordination to the Father, "far be it from us to call God the Father an angel, lest He would be subordinate to another whose angel He would be. But . . . we ought to understand . . . God the Son, who, because He is of God, is rightly called God, because He is the Son of God. But, because He is subjected to the Father, and the Announcer of the Father's will, He is declared

to be the Angel of Great Counsel." Novatian, "Treatise Concerning the Trinity," Chapter 8, in Roberts and Donaldson, eds., *Ante-Nicene Fathers*, 5:628.

5. Joseph F. Smith, Anthon H. Lund, and Charles W. Penrose, "The Origin of Man," in James R. Clark, ed., *Messages of the First Presidency*, 6 vols. (Salt Lake City, UT: Deseret Book, 1966), 4:203.

6. At the risk of opening a can of worms, Latter-day Saints do accept the biblical declaration that Adam was a "son of God" (Luke 3:38). However, in LDS theology Adam was created in an immortal (not mortal) state. Through his Fall he became mortal, and subject to the vicissitudes of life. Thus, while God fathered Jesus's mortal body (according to LDS thought), He was the father of Adam's immortal (or Terrestrial) body. Consequently, Jesus is set apart from Adam in the nature of His earthly tabernacle.

7. As a good resource for the doctrine of deification in the various denominations of Christianity, see Michael J. Christensen and Jeffery A. Wittung, eds., *Partakers of the Divine Nature: The History and Development of Deification in the Christian Traditions* (Grand Rapids, MI: Baker Academic, 2008). For a general look at the history, importance, and implications of this doctrine in Christianity, see Panayiotis Nellas, *Deification in Christ: The Nature of the Human Person* (Crestwood, NY: St. Vladimir's Seminary Press, 1997); Veli-Matti Kärkkäinen, *One with God: Salvation as Deification and Justification* (Collegeville, MN: Liturgical Press, 2004); Christoforos Stavropoulos, *Partakers of Divine Nature* (Minneapolis, MN: Light and Life Publishing, 1976); Vladimir Lossky, *The Vision of God* (Bedfordshire: The Faith Press, 1973).

8. These words are used in the Roman Office of Readings on Saturday of the 15th week in ordinary time. For a modern translation, see Boniface Ramsey O.P., *Ambrose* (New York: Routledge, 1997), 158.

9. Brad Gooch, *Flannery: A Life of Flannery O'Connor* (New York: Little, Brown and Company, 2009), 174.

10. This position is sometimes called the Primacy of Christ and was associated with St. Francis. See Damian McElrath, ed., *Franciscan Christology* (New York: Institute of St. Bonaventure University, 1980). For an excellent discussion of the need to rethink Christian cosmology in the light of changing views of matter, see David Wilkinson, *Christian Eschatology and the Physical Universe* (New York: Continuum, 2010).

11. An inspired expansion on the book of Genesis, given by the Prophet Joseph, and held by Latter-day Saints as canonical.

12. Ada R. Habershon, *Study of the Types* (Grand Rapids, MI: Kregel Publications, 1974), 35.

13. See, e.g., John 1:29 and 36; 1 Nephi 10:10; 11:21, 27, and 31–32; 12:6, 10–11, and 18; 13:24, 28–29, 33–34, 38, and 40; 14:1–3, 6–7, 10–14, and 25; 2 Nephi 31:4–6; 33:14; Alma 7:14; Mormon 9:2–3; D&C 88:106. See also Genesis 22:7–8; Exodus 12:3–5 and 21, etc.

14. Raymond E. Brown, *The Birth of the Messiah*, new updated edn. (New York: Doubleday, 1993), 124 and 125.

15. It has been argued by some that Latter-day Saints think that God and Mary had sexual relations in order to conceive Jesus. I cannot emphasize enough that Mormonism has no such doctrine. How exactly the conception of Christ took place is unknown. And regardless of any theories posited by any given individual, The Church of Jesus Christ of Latter-day Saints does not seek to define what God has Himself left a mystery.

CHAPTER 8

1. Paul Althaus, *The Theology of Martin Luther* (Philadelphia, PA: Fortress Press, 1966), 425.

2. See David L. Whidden III, *Christ the Light: The Theology of Light and Illumination in Thomas Aquinas* (Minneapolis, MN: Fortress Press, 2014). For a fascinating Mormon perspective on light, see David A. Grandy, "Physical Light and the Light of Christ," *BYU Studies Quarterly* 53, no. 4 (2014): 7–36.

3. See, e.g., Colin Kruse, *Tyndale New Testament Commentaries: 2 Corinthians* (Grand Rapids, MI: Eerdmans, 1998), 201–202; I. Howard Marshall, *The IVP New Testament Commentary Series: 1 Peter* (Downers Grove, IL: InterVarsity Press, 1991), 125; Raymond E. Brown, *The Anchor Bible: John XIII–XXI* (New York: Doubleday, 1970), 619. See also Raymond E. Brown, Joseph A. Fitzmyer, and Roland E. Murphy, eds., *The New Jerome Biblical Commentary* (Englewood Cliffs, NJ: Prentice Hall, 1990), 828.

4. Brown, *Anchor Bible*, 619.

5. See Clement of Alexandria, "The Stromata," Book 6, Chapter 14, in Alexander Roberts and James Donaldson, eds., *Ante-Nicene Fathers*, 10 vols. (Peabody, MA: Hendrickson Publishers, 1994), 2:506; Irenaeus, "Against Heresies," chapter 36, verses 1–2, in Alexander Roberts and James Donaldson, eds., *Ante-Nicene Fathers*, 10 vols. (Peabody, MA: Hendrickson Publishers, 1994), 1:567; Papias, "Fragments," V, in Alexander Roberts and James Donaldson, eds., *Ante-Nicene Fathers*, 10 vols. (Peabody, MA: Hendrickson Publishers, 1994), 1:154.

6. John R. Sachs, "Hell," in Richard P. McBrien, ed., *HarperCollins Encyclopedia of Catholicism* (San Francisco, CA: Harper San Francisco, 1995), 608.

7. Clement of Alexandria, *"Stromata,"* Book 7, Chapter 10, in Roberts and Donaldson, *Ante-Nicene Fathers*, 2:539.

8. Augustine, "Exposition of the Psalms," Psalm 50, exposition paragraphs 1 and 2, in Philip Schaff, ed., *Nicene and Post-Nicene Fathers*, first series (Peabody, MA: Hendrickson Publishers, 1994), 8:177 and 178.

9. Thomas Aquinas, Opusc. 57 in festo Corp. Christi, 1, cited on the Vatican's website, http://www.vatican.va/jubilee_2000/magazine/documents/ju_mag_01061998_p-10_en.html.

10. Stephen H. Webb, *On God and Dogs: A Christian Theology of Compassion for Animals* (New York: Oxford University Press, 1998) and Webb, *Good Eating: The Bible, Diet, and the Proper Love of Animals* (Grand Rapids, MI: Brazos Press, 2001).

11. Joseph Smith, *Teachings of the Prophet Joseph Smith*, compiled by Joseph Fielding Smith (Salt Lake City, UT: Deseret Book, 1976), 291.

12. Joseph Fielding Smith Jr., *Doctrines of Salvation*, 3 vols. (Salt Lake City, UT: Bookcraft, 1998), 1:74.

CHAPTER 9

1. See Miranda Wilcox and John D. Young, eds., *Standing Apart: Mormon Historical Consciousness and the Concept of Apostasy* (New York: Oxford University Press, 2014). This important book shows a new interest by LDS scholars to reflect on the diversity and limits of traditional Mormon understandings of apostasy.

2. Spencer W. Kimball, "Circles of Exaltation," an address to religious educators, June 28, 1968, in *Charge to Religious Educators*, 2nd edn. (Salt Lake City, UT: The Church of Jesus Christ of Latter-day Saints, 1982), 12.

3. George Santayana, *The Life of Reason; or, The Phases of Human Progress* (New York: Charles Scribner's Sons, 1920), 284.

4. E.g., Alonzo L. Gaskill, *The Lost Language of Symbolism: An Essential Guide for Recognizing and Interpreting Symbols of the Gospel* (Salt Lake City, UT: Deseret Book, 2003); Gaskill, *Sacred Symbols: Finding Meaning in Rites, Rituals, and Ordinances* (Springville, UT: Cedar Fort, 2011); Gaskill, *The Truth about Eden: Understanding the Fall and our Temple Experience* (Springville, UT: Cedar Fort, 2013); and Gaskill, *Miracles of the New Testament: A Guide to the Symbolic Messages* (Springville, UT: Cedar Fort, 2014).

5. See, e.g., Bargil Pixner, *Paths of the Messiah and Sites of the Early Church from Galilee to Jerusalem: Jesus and Jewish Christianity in Light of Archaeological Discoveries* (San Francisco, CA: Ignatius Press, 2010); Jeffrey R. Chadwick, "Revisiting Golgotha and the Garden Tomb," *Religious Educator*, no. 1 (2003): 13–48.

6. Charles H. Gabriel, "I Stand all Amazed," in *Hymns of The Church of Jesus Christ of Latter-day Saints* (Salt Lake City, UT: Deseret Book, 1985), hymn 193.

7. Paul Ricoeur, *Memory, History, Forgetting*, translated by Kathleen Blamey and David Pellauer (Chicago: University of Chicago Press, 2004).

8. See Leonard J. Arrington and Davis Bitton, *The Mormon Experience: A History of the Latter-day Saints* (Boston: George Allen & Unwin Ltd, 1979), 193.

9. David McCullough, "History in the Making," lecture delivered at a Hillsdale College in 2005. See *The Free Library*, s.v. "History in the Making," http://www.thefreelibrary.com/History+in+the+making.-a0263519053.

CHAPTER 10

1. I am following here the work of Robert O'Connell, *The Origin of the Soul in St. Augustine's Later Works* (New York: Fordham University Press, 1987). Also see Ronnie J. Rombs, *Saint Augustine and the Fall of the Soul: Beyond O'Connell and his Critics* (Washington, DC: The Catholic University of America Press, 2006).

2. Eric Osborn, *Tertullian: First Theologian of the West* (Cambridge: Cambridge University Press, 2003). For background, see David Sedley, "Stoic Physics and Metaphysics," in Keimpe Algra, Jonathan Barnes, Jaap Mansfeld, and Malcolm Schofield, eds., *The Cambridge History of Hellenistic Philosophy* (Cambridge: Cambridge University Press, 1999), 382–411.

3. J. H. S. Burleigh, ed. and trans., *Augustine: Earlier Writings* (Louisville, KY: Westminster John Knox Press, 2006), 55.

4. Burleigh, *Augustine: Earlier Writings*, 206.

5. Burleigh, *Augustine: Earlier Writings*, 206.

6. See Terryl L. Givens, *When Souls Had Wings: Pre-Mortal Existence in Western Thought* (New York: Oxford University Press, 2010), 219. Also see his remarkable book, written with Fiona Givens, *The God Who Weeps: How Mormonism Makes Sense of Life* (Salt Lake City, UT: Ensign Peak, 2012).

7. Attributed to Joseph Smith is the following idea (recorded by W. W. Phelps, secretary/clerk to the Prophet): "eternity . . . has been going on in this system, (not this world) almost two thousand five hundred and fifty five millions of years." See W. W. Phelps, letter to William Smith, Nauvoo, IL, December 25, 1844, in *The Times and Seasons*, 6 vols. (Independence, MO: Independence Press, 1986), 5:758.

8. Edward Young, the twentieth-century Hebrew Bible scholar, pointed out that "Tertullian, Gregory the Great, and others have referred this verse to the fall of Satan, described in Luke 10:18." See Edward J. Young, *The Book of Isaiah*, 3 vols. (Grand Rapids, MI: Eerdmans, 1997), 1:441.

9. See Merrill C. Tenney, *John: The Gospel of Belief* (Grand Rapids, MI: Eerdmans, 1948), 153; Charles F. Pfeiffer and Everett F. Harrison, eds., *The Wycliffe Bible Commentary* (Chicago, IL: Moody Press, 1975), 1092; W. Robertson Nicoll, *The Expositor's Greek Testament*, 5 vols. (Grand Rapids, MI: Eerdmans, 1983), 1:782; R. V. G. Tasker, *Tyndale New Testament Commentaries—John* (Grand Rapids, MI: Eerdmans, 1997), 126; Leslie F. Church, ed., *The NIV Matthew Henry Commentary* (Grand Rapids, MI: Zondervan, 1992), NT 363; J. H. Bernard, *The International Critical Commentary—A Critical and Exegetical Commentary on the Gospel According to St. John*, 2 vols. (Edinburgh: T & T Clark, 1976), 2:325; Brooke Foss Westcott, *The Gospel According to St. John—The Greek Text with Introduction and Notes* (Grand Rapids, MI: Baker Book House, 1980), 31.

10. Elder B. H. Roberts, of the First Council of the Seventy, emphasized that "conditions in this life are influenced and fixed by the degree of faithfulness, by

the degree of development in the pre-existent stated. Otherwise the diversified conditions in which men find themselves placed cannot be reconciled with the justice of God." However, he added "Then how blessed, indeed, some one [*sic*] will exclaim, must they be who are born to riches, who were born to titles . . .! How faithful must they have been who inherit these privileges and blessings! whose life is one continual summer, whose existence is as a sea without a ripple! Nay, I pray you, take no such view of it as that. This class that I have described is not the most blessed among men. When you would point to those who are the favored sons of God, and who enjoy the best and highest privileges in this life, you must take into account the object for which man came here. That object is to gain an experience. Hence, those are the most blessed who live in the midst of conditions that give the widest experience. The favored sons of God are not those furthest removed from trial, from sorrow, from affliction. It is the fate, apparently, of those whom God most loves that they suffer most, that they might gain the experience for which men came into this world. It is not the smooth seas and the favorable winds that make your best sea-men. It is experience in stormy weather; it is the ocean lashed into a fury by the winds, until the fretted waves roll mountain high and make the 'laboring bark climb hills of sea and duck again and again, as low as hell is from heaven.' It is when the lightning splits the clouds, when the masts are splintered, when the ropes are tangled, and all is confusion, that the sailor learns to control his fear and stand unmoved and calm in the midst of the threatening difficulties about him. Those are the experiences that make good sailors. And so the sorrows, the afflictions, the trials, the poverty, the imprisonment, the mobbings, the hatred of mankind, are experiences that furnish men an opportunity to prove whether or not the material is in them to outride the storms of life, prove their right and title to that exaltation and glory which God has in reserve for the faithful." B. H. Roberts, "What Is Man?", in *Collected Discourses*, compiled by Brian H. Stuy, 5 vols. (Salt Lake City, UT: BHS Publishing, 1991), 4:237. Roberts's point was simply that even if (in LDS thought) one's pre-mortal choices determined their circumstances in mortality, one should not extrapolate from that that those who suffer were somehow bad or unfaithful in their pre-mortal existence. While choices made there influence the circumstances of our lives here, nevertheless, it is not always true that the good receive good and the bad receive bad based on their preexistence.

11. Indeed, Joseph Smith is quoted as having said that reincarnation is a "doctrine of the devil." See Joseph Smith, *Teachings of the Prophet Joseph Smith*, compiled by Joseph Fielding Smith (Salt Lake City, UT: Deseret Book, 1976), 105.

CONCLUSION

1. J. Spencer Fluhman, *A Peculiar People: Anti-Mormonism and the Making of Religion in Nineteenth-Century America* (Chapel Hill: University of North Carolina Press, 2012). Also see Gregory A. Prince and Gary Topping, "A Turbulent Coexistence: Duane Hunt, David O. McKay, and a Quarter-Century of Catholic-Mormon Relations," *Journal of Mormon History* 31, no. 1 (Spring 2005): 142–163, and Matthew J. Grow, "The Whore of Babylon and the Abomination of Abominations: Nineteenth-Century Catholic and Mormon Mutual Perceptions and Religious Identity," *Church History* 73, no. 1 (March 1, 2004): 139–167.

2. Quoted in Mark A. Noll, "A Jesuit Interpretation of Mid-Nineteenth-Century America," *BYU Studies* 45, no. 3 (November 2006): 45.

3. Noll, "A Jesuit Interpretation of Mid-Nineteenth-Century America," 52. For another historian's perspective, note this comment: "In Reisach's view, the 'pseudo-church' of Mormonism represented simply a sect writ large, a symptom of American Protestantism, not its cure, and thereby a powerful, inadvertent witness for the Catholic Church as the authentic bulwark of religious truth and social cohesion." Thomas Albert Howard, *God and the Atlantic: America, Europe, and the Religious Divide* (New York: Oxford University Press, 2011), 72.

4. Fluhman, *A Peculiar People*, 45.

Index

216

Index